Tracing Asylum Journeys

This book explores the asylum journey of non-European asylum applicants who seek asylum in Turkey before resettling in Canada with the aid of the Canadian government's assisted resettlement programme. Based on ethnographic research among Syrian, Afghan, Eritrean, Ethiopian, Iraqi, Iranian, Somali, Sudanese and Congolese nationals it considers the interactions of asylum seekers with both UNHCR's refugee status determination and Canada's refugee resettlement programme. With attention to the practices of migrants, the author shows how the asylum journey contains both mobility and stasis and constitutes a micro-political image of the fluidity and relativity of attributed identities and labels on the part of state migration systems. A multi-sited ethnography that shows how the migration journey is linked to the production and reproduction of knowledge, as well as the diffusion of produced knowledge among past, present, and future asylum seekers who form trans-local social networks in the course of their route, in Turkey, and in Canada. *Tracing Asylum Journeys* will appeal to sociologists and political scientists with interests in migration and transnational studies, and refugee and asylum settlement.

Uğur Yıldız is Lecturer in the Department of International Relations at Aksaray University, Turkey.

Studies in Migration and Diaspora

Series Editor: Anne J. Kershen, Queen Mary University of London, UK

Studies in Migration and Diaspora is a series designed to showcase the interdisciplinary and multidisciplinary nature of research in this important field. Volumes in the series cover local, national and global issues and engage with both historical and contemporary events. The books will appeal to scholars, students and all those engaged in the study of migration and diaspora. Amongst the topics covered are minority ethnic relations, transnational movements and the cultural, social and political implications of moving from 'over there', to 'over here'.

Undoing Homogeneity in the Nordic Region
Migration, Difference and the Politics of Solidarity
Edited by Suvi Keskinen, Unnur Dís Skaptadóttir and Mari Toivanen

Wellbeing of Transnational Muslim Families
Marriage, Law and Gender
Edited by Marja Tiilikainen, Mulki Al-Sharmani and Sanna Mustasaari

Tracing Asylum Journeys
Transnational Mobility of non-European Refugees to Canada via Turkey
Uğur Yıldız

Convivial Cultures in Multicultural Cities
Polish Migrant Women in Manchester and Barcelona
Alina Rzepnikowska

Democracy, Diaspora, Territory
Europe and Cross-Border Politics
Olga Oleinikova and Jumana Bayeh

For more information about this series, please visit: https://www.routledge.com/sociology/series/ASHSER1049

Tracing Asylum Journeys
Transnational Mobility of Non-European Refugees to Canada via Turkey

Uğur Yıldız

LONDON AND NEW YORK

First published 2020
by Routledge
2 Park Square, Milton Park, Abingdon, Oxon OX14 4RN

and by Routledge
52 Vanderbilt Avenue, New York, NY 10017

Routledge is an imprint of the Taylor & Francis Group, an informa business

© 2020 Uğur Yıldız

The right of Uğur Yıldız to be identified as author of this work has been asserted by him in accordance with sections 77 and 78 of the Copyright, Designs and Patents Act 1988.

All rights reserved. No part of this book may be reprinted or reproduced or utilised in any form or by any electronic, mechanical, or other means, now known or hereafter invented, including photocopying and recording, or in any information storage or retrieval system, without permission in writing from the publishers.

Trademark notice: Product or corporate names may be trademarks or registered trademarks, and are used only for identification and explanation without intent to infringe.

British Library Cataloguing-in-Publication Data
A catalogue record for this book is available from the British Library

Library of Congress Cataloging-in-Publication Data
A catalog record has been requested for this book

ISBN: 978-1-138-36455-4 (hbk)
ISBN: 978-0-429-43130-2 (ebk)

Typeset in Times New Roman
by Taylor & Francis Books

Contents

List of illustrations	vi
Series editor's preface	vii
Acknowledgements	x
Table of abbreviations	xii

	Introduction: The asylum journey en route to Canada via Turkey	1
1	The asylum journey and the governance of transnational refugee mobility	21
2	Asylum and resettlement policies as an 'abstract model' for the asylum journey	38
3	The separation phase of the asylum journey	62
4	Practicing liminal space in the 'journey of hope'	83
5	The journey of hope and the incorporation phase of the asylum journey	102
	Conclusion: The asylum journey as the 'journey of hope'	119

Appendix: Interview list	128
References	131
Index	140

Illustrations

Figures

1.1 Mobility's political imagination under sedentarist and nomadic thinkings 36
2.1 The stacked-Venn diagramme illustrating the relational and processual asylum journey en route to Canada via Turkey 39
3.1 Razi train station, the Iranian-Turkish border 75
5.1 Tracing the transnational refugee mobility to Canada via Turkey 102
5.2 Asylum process from arrival in Turkey to resettlement in Canada 103
5.3 Time to fly to Canada, at Istanbul Atatürk Airport 107
5.4 An Iranian singer, Andi, performing at a concert in Ottawa, Canada 115

Maps

3.1 The mapped asylum journey of an Iranian traveller 76
3.2 An Iranian asylum traveller drawing the border crossing via 'illegal' routes 77
3.3 Multitude of routes en route to Canada via Turkey 79
3.4 An Eritrean asylum traveller's mapping of her journey 80

Tables

2.1 Turkey's asylum seekers and refugees based on the country of origin (2010–2017) 49
2.2 Numbers on resettlement of Syrians via Turkey between 2011 and 2018 50
2.3 Canada's resettlement numbers through 31 May, 2018 53
2.4 Resettlement to Canada via Turkey through UNHCR's collaboration through 31 May 2018 56

Series editor's preface

In recent years there has been an increasing amount of research into the 'migrant experience'. This has grown to include not only studies of the point of arrival and settlement but additionally, to focus on the place of departure and the impact of emigration on the sending society. Yet, as Ugur Yıldız so accurately points out in this volume, the migrant journey, a significant constituent of that 'experience', has been somewhat neglected, in spite of being one which frequently determines the eventual destination. The author has sought to enhance what work has been done by putting the migrant odyssey under the theoretical, methodological and empirical microscope. Yıldız favours the term odyssey—defined as meaning 'a long adventurous journey' and 'extended process of change'[1]—to describe the voyage of those who feature in his study, as the word accurately encapsulates the reality of what his subjects undergo in order to reach their promised land. He stresses that the route from departure to arrival is rarely linear; it is often circumlocutionary with stops which may last months or even years before an asylum seeker can become a registered/recognised refugee, and thus able to complete the journey. During this period the individual lives in a liminal state of what Yıldız has termed 'mobistasis'—mobile yet immobile.

One of the main countries to provide a waiting room for those seeking to make the transition from asylum seeker to official refugee is Turkey; the country which provides the hub for the author's research. According to current figures from the UNHCR, at the time of writing Turkey currently hosts 3.6 million registered refugees from Syria, plus 365,000 'persons of concern'[2]—in other words, asylum seekers, or as the author prefers to call them, asylum travellers. The latter have journeyed from a range of countries in the Middle East and North Africa including Iraq, Afghanistan, Iran, Sudan, Eritrea and Somalia. Asylum seekers are unable to take up permanent residence in Turkey but in accordance with the geographical limitation laid down under the Geneva Convention of 1951 they can apply for confirmed refugee status. Once confirmed status is awarded the 'refugee' can begin the process of moving onwards to the final destination and a new life in countries such as Canada, Australia or the

United States. For the purposes of his research the author focused on those who had selected Canada as the chosen goal of their migrant odyssey. He interviewed migrants in countries of departure such as Iran, those in waiting for status decisions in Turkey and (re)settled refugees in Canada.

It is the field work carried out by Yıldız—70 interviews plus participant observation—which puts meat on the bones of the recorded migrant experiences. He explores 'interactions, negotiations and encounters' en route and the reactions to the transnational life in waiting; all these stages in the migrants' journey contributing to the persons that emerge at the end of the odyssey. The interviewees reveal their various motivations for departure; some generated by economic or intellectual ambition, others from fear of persecution on grounds of religion, gender or sexual proclivities. In certain instances, journeys were undertaken legally, while in other cases, unlawful exit had to be negotiated through the purchase of forged documents or with the aid of illegal travel agents or people traffickers.

Arrival at the mobistasis stage brings with it both pleasure and pain. The 'journey of hope' as one interviewee called it is followed by the need to confront bureaucracy and begin the process of acquiring official recognition. Then follows the wait which, as has been noted, can take months or even years—periods of liminality during which joy all too often becomes despair. The final leg of the odyssey is the *incorporation* stage during which the successful applicants, having proved their suitability for settlement in Canada, undergo cultural orientation. However, arrival in Canada is not always a time of happiness: one refugee from Rwanda recalled that it was 'the saddest experience of my life'. Resettlement, and the accompanying life changes in schooling, working and living in a new environment, is a process which is helped by the presence of familial ties and networks. During this time new arrivals will continue to live a transnational existence, maintaining links with the past whilst creating a new life in a new world. At the same time resettled migrants assume a new role, having experienced 'the journey', they can pass on their knowledge to would-be emigrants seeking to make their odysseys.

At a time when, increasingly, migration and migrants are perceived as negatives, this volume highlights the valid reasons for departure and graphically describes the hardships and struggles of the migrant odyssey. The journey is not one undertaken lightly. It is either commenced because emigrants are under immediate threat and, as in the case of Syrian refugees, are fleeing a devastating civil war, or it is begun because individuals are searching for a fulfilling future in a land free from intolerance, limited freedoms and paucity of economic opportunity. A reading of this book informs us of the privations, bureaucracy and disappointments of the migrant journey and introduces us to some of those that have taken on the burden in order to become formally accepted as refugees, and have thus been able to pass through the gateway to a stable future. This is a book which should be read by all those engaged in the field of migration studies and additionally by those who have little understanding of what it means to make the asylum journey.

Anne J Kershen
Queen Mary University of London

Notes

1 See *SOED* (5th Edition). CD. Rom Version.
2 www.UNHCR.org/tr/en/refugees-and-asylum-seekers-in-turkey accessed 26/04/2019

Acknowledgements

This book is the product of a long journey that has proceeded in several phases. I would not have been able to reach my destination without the support and encouragement of the many friends, colleagues, and mentors that I have had the opportunity to meet and work with.

My journey began with my master's degree at Koc University in Istanbul. One of the class readings was William Walters' article on undocumented migrants in the Calais migrant camp; I was tasked with writing a response paper and leading the class discussion about Giorgio Agamben's notion of *homo sacer*, which Walters' article questions. That class discussion turned into a much longer academic endeavour but Agamben's notion of *homo sacer* stayed with me as I began to study the ambiguous and uncertain conditions and experiences of asylum seekers in Turkey. For my research, I conducted semi-structured interviews with asylum applicants and asylum seekers from different countries of origin. With the intention of deepening my understanding, as part of my fieldwork I started to work as an intern at the Association for Solidarity with Asylum Seekers and Refugees (ASAM) in Istanbul from 2011 until the end of my master's degree. At the ASAM office, I taught Turkish to migrant residents in Istanbul from many places: Ethiopia, Iraq, Iran, Somalia, Sudan, the Democratic Republic of Congo among others. Some were asylum seekers, but others were undocumented or 'illegal' migrants who were working to improve their Turkish language skills. I was able to interact with them and to observe and become familiar with their daily routines and experiences, but also the legal, social, financial and psychological difficulties they faced during their stay in Turkey. Towards the end of my master's degree, I also witnessed the resettlement processes of many of my refugee and asylum seeker friends. Due to Turkey's geographical limitation, none could settle permanently in the country. Some were resettled to the United States, others to Canada or Australia.

The second phase of my journey began when I decided to extend my research and to follow further the resettlement and asylum journeys of some of these refugee friends. In 2012, I contacted Professor William Walters, who would become my PhD supervisor, and ran my dissertation project by him. For five years, I pursued many paths—and a few detours along the way—to reach my destination. There have been several challenges and contingencies on the road—PhD courses to complete, comprehensive exams to pass, fieldwork in several countries across different cities to finish, and conferences to attend. At the end of the journey in 2017, I defended my dissertation.

Many thanks are due to those who helped me along the way. First and foremost, I would like to thank the protagonists of this work: the millions of asylum seekers and refugees, past, present and future—most of all, my refugee friends, who shared their experiences along their journey of hope and asylum, so that this work and my journey would be possible. I sincerely wish all of them all the very best.

Special thanks also go to my academic inspiration, Professor William Walters, and my great mentor Professor Deniz Sert. I am grateful to Dr Simon Watmough for his patience in revising the manuscript and providing insightful comments that helped me finalize the polished version of this book. I would like to thank Professor James Millner and Professor Peter Nyers as my committee members for their very insightful comments, my family, my friends Deniz Karci and Aysen Ustubici at Koc University, my friends JP, Jamie, Darlene and Kellen who hosted me during my PhD journey in Ottawa, and my friend Mustafa who listened to me almost every day with patience.

And, finally, it is the end of this journey, but not the odyssey. A special thanks to my wife, Ilkay, this gruelling journey would be unimaginable without her. Thanks for caring for me and providing a comfortable life for us.

Table of abbreviations

ASAM	Association for Solidarity with Asylum Seekers and Refugees
BIHE	Baha'i Institute for Higher Education
CBP	United States Customs and Border Protection
CIC	Canadian Department of Citizenship and Immigration
CCI	Catholic Centre for Immigrants
DGMM	Directorate General of Migration Management
DRC	Democratic Republic of the Congo
GRE	Graduate Record Exam
IOM	International Organisation for Migration
IRPA	Immigration and Refugee Protection Act
IRB	Immigration Review Board
LFIP	Law on Foreigners and International Protection
KADER	Chaldean Assyrian International Humanitarian Association
LGBTQ	Lesbian, Gay, Bisexual, Transgender & Queer
LINC	Language Instruction for the Newcomers to Canada
MoI	Turkish Ministry of Interior
NGO	Non-Government Organisation
RAP	Resettlement Assistance Program
UDHR	Universal Declaration of Human Rights
UNHCR	United Nations High Commissioner for Refugees

Introduction
The asylum journey en route to Canada via Turkey

The mass movement of Syrians towards 'safe' countries since 2011 has cast the long—and often dangerous—journeys taken by refugees en route to destination countries into sharp relief. Governments, policymakers and local and international non-governmental organizations (NGOs) all clamour to direct attention to the challenge posed by millions of refugees seeking refuge from the horrors of violent conflict. In the academy, the refugee 'crisis' has captured the attention of disciplines as diverse as political science, law, international relations, sociology, and anthropology. At the same time, people on the move need aid and logistical services and the operations the many local and international NGOs providing such assistance have mushroomed accordingly. In short, the refugee 'crisis' has become ubiquitous. More to the point, all this activity and interest is focused on—and directly related to—the question of refugee movement. And this has paved the way for a new body of research with a distinct focus of interest to emerge within the field of refugee studies: refugee journeys.

Research in the field of migration and refugee studies has been largely *policy-focused*, specifically examining the policies of settlement and resettlement countries (Joly, 1996; Squire, 2009; Mountz, 2010; Hamlin, 2014; Abass & Ippolito, 2014). At the same time, it has been *destination-oriented*, looking at the experiences of refugees once they reach their country of resettlement. Yet the journey taken by refugees *as an experience in itself* has received comparatively little attention. This is puzzling. After all, mass refugee and asylum migration towards Europe from Africa and the Middle East is widely recognized as involving both novel and established translocal networks and social ties among those on the move en route to the countries of resettlement. More to the point, it involves terrible tragedy. Almost every day in 2015 and 2016, we saw media reports of migrant boats capsized in the Mediterranean Sea with the loss of thousands of lives. This tragedy underscores the necessity of exploring migrant journeys anew: empirically, methodologically and theoretically.

Tracing the Asylum Journey is about the transnational odyssey of refugees, their practices and experiences en route, and the various pathways and approaches these travellers take along the way. In particular, it charts the

2   Introduction

passage from various 'refugee-producing' countries of origin to one particular 'refugee-receiving' country of resettlement (in this case, Canada) via a single country of asylum (Turkey). In so doing, it details the series of negotiations that take place through the refugee odyssey—namely, between the practices of asylum seeking in Turkey and resettlement to Canada, and between asylum travellers and the various states they come into contact with as they travel. It also outlines the interaction among asylum travellers themselves while en route, in Turkey (as the country of asylum) and in Canada (as the country of resettlement).

While the Syrian crisis serves to frame the discussion, the monograph does not focus specifically on Syrian refugees. It draws, rather, on the asylum experience of travellers from a diverse range of countries, including Afghanistan, Iran, Iraq, the Democratic Republic of the Congo (DRC), Eritrea, Ethiopia, Somalia, and Sudan, through the method of in-depth, semi-structured interviews with nationals from these countries. And while the book focuses very much on the contemporary experience, it also considers the historical context—namely, a series of waves of non-European asylum travellers to Canada via Turkey since at least the early 1980s. At that time, a massive flow of Iranian citizens was departing for 'safe' or third countries via Turkey in the wake of Khomeini's Islamic Revolution. Then, from the early 1990s—after the first Gulf War—and again following the 2003 US invasion of Iraq, mass movements of Iraqi nationals towards third countries via Turkey were again observed. More recently, after the Syrian crisis erupted in 2011, the largest ever migration flow to Turkey—some three million people and counting—fled in search of protection from war and violent chaos.

The empirical focus in this volume is necessarily limited. It focuses on the cases of Turkey and Canada—and the collaboration of both with the United Nations High Commissioner for Refugees (UNHCR). It does so for one specific reason: Turkey's geographical limitation[1] on asylum travellers who arrive in Turkey from non-European countries of origin and who cannot remain indefinitely in Turkey or settle permanently. As will be detailed further through the book, Turkey's policy of geographical limitation acts as the delimiting factor here, insofar as it creates the conditions whereby refugees from outside Europe who arrive in Turkey and are recognized by the UNHCR have only temporary protection and must be resettled to third countries. Canada has been a long-established partner with Turkey and the UNHCR in this schema of transnational asylum governance. Canada resettles UNHCR-recognized refugees from Turkey through both government-assisted and privately sponsored refugee resettlement programmes. The selection process is based on interviews conducted by visa officers at the Canadian embassy in Ankara. A similar framework applies for other resettlement countries like the United States and Australia. Like Canada, both countries operate refugee resettlement programmes via Turkey through the UNHCR's Ankara office. And the UNHCR runs a similar programme for resettlement of refugees living in camps in Lebanon and Jordan. It covers before the period of September 2018 when the UNHCR has handed over the responsibility of refugee status determination for non-European asylum applicants to the Turkish Directorate General of Migration Management (DGMM).[2] All that being said, it is crucial to note that this is one particular dimension of the global refugee protection regime and it operates differently in other regions, although those are beyond the scope of the present book.

Tracing the Asylum Journey thus places the journey taken by asylum travellers at the centre of a series of research fields—political science, sociology, and refugee studies—by adopting a novel *journey as method* approach. A growing literature now examines migrant and refugee journeys as experiences in themselves, including these recent books (Khosravi, 2010; Andersson, 2014; Kaytaz, 2016; Schapendonk, 2016; Suter, 2017). *Tracing the Asylum Journey* therefore does not promise to reinvent the wheel on this question or reveal hidden secrets in the domain of the global refugee regime. What it does offer are robust theoretical and methodological reflections on—and empirical analysis of—the asylum journey, in which the production, reproduction and diffusion of knowledge—what Brigden (2013) has helpfully termed 'mobile knowledge'—is embedded. Most current research treats the mobility of refugees and 'irregular' migrants as relatively self-evident. In this book, the journey is approached as a *method*, and treated as a puzzle that needs to be solved. But what *precisely* is a journey? And what is an *asylum journey*? What are the various heterogeneous practices, interactions and negotiations, that asylum applicants encounter? How is the journey—understood in part as a site of mobile knowledge—produced and reproduced in time and space? What are the bureaucratic mechanisms, practices, and negotiations that officially designate the direction of the asylum journey?

One innovative aspect in the present book is its examination of the production of knowledge and its exchange among past, present, and future asylum travellers. Mobility has typically been framed and theorized within a distinct conceptual repertoire, one that emphasizes *force* and *involuntary departure* (Turton, 2003; Hathaway, 2007). What might the refugee literature gain if we move beyond this idea of forced, involuntary movement and approach the journey as method and 'as a living, micro-cultural, micro-political system in motion' (Gilroy, 1993, p. 3)? Indeed, shifting to the idea of a 'system in motion' foregrounds a series of questions about the journey regarding *sites and practices of governance* (border regimes and institutions encountered by travellers); the *shifting labels and identities* attributed to travellers as they pass through the various stages of the odyssey; the *production and reproduction of relevant knowledge*; and the *tactics of travellers* on the route. Thinking of the refugee odyssey in this way foregrounds the notion of *asylum habitus*, understood in the Bourdieusian sense as 'systems of durable, transposable dispositions, structured structures' (Bourdieu, 1977, p. 72). I will detail how habitus is to be employed in the book further in Chapter 1.

4   Introduction

In this book, I argue that the standard way of viewing the journey—i.e. as a homogeneous phenomenon—masks the existence of something very important. Namely, that the odyssey is always a multiplicity of routes and encounters, in which repercussions of the visible and the invisible, the forced and the unforced, and the calculated and the hasty have been historically formed, structured, and negotiated—not only among asylum travellers and institutional mechanisms, but also between past, present, and future travellers in an infinite asylum journey. In so doing, I recognize that each asylum odyssey contains multiple journeys within it and multitudes of routes that are followed and experienced. In short, while the frame of 'asylum journey' may seem to imply homogeneity, the diversified routes and differentiated pathways that each traveller undertakes en route to Canada via Turkey, mean that each is a unique experience in itself—that is to say, a heterogeneous, complex, and varied phenomenon.

This is not to say that each traveller's experience during the asylum journey is purely episodic. Rather, as my empirical chapters illustrate, one experience may differ significantly from another due to changing bureaucratic regulations, new border technologies, or updated information (or, indeed, misinformation) travellers gather—say, regarding safer (or riskier) routes or better options for resettlement. This may be the case, even as the underlying reasoning for the journey remains the same: resettlement to Canada by seeking asylum in Turkey.

Conventional approaches to the mobility of refugees tend to foreground certain aspects, such as the regulations in a given state's system of asylum governance and the experiences of individuals—as well as presenting the move as direct and linear, i.e., from refugee-producing to refugee-receiving country. *Tracing the Asylum Journey*, in contrast, draws attention to the route itself, in the process revealing the importance of the paths taken along it—as well as the landscapes traversed, and the identities/labels arbitrarily attributed, along the way. The book in no way underestimates the importance of the bureaucratic aspects of the journey—namely Turkey and Canada's immigration and asylum regulations and the global refugee regime structured by the Geneva Convention, the UNHCR, and its signatory states. At the same time, it does not place the legal asylum and immigration regime at the centre of analysis of transnational refugee mobility to Canada via Turkey. Rather, it presents the journey as a series of contingencies—that is to say, *interactions, negotiations* and *encounters*.

Let us briefly consider these different types of contingent events, starting with *interactions*. The asylum journey to Canada via Turkey is based first on interactions between asylum travellers themselves, both in time and in space. In other words, interactions between travellers of the *past* who have already experienced the journey, have reached the destination, and have much knowledge/information about it to pass on; those experiencing it in the *present*; and those who are yet to depart but who will do so in *future* and who will seek knowledge about the journey from those who have ventured before and who will make choices along the way based on the information/misinformation so acquired.

Second, the asylum journey is a series of *negotiations*. These are multiple, occurring between institutions and agencies, states and the asylum travellers themselves. So, we observe, for example, negotiations between the key migration agencies (the UNHCR and the International Organization for Migration (IOM), but also others) and the relevant countries (Turkey and Canada), but also between the countries themselves and between asylum travellers and the agencies and the two states.

Third, the asylum journey occurs through a series of *bureaucratic encounters* between asylum travellers and border mechanisms, the administrative apparatus in Turkey as the country of asylum (and that of Canada, the country of resettlement), and, of course, the UNHCR. As introduced above, in this volume, I argue that this series of interactions, negotiations, and encounters is largely formed and shaped through the production and reproduction of knowledge, and the diffusion of that produced and reproduced knowledge through time and space—in other words, mobile knowledge. This mobile knowledge, moreover, is not fixed and homogeneous. Mobile knowledge is, rather, flexible and dynamic. And it is produced and diffused in multiple ways as information/misinformation is generated and circulated among asylum travellers.

This book sets out to make a significant contribution to methodological debates and research practices. It bears repeating that the researcher faces a series of challenges in the field when studying the refugee/asylum odyssey. The journey itself is a densely packed assemblage of contingencies, as mentioned above. How, for example, is the researcher to unpack these contingencies, to navigate the many varieties of regulations and arbitrary interpretations of what or who a refugee is in different domains of governance? Moreover, the researcher is faced with the challenge of studying a phenomenon that is not fixed but rather a living micro-cultural and micro-political system in constant motion and perpetual becoming. This is Gilroy's 'system in motion', mentioned above. I argue throughout that focusing on the experiences and narratives of asylum travellers is one key methodological response to these challenges. It allows for a closer interrogation of arbitrarily attributed labels as well as the complex and diversified practices of institutions and asylum travellers themselves (Zetter, 2007). I argue that once asylum infrastructure is 'unpacked' or 'unfolded', key theoretical and methodological advances can be made in research on the refugee journey. Those advances can be normative as well, when a more sophisticated approach sheds much-needed light on the exclusionary, inclusionary, and transformative domain of asylum. Disaggregating the journey in this way highlights the significance of micro calculations, negotiations, encounters, and practices which may otherwise be obscured—or at least difficult to see.

More concretely, *Tracing the Asylum Journey* has three specific aims. First, it presents an advance on our theoretical and methodological approach to the

6 Introduction

analysis of refugee journeys. There is a vibrant debate in migration and refugee studies on the mobility of refugees. However, the conceptual field is rather thin and limited. Building on insights from several fields—refugee and migration studies, border and security studies, and transnationalism studies—and conceptual toolkits drawn from sociology, political science, international relations, and anthropology, the book seeks to enrich the conceptual field and advance the theoretical horizon of refugee journey analysis.

Second, it offers a significant intervention in—and an important contribution to—the mobility–immobility nexus in refugee studies. Understanding the fluid dynamics of asylum seeking and resettlement is not possible if we treat the refugee odyssey as a linear, straightforward movement from point A to point B, from sending country to receiving one. Rather, it involves multiple paths, gateways, entry and exit points, and territories en route to the country of resettlement. Crucially, the journey involves not only mobility, but also immobility and/or periods of stasis—breaks that are, in many cases, a natural part of the journey. A detailed, microanalysis of the act of asylum seeking and resettlement is important if we are to understand the regular, flexible and contingent practices, forms, and norms in the course of the asylum journey. This book thus challenges how we imagine the refugee mobility under the conceptual frame of 'forced migration'—as a linear movement from the country of origin to a safe one. It also critically interrogates the concept of 'transit' migration and associated attributed labels—namely, how we categorize individuals as 'transit migrants', and how we classify both 'transit' and 'destination' countries.

Third, this volume aims to advance a more detailed understanding of the asylum journey as an empirical phenomenon, combining theory and an empirical case study with a highly elaborated methodological and conceptual toolkit. This book thus offers a comprehensive resource for migration and refugee scholars and students conducting research in this area. The empirical case study it provides—asylum seeking in Turkey and resettlement to Canada—is both relevant and illustrative. As the book will explore in greater depth in later chapters, Turkey is a liminal space in the migratory process of asylum travellers on the way to resettle in Canada. However, asserting that Turkey is, in fact, best thought of as merely a transit or stepping stone for refugees is untenable.

The volume draws on multi-sited ethnographic fieldwork by the author—semi-structured interviews and participant observation—conducted in Istanbul (Turkey), Ottawa (Canada), and Tehran (Iran). Each chapter focuses on one dimension of the asylum journey, largely but not exclusively, framed in terms of bureaucratic stages. The first is the stage of *separation*, undertaken when the asylum traveller departs the country of origin. The second is the *liminal* phase in Turkey, and the third is the *incorporation* phase in Canada. Some of the individual journeys that are detailed in the present volume are used to provide an illustration of the odyssey, based on the narrative of the personal experience and practices along the way. Rather than seeing this as a mapping of the journey, it instead should be read as a form of what critical scholars have called *anti-mapping*, a concept that will be discussed in further detail later in the chapter. In anti-mapping, the asylum travellers' own interpretations of movement from home country to resettlement country is set against the official mapping of that mobility through the various points of asylum regime governance—that of the states and the international agencies—along the way.

The present chapter proceeds as follows. The first section briefly details the concepts that the reader will encounter throughout the book. The second presents the research rationale for treating asylum as an assembled journey and outlines in more detail what the monograph is about. The subsequent section presents the research questions. Section four details the choice of empirical cases for the book: Turkey and Canada. The overall research methodology and the methods used throughout the fieldwork are presented in the fifth section. The concluding section provides a brief outline of the structure of the book.

The use of concepts

The intention in this book is to map the mobility of refugees as they endeavour to realize resettlement in Canada by seeking asylum in Turkey. In so doing, it hopes to reveal how transnational mobility 'engages the whole of the senses in bending time and space...taps into the long and variegated history of the unleashing of performance, leads us to understand movement as a potential, challenges the privileging of meaning' (Thrift, 2008, p. 14). Moreover, it suggests that mobility is not simply a physical movement in the literal sense.

We begin with the two central concepts—*refugee* and *asylum seeker*—that the reader will encounter throughout the book. The term refugee[3] is used in line with contemporary usage, as laid out in the 1951 Convention relating to the Status of Refugees (hereafter the Geneva Convention), introduced after the establishment of the UNHCR in 1950. The definition of 'refugee' as laid out in the original Convention document—under the now famous rubric of a 'well-founded fear of persecution'—was limited in terms of geography, referring then to any person fleeing a European country due to events prior to 1951. The UNHCR sought to revise the 1951 definition to remove these limits of time and geography through the 1967 Additional Protocol to the Convention, however leaving the decision to remove the limitations to signatory states.[4] More concretely, the Convention defined a refugee as a person who leaves his/her country of origin based on a well 'fear of persecution' on account of his or her nationality, religion, ethnicity or membership of a particular social or political group. It is crucial, then, to be clear that refugee status is a *legal identity* for persons who depart their country of origin to countries of refuge in accordance with the definition of the 1951 Geneva Convention.

8 *Introduction*

In contrast, the term *asylum seeker* is a bureaucratic—and not a legal—one. It is applied to a person who has formally lodged an application for asylum and for whom the bureaucratic process of refugee status determination has begun (Goodwin-Gill, 2008). The individual concerned will have left his or her country of origin to seek refuge or sanctuary but is waiting for his or her legal recognition as a refugee by the UNHCR. Moreover, across the world today the number of asylum seekers well exceeds the number of refugees within the contemporary refugee regime.

Most of my respondents are not aware of these fine conceptual distinctions. They simply call themselves refugees, whether or not they have yet lodged an application with the UNHCR for asylum. Therefore, I use the term *asylum traveller* to refer to individuals who have commenced (or are preparing for) the asylum journey as a way to cut through the fact that the identities attributed to persons en route—such as *undocumented/documented, irregular/regular, illegal/legal,* and *asylum seeker/refugee*—are not fixed and static (Crawley & Skleparis, 2018). Using the term asylum traveller thus moves us beyond these attributed distinctions and labels, which seek to divide people into strict categories. There is also an analytical rationale. Combining two labels underlines the relational, relative, spatial—as well as situational—nature of the phenomenon. The term asylum highlights the bureaucratic aspect in the odyssey, while the label *traveller* connotes the agency involved in the process—the fact that choices are made by people in starting and proceeding along the journey. Thus, asylum traveller is a more appropriate term, since it emphasizes both the agency of individuals and the autonomy of the journey. This is in line with Nelly Richard's depiction of the body as 'the physical agent of the structures of everyday experiences' and as 'the producer of dreams, the transmitter and receiver of cultural messages, a creature of habits, a desiring machine, a repository of memories, an actor in the theater of power, a tissue of affects and feelings' (Richard, 2000, p. 188).

Another concept—and one that makes an innovative contribution to the field—is that of *mobistasis*. This notion is based on the nexus between stasis and mobility, as well as the uncertain and indeterminate breaks, pauses, and stops in the course of the ongoing asylum journey. More concretely, mobistasis refers to an episodic passage of stillness and perpetual becoming in terms of legal statuses and social identit(ies), and the ongoing production, reproduction and diffusion of knowledge and transnational/translocal networks in a state of stasis/immobility during as-yet-unconcluded journeys (Yıldız & Sert, 2019). Thus, as foreshadowed above, instead of labelling Turkey as a 'transit country' en route to Canada, in this volume I frame it as a space of mobistasis. This more properly locates Turkey as a country of asylum located 'between' a non-European 'home' country—such as Iran, Iraq, Afghanistan, Eritrea, Ethiopia, Somalia, Sudan, Syria, and the DRC—and the country of resettlement. In this asylum journey, upon their arrival in Turkey and interview with the UNHCR asylum travellers have to stay in one of the satellite cities designated by Turkey's Ministry of Interior (MoI).[5] Seeking asylum in Turkey is the commonality of individuals from different countries of origin during the asylum journey towards the country of resettlement.

I approach the practice of seeking asylum in Turkey to realize resettlement in Canada via the UNHCR's operations in Turkey through Pierre Bourdieu's (1977, p. 72) concept of habitus, which refers to 'systems of durable, transposable dispositions, structured structures'.[6] In adopting the concept of habitus as a framing device, the spatial and specific attention to the journey of refugees produces an empirical image of how refugees arrive at borders, to the vehicles and networks, and to the country of asylum and the country of resettlement through the formation of an asylum habitus. Throughout the book, asylum habitus refers to the routinization of seeking asylum in the context of journeys of refugees towards Canada via Turkey. The concept addresses a structured and motivating structure of asylum travellers who produce, reproduce, and diffuse knowledge on the asylum journey among past, present, and future asylum travellers with their established translocal solidarity networks based on sharing produced knowledge. By following the odyssey from 'home' country towards Canada via Turkey, I demonstrate how asylum travellers produce, reproduce, and diffuse knowledge en route by shifting tactics to either *comport with* or *mitigate* the official and bureaucratic governance strategies of asylum, which formally manage and regulate the asylum journey at the transnational level, and adjust the speed of mobility.

In addition, I use terms such as *journey* and *routes* in specific ways. First, they allow me to address the physical mobility of travellers and their interaction with other actors within the refugee mobility system—including local and international organizations and human smugglers as 'travel agents'. More than this, they permit me to shed much-needed light on the encounters, negotiations, and contestations of which form part of the global refugee protection system. The second reason I use these terms is to ground the analytical framework of journey as method, which is an attempt to move beyond the political imaginary of refugee mobility as the refugee-producing and refugee-receiving states. The formulation of the asylum journey with its route in the transnational refugee journey helps us to think of migration beyond the beyond the standard political imaginary, which reduces refugee mobility to a simple and linear transit from point A to point B, from refugee-producing to refugee-receiving state (Hyndman, 1997). It emphasizes the importance of routes, pathways, cities, hubs, and complex landscapes in the migration system.

Most of the journeys taken by the various respondents who have participated in this research have no clear starting point. Moreover, a traveller who undertakes the asylum odyssey experiences multiple passages and crossings within one overall journey. This also implies the same person will experience mobistasis along the way—namely, several pauses and periods of waiting throughout his/her asylum journey (Brigden & Mainwaring, 2016). In other words, the first, second—or even third—port of call may not be the final destination for any given asylum traveller. The traveller can thus 'arrive' many times in a new landing point without yet arriving at her final destination. Therefore, this specific journey en route to Canada via Turkey is important to move beyond the temporal, time-limited and physical aspect of the journey due to the uncertainty in stopping, waiting, and continuing the mobility.

Asylum as an assembled journey

Refugee journeys have their own codes and norms at the transnational level that are framed by the global refugee protection system, which is itself underpinned by the relevant conventions, the UNHCR, and the practices of its signatory states. And, as foreshadowed earlier in the chapter, even though journeys are regulated and in many ways routinized at the transnational level, they are neither linear nor direct movements from point A to point B. Rather, they embody multiple border crossings, pauses and interruptions, periods of movement and stillness, and various detours, back and forth, with or without proper travel documents. Furthermore, as mentioned, journeys consist of a series of encounters—between asylum travellers and border mechanisms, the administrative apparatus in Turkey, the country of asylum (and that of Canada, the country of resettlement), and of course the UNHCR—in which the (re-)production and diffusion of knowledge structured by an asylum habitus are key.

As mentioned above, when we speak of the asylum journey, we tend to regard it as a linear movement from the country of origin to the country of asylum and/or resettlement. This view, no doubt a product of a limited political imaginary, obscures the fact that the asylum odyssey is not some point-to-point step but rather—as laid out above—an *assemblage*—a collection of *interactions, negotiations* and *encounters*. This assemblage therefore calls for disaggregation. Thus, we must 'unpack' or 'unfold' the involvement of agents and actors such as UNHCR and countries of asylum/resettlement along with IOM, the domestic and global NGOs, human smugglers, and border politics. In so doing we find, first, that the UNHCR's global refugee norms determine the eligibility of an asylum applicant to continue the 'journey of hope' (an idea that will be explored in further detail in later chapters) to Canada. Second, Turkey's asylum governance excludes non-European asylum applicants by including them in accordance with Turkey's geographical limitation on non-European asylum applicants. Third, Canada's resettlement governance accepts some of the UNHCR-recognized refugees into Canada's territorial space through the process of selection based on the refugees' potential self-sufficiency and her or his language abilities, profession, age, health, and family ties and social support network in the potential place of resettlement. These are the criteria that Canada's visa officers abroad use to screen potential UNHCR-recognized refugees applying to resettle there (UNHCR, 2013).

Therefore, this is a journey of encounters that entails jumping through what in the vernacular we might call 'bureaucratic hoops'. Disaggregating the journey is thus crucial if we are to fully grasp the micro practices of asylum travellers en route as they essentially negotiate these obstacles—underpinned by information/knowledge derived from past and present asylum travellers—as well as their experiences in the country of asylum and resettlement more generally. Moreover, the journey needs to be de-generalized since—as has been reiterated throughout the chapter—the odyssey often involves multiple passages and crossings within a journey, and one traveller's path will differ from another's. More importantly, the practices that each traveller engages during their journey will likely differ from those of others as mobile knowledge shifts for different asylum journeys in time and space.

What is an asylum journey?

Considering the intention of *Tracing the Asylum Journey* to unpack the asylum odyssey and to shed much-needed light on the various encounters, passages and crossings within, a simple but crucial question arises: what *precisely is an asylum journey*? Following Mainwaring and Brigden (2016, p. 244), I define the asylum journey as 'an experience with indeterminate beginnings and ends' that 'transcends easy conceptual borders, as well as physical ones'. In other words, a traveller who has crossed the border without documents can obtain legal status, at least until the completion of the UNHCR's refugee status-determination process.

In *Border as Method, or the Multiplication of Labor*, Mezzadra and Neilson (2013) question the conventional view of 'the border as a neutral line' and that the 'method is a set of pregiven, neutral techniques that can be applied to diverse objects without fundamentally altering the ways in which they are constructed and understood' (p. 17). They then lay out their 'border as method' approach which 'provides productive insights on the tensions and conflicts that blur the line between inclusion and exclusion, as well as on the profoundly changing code of social inclusion in the present' (Mezzadra & Neilson, 2013, p. viii). In line with their border as method approach, I take a journey as method approach to explore the asylum journeys of non-European asylum travellers en route to Canada via Turkey. Like border as method, journey as method is 'something more than methodological' (Mezzadra & Neilson, 2013, p. 17). It also offers an opportunity for critical interrogation. Through the border as method formula, Mezzadra and Neilson (2013) adopt what they call 'militant investigation', which is appraised by activists and critical scholars in the domain of migration studies.

Militant investigation works against the 'profiling of migrations as stable targets of research' and it aims to reveal 'the turbulence of migration practices, the contested politics migrants encounter and produce, the contingent "existence strategies"' (Gapelli, Tazzioli, Mezzadra, Kasparek & Peano, 2015, p. 63). Second, militant investigation accords with the need to shed light on what Walters has usefully termed 'viapolitics', unearthing the 'power asymmetries that make migrants into subjects of migration knowledge production' (Walters, 2015, p. 64). Both aims are significant to foreground the agency and autonomy of asylum travellers' mobility by detailing the specific tactics they pursue and the elaborated decisions they make in negotiating their journey. A militant investigation that adopts the approach of the journey as method is thus concerned with the 'question of politics [and] the kinds of social worlds and subjectivities produced' en route (Mezzadra & Neilson, 2013, p. 17).

I do this for two reasons: one broadly empirical–methodological and the other critical– theoretical. Adopting the approach of journey as method allows me to move beyond 'tricky conceptual overlapping and confusion through the punctual analysis of concrete borderscapes' (Mezzadra & Neilson, 2013, p. 16). In other words, the journey itself is a method that helps us better understand the concrete experiences and practices occurring through interactions and negotiations among migrants themselves, and between asylum travellers and the various bureaucratic mechanisms they encounter.

It is also significant in critical–theoretical terms, allowing me to shed much-needed light on the processes of power at play and to critically contemplate the interaction and encounter between the tactics of migrants devised en route. This foregrounds the underlying politics of the odyssey—in other words, the viapolitics. The notion of viapolitics speaks not only to hardships encountered along the journey, but also contemplates the factors that the see the status of legal/illegal imposed on—or attributed to—travellers' behaviour and circumstances as they negotiate the strategies of control deployed by national and global asylum policies (Walters, 2015). It also reminds us that the journey and its various passages and crossings are, in Gilroy's terms (1993), a micro-political 'system in motion'. The asylum journey is, then, a moving encounter between states and migrants. During this encounter, it is not only refugees and asylum seekers that are 'on the move', but also institutional and state practices/regulations on asylum and immigration, which are constantly changing to meet new political and logistical circumstances (Nyers, 2006).

Methodology

Given the idea of the asylum odyssey as a 'system in motion', the methodological focus of the book is an empirical case study that draws on qualitative data collection with semi-structured interviews conducted with asylum travellers in Turkey and Canada. The intention with the qualitative research method is to capture the unique practices and experiences during the asylum journeys of non-European asylum travellers who seek asylum in Turkey for resettlement to Canada. It is also my intention to trace these journeys, and to present as far as possible the authentic and novel journey narratives of the respondents themselves.

In this sense, I conducted two periods of fieldwork in Turkey and Canada that I will detail below. The first field trip took place from 2014 to 2016 as part of my doctoral dissertation project. During the first field trip, I was participant observer in Istanbul (Turkey) and Ottawa (Canada), and took a train from Kayseri (Turkey) to Iran's capital Tehran, spending around two weeks in total there. By tracing the routes of asylum travellers, my own research odyssey—from Canada to Turkey and from Turkey to Iran, and then from Tehran towards Ottawa via Turkey—has produced a multi-sited ethnographic project and an *ethnographic journey* in itself. This contributes to our understanding of the transnational mobility of refugees by pushing the methodological boundaries of the discipline of political science.

The second tranche of fieldwork, in 2017–2018, followed the completion of my PhD and my return to Turkey. During the second tranche, I conducted interviews with Syrian refugees in Istanbul and Aksaray.[7] Semi-structured interviews in both field sites are the main techniques utilized for this project to collect information on the cases to bring narratives, practices, and tactics of travellers and strategies of migration governance during their encounters and negotiations.

In addition to the semi-structured interviews, the book foregrounds the maps drawn by some respondents' personal asylum odysseys to reveal complicated, diverse, and heterogenous dimensions of each journey. As touched on above, the personal drawings of asylum journeys can be regarded as an example of 'anti-mapping'.[8] It is anti-mapping since it necessarily eschews abstract standardization (the concluding theme of map-making) in favour of individualization, diversity and heterogeneity in the representations of travellers. In line with Henri Lefebvre's (1991) neo-Marxist reading on the production of space as 'the perceived', 'the conceived', and 'the lived', asylum travellers' drawings of the journey illustrate how space is produced and reproduced and lived and practiced by them an as opposed to the abstract maps drawn by policy makers other institutions. It is therefore anti-mapping since it opposes the asylum journey's linear image as the movement between refugee-sending and refugee-receiving countries. The maps drawn by asylum travellers emphasize the necessity of paying greater attention to the practices/tactics employed by the latter themselves. They also demonstrate that the asylum journey is an aggregation of encounters and negotiations played out on a canvas made up of formal/abstract mapping (bureaucratic regulations that formally structure movement) and informal representations of the journey (the lived experience of individuals on the odyssey) in the transnational journey to Canada via Turkey.

Interviews along with the personal maps are significant tools 'to uncover a deeper level of information to capture meaning, process, and context, where explanation involves describing and understanding people as conscious and social human beings' (Landman, 2008, p. 21). Interviews conducted with asylum travellers provide access to the 'memories' of past travellers—of my respondents' friends and family members who took the same journey long ago. This highlights the multi-layered aspect of the asylum journey and demonstrates how the particular routes in the odyssey change over time (e.g., in the past, Pakistan, not Turkey, was a first port of call in seeking asylum for resettlement to Canada).

Finally, I also covered the secondary literature on regulations in the domain of migration and the refugee policies of Turkey and Canada. In terms of statistical data, I benefited from Turkey's Directorate General for Migration Management (DGMM), Citizenship and Immigration Canada (CIC), and the UNHCR's population and demography statistics on asylum seekers and refugees in Turkey and resettlement statistics for Canada.

Choosing the cases: Turkey and Canada

Let me turn now to briefly lay out why I have chosen to focus on Turkey and Canada for the present book. Limits of time and space mean that no book can cover all aspects of the global refugee regime. Thus, rather than adopting a comparative case study design, *Tracing the Asylum Journey* zeroes in on a narrower empirical frame of reference—namely, one country of asylum (Turkey) and one of resettlement (Canada). As will be seen in detail in later chapters, a central theme in the book is the idea of geographical limitation on refugee status determination. For now, it suffices to say that this is a factor that strongly favours the selection of Turkey in the study. In terms of the generalisability of the findings presented in this volume, my claims are necessarily limited. For example, I do not claim that the selected cases represent the global refugee regime in its totality.

More concretely, case selection is designed to support the methodology outlined above and thus to move the book beyond the traditional paradigm of refugee mobility as linear transit from 'sending' to 'receiving' country. It also aims to reinforce my treatment of the asylum journey as an assemblage that needs to be disaggregated to demonstrate the multiplication of routes and transit points.

Furthermore, selecting Turkey and Canada as case countries allows me to present the practices and experiences of asylum travellers both in the country of asylum and the country of resettlement. In terms of the two country's geographical location, whereas Turkey is located between the Middle East and Europe (and, in fact, bridges the two), Canada has only the United States as a neighbour to the south. These geopolitical differences have a direct impact on patterns of migration and mobility for both countries.

More concretely, I chose Turkey mainly for the geographic reasons sketched above. In the nexus of mobility and space, Turkey's physical location 'between' the Middle East and Africa and Europe matters. Three related dimensions of this are relevant. In the first place, Turkey's geopolitical location means it is a 'natural' space of migration along the route towards Europe. However, Turkey is also a space of asylum on the way to resettlement into the United States, Canada, and/or Australia. In other words, the country has historically attracted thousands of asylum applicants and has become a hub for non-European asylum applicants including Iranians, Iraqis, Afghanis, and recently Syrians.

This leads to the second element, which is Turkey's geographical limitation on refugee status determination. As mentioned briefly above and will be elaborated in more detail in Chapter 2, the original 1951 Geneva Convention contained both temporal and geographic limitations built in. The Convention defined a refugee as a person fleeing one of the European states due to events before 1 January 1951. The Convention's 1967 Additional Protocol was developed to revise these restrictions to make the scope more general. Turkey chose to retain the geographical limitation against non-European asylum applicants but did accede to lifting the temporal one, as was its sovereign right under the terms of the 1967 agreement (Kirişci, 1996a). The third element, then, derives from the second—namely, that Turkey's geographical limitation has led UNHCR to be more active within Turkey in processing refugee status determination and refugee resettlement to third countries. Thus, Turkey is a major collaborative partner in a regional asylum governance system.

I chose Canada on the grounds of its complementary place within the aforementioned global asylum governance structures. Canada has long been a resettlement country operating through its visa officers abroad, who work in close collaboration with the UNHCR and the IOM. UNHCR's involvement in the refugee status-determination process in Turkey provides a type of filtration process for Canada to operate its government-assisted refugee resettlement in a more controlled and regulated way in the selection of UNHCR-recognized refugees from Turkey. Thus, Canada's government-assisted refugee resettlement programme can be regarded as an extension of Canada's inland asylum governance abroad, in this case to Turkey. More importantly, Turkey's geographical limitation combined with Canada's refugee resettlement programme establishes a transnational border crossing structure under the global refugee regime.

This structure of case selection thus disaggregates a system of global refugee governance into its constituent parts, which thus supports the methodology of journey as method outlined above. However, there are additional, more quotidian reasons to select the two countries that reflect my personal experience and research trajectory. It has been much easier to pursue doctoral research in Canada and return to Turkey for field trips on professional, practical and logistical grounds.

Conducting interviews and access to data

The present research grew out of two separate tranches of fieldwork, with a total of seventy semi-structured interviews conducted in three countries. As mentioned, the first tranche took place during my dissertation research, with fieldwork between April 2014 and September 2016 in Istanbul (Turkey) and Ottawa (Canada), as well as a short train trip to Tehran (Iran). The second phase of the research took place in Istanbul and Aksaray (Turkey) upon the completion of my PhD in 2017, when I returned to Turkey as was able to conduct further interviews with Syrian individuals. Interviews were conducted prior to the change in September 2018 asylum governance in which the UNHCR has handed over the responsibility of registration of non-Syrian applicants to the DGMM (see endnote 2).

First tranche (2014–2016)

The first tranche of fieldwork (2014–2016) involved multi-sited field visits in Turkey, Canada and Iran. At this time, the bulk of Canada's resettlement programme via Turkey involved resettling the Iranian and Iraqi refugees. Canada only began to resettle large numbers of Syrians from Turkey, Lebanon and Jordan in late 2015. Therefore, the first tranche of fieldwork focused mostly on Iranian and Iraqi asylum travellers. I conducted 45 semi-structured interviews in this time: 16 semi-structured interviews in Istanbul and 22 in Ottawa, with an additional two informal interviews in Tehran, and five interviews with fieldworkers working for NGOs.[9] In 2014, I travelled from Ottawa to Istanbul, and attended the IOM's Cultural Orientation Program there, which is sponsored by the Canadian government. After returning to Ottawa, I conducted interviews with resettled refugees who had applied for asylum in Turkey. In 2015, I conducted my second field trip in Turkey. I took the train from Kayseri to Tehran and after staying two weeks there, I took a return train journey from Tehran to Ankara to engage in active participant observation of the asylum journey undertaken by the travellers themselves. On my return to Canada in 2015 and during 2016, I conducted interviews with refugees who had been resettled from Turkey, some of whom were respondents that I had previously interviewed for my master's research in Turkey in 2012. I was able to make further contacts in Canada through some of the interviewees I had met at the IOM's Cultural Orientation Program in Istanbul and thus conducted further interviews with them in Ottawa.

I accessed respondents through a snowball technique, mainly through personal networks and refugee and migration related NGOs. At the end of each interview, I would ask my respondents about the possibility of reaching other candidates for interview with the help of their networks.

Second tranche (2017–2018)

I returned to Turkey after completing my PhD. in Canada and conducted twenty-five additional interviews from May 2017 to July 2018. These were conducted exclusively with Syrian travellers—ten in Istanbul and 15 in Aksaray. It is crucial to note that the asylum journey of the Syrian respondents is rather different to that of the non-Syrians. The Syrian travellers I interviewed had not yet applied for asylum and had not yet even considered seeking asylum in Turkey for resettlement to other countries. Nine respondents were—at the time of the interviews—about to receive their Turkish citizenship, while a further 12 respondents were waiting for citizenship opportunities. The remainder were assessing a range of other options, specifically looking into opportunities to return Syria, to stay in Turkey, or to find a way to move on to other countries. For Syrian respondents waiting for Turkish citizenship, there is no journey to UNHCR Turkey. Instead, it is to Turkey's DGMM that these applicants must travel to receive the ID card issued to all Syrian newcomers. For those Syrians who are taking the route of applying for refugee status and resettlement, their journey is much like the other travellers covered in this study in that they must journey to the UNHCR Office in Ankara and register as asylum seekers there. In this sense, including Syrians in the research provides an opportunity to compare and test some of the core concepts in the book, including mobistasis and the asylum habitus.

To respect the valuable time of respondents, I limited each interview in Turkey and Canada to around 60 minutes. I was not always able to record conversations due to the concerns of respondents. At the end of each interview, I asked some of my interviewees to draw a map of their personal odyssey, including the routes they had taken and the crossings they had made along the way. These semi-structured interviews were all conducted with adults (persons 18-years old and above), both male and female. All the respondents had arrived from different non-European countries such as Afghanistan, Iran, Iraq, the DRC, Ethiopia, Somalia, Sudan, and Syria. The respondents came from a diverse range of backgrounds, with varying levels of education, marital status, and religion and individual tactics and practices along the way. Each interviewee has been assigned a Western and/or Latin pseudonym—on purpose—to underscore the fact that anyone can find him or herself embarking on the asylum odyssey. It is also part of my personal motivation to move beyond the Western-centric approach in the domain of refugee politics, which casts 'the West' against 'the rest'.

Ethical issues and problems in the field

Ethical precautions were taken to ensure the rights of respondents were respected and to protect them from potential physical and psychological harm due to their direct or indirect involvement in the research. The informed consent of all the respondents was taken before the interviews began and a tape-recorder was used with their express permission. Recording was an issue for several respondents, and in those cases, I took extensive notes during the interviews in lieu of recordings. The recording and personal interview notes were stored securely. This set of precautions ensured that respondents' anonymity was ensured and their personal data secure.

Minor access issues arose during the research. This was mainly due to the financial constraints and restricted time available for the research. The principal issue in accessing potential respondents related to questions of rapport and trust. The refugee and asylum seeker population is typically treated as if it were a set of entirely 'vulnerable' and 'fragile' human beings—officials reiterate this notion and warn refugees against sharing 'secret' or 'sensitive' information, which might cause them psychological harm. It is thus challenging at times to build rapport and trust with asylum travellers, especially unless one has significant amounts of time to develop these relationships. This was especially true with Syrian travellers living in Aksaray. Of course, none of this is to say that we should ignore the very real concerns and fears that asylum travellers face along the way or to downplay the risk of psychological trauma.

The second issue is that arises in relation to access concerns the places of residence of those waiting for their refugee status to be determined. After their initial interviews with the UNHCR, asylum travellers in Turkey are resettled into one of 62 designated 'satellite cities' by Turkey's MoI and these cities are spread all across the country. This made it difficult to conduct fieldwork and interviews in each location to reflect the narratives, practices, and experiences of refugees in all regions due to time and financial constraints. Third, since this research is about the routes and journey of refugees with their resettlement, it was difficult to track refugees who were resettled in different provinces across Canada for further interviews with these same respondents in their new resettlement environment.

While the research touches upon significant moral concerns—the manner in which states interact with the human beings who cross their borders seeking asylum and the choice of some travellers to use unlawful human smuggling networks—this project's concerns in these respects are limited. The project does not aim to provide a guideline for states to improve their security practices along the way or their particular treatment of asylum travellers. It is further not a guideline for refugees and asylum travellers about which routes to take or what options to pursue or not pursue. I am also cognisant of the ethical dimensions associated with the specific interventions in the asylum journey made by the present research. For example, I remain aware of the potential risks in asking some of my interviewees to map their personal journeys and the routes taken as they travel along their path—this has some concern since it may offer information that can impact how the systems of border checks and control regimes are developed. The publication of research on the specific transnational route covered here—with the UNHCR in Turkey for travellers en route to Canada—may expose future travellers within this nexus to heightened suspicion and/or surveillance. These risks are must of course be balanced against the value of unpacking what has remained to date a very misunderstood asylum journey.

Structure of the book

As foreshadowed earlier in the introduction, the book contains five chapters. The first is largely theoretical, framing the current debates in the literature

Introduction 19

and providing an outline of the theory and methodology. It begins with a brief literature review—a survey of the key strands of research in the fields of critical refugee studies, forced migration studies, transit migration, and transnationalism studies that bear on the refugee journey—then details the theoretical and conceptual toolkits utilized throughout the book. The remainder of Chapter 1 addresses method and methodology, as well as ethical concerns.

Chapter 2 details the key bureaucratic aspects of asylum seeking and resettlement, focusing on the contemporary global system of refugee governance as well as the regimes of the two country cases: Turkey and Canada. It begins with a brief historical background on the UNHCR, the 1951 Geneva Convention and the 1967 Additional Protocol. It then provides a brief historical overview of Turkey's asylum policies and how the country acts as a 'bridge' in a transnational asylum governance structure that is underpinned by its geographical limitation on asylum seekers from non-European countries. It concludes with an overview of Canada's refugee resettlement programme and its policy of 'selective inclusion'.

Chapters 3, 4 and 5 present the bulk of the empirical analysis of the book. The underlying structure draws its inspiration from van Gennep's (1960) notion of 'rites of passage'. Accordingly, I adapt this idea and present the *three phases of the asylum journey*—each with its own dedicated chapter. Chapter 3 focuses on the practices and experiences of asylum travellers prior to their arrival in Turkey—the *separation phase* of the asylum journey. This involves decision-making around leaving the country of origin, gathering information and picking up misinformation about formal procedures, and access or difficulty in accessing documents related to the journey.

Chapter 4 follows the second phase of the journey—the *transition* or *liminal phase*—when the traveller arrives in Turkey in order to seek asylum. The chapter analyses asylum seeking practices and experiences of asylum travellers in Turkey and their encounters with Turkey's geographically exclusionary asylum system. It details the various contingent events— interactions, contestations, negotiations, and encounters—experienced by travellers as they negotiate the series of requirements before them in their attempt to realize the objective of being resettled to Canada.

Chapter 5 covers the *incorporation phase* of the journey, the resettlement of those refugees who have been screened and approved for entry into Canada. The chapter details the various aspects of Canada's resettlement programme and the experiences of asylum travellers in Canada after the completion of their resettlement.

The final chapter concludes the book. It draws together all the various strands covered in the book, summarizes the key claims and findings and reiterates the core themes of the asylum habitus, mobile knowledge and mobistasis.

Notes

1 Geographical limitation restricts non-European asylum applicants from being granted refugee status, which I will detail the regulation in the Selection of Cases section and in Chapter 2. As of 1 July 2016, according to the UNHCR, Turkey is one of four countries—including Congo, Madagascar, and Monaco—applying a geographical limitation to non-European asylum seekers.
2 As of 10 September 2018, UNHCR stopped the registration and application of foreign individuals for protection in Turkey. This crucial change in asylum bureaucracy does not affect the main arguments of this study as the fieldwork was completed prior to the change. For the details of change, see https://help.unhcr.org/turkey/information-for-non-syrians/registration-rsd-with-unhcr accessed May 2019.
3 The first appearance of the term in the English language dates to the Revocation of the Edict of Nantes in 1685 and was applied to the Huguenots who were denied the practice of Calvinism in France and fled to other countries (D'Orsi, 2016).
4 Further elaboration on the difference between the terms 'refugee' and 'asylum seeker' and a discussion on the formation of the UNHCR and ratification of both the 1951 Geneva Convention and the 1967 Additional Protocol are presented in Chapter 2.
5 There are currently 62 provinces in Turkey that are designated destinations for asylum seekers to remain while they wait for the completion of the resettlement process. Notably, the three largest metropolitan cities—Istanbul, Ankara and Izmir—are excluded. See: www.egm.gov.tr/Sayfalar/iltica-goc-islemleri.aspx
6 Chapter 1 details my use of the notion of asylum habitus in much greater detail.
7 Aksaray is a province in the central part of Turkey. It should not be confused with Istanbul's Aksaray neighbourhood.
8 By foregrounding travellers' own choices in how they map the journey, book is very much in line two critical research groups—'anti Atlas of Borders' and the 'counter-cartographies collective'. For further information on 'antiAtlas of Borders', see www.antiatlas.net/en/ For the 'counter-cartographies collective', see www.countercartographies.org/
9 I was required to complete the Carleton University Research Ethics Board's ethics clearance form to meet ethical standards in accordance with the Tri-Council Policy Statement: Ethical Conduct for Research Involving Human and the Carleton University Policies and Procedures for the Ethical Conduct of Research, which was completed in May 2014 and renewed in May 2015.

1 The asylum journey and the governance of transnational refugee mobility

Refugee movements have been examined in various ways (the legal asylum regulations of states and the experiences of refugees in the country of asylum and/or resettlement) in a number of different disciplines (political science, sociology, international relations, legal studies, and anthropology). However, the 'journey as method' approach has remained limited in the literature. Considering the diversified practices employed by asylum travellers and the changing regulations imposed by states—not to mention the different perspectives offered by each of the abovementioned disciplines—I approach the asylum odyssey as an inter- and multi-disciplinary phenomenon.

In general, the global refugee system—i.e., the 1951 Geneva Convention and related protocols, primarily based on humanitarian needs—provides one of the most highly regulated schemas of mobility. In fact, the system seems to operate in a multi-layered environment where nation-states, refugees, and local and international NGOs encounter—and negotiate with—each other. Refugee movements are not limited to the border crossing practices of travellers. They are also shaped in any number of ways by the policymakers and asylum bureaucracies that regulate, adjust, and map the journey and impose various bureaucratic statuses and fluid interpellations on travellers along the way. Therefore, research on refugee movement is not only multi-disciplinary, but also multi-dimensional in the empirical sense, embodying a variety of agents and structures.

This chapter begins with a brief overview of the various ways the image of the contemporary refugee has been approached by three research fields: transnationalism, autonomy of migration, and critical migration studies. Different as they are, all of these fields of study invariably advise scholars to exercise caution in the application of certain concepts in the study of transnational migration, including the descriptors 'transit', 'forced' and 'voluntary'. After framing the debate in the literature on refugee journeys, the chapter turns to detail the conceptualizations and theoretical frames that will be utilized throughout the book.

The general image of the refugee in migration studies

'It is the refugee', according to Melaku Kifle, the Refugee Secretary of the All-Africa Council of Churches, 'who reveals to us the defective society in which we live. He [sic] is a kind of mirror through whose suffering we can see the injustice, the oppression and the maltreatment of the powerless by the powerful' (cited in Malkki, 1995a, p. 12). The statement underlines the multi-dimensional—and inter- and multi-disciplinary—nature of studies on refugees. Kifle also raises broader themes here: *defective society, injustice* versus *justice, oppression* and *maltreatment*, and the *powerless* versus the *powerful*. This implies that the migration literature should consider conceptualizations of nationalism, the nation-state, citizenship, inclusion and exclusion, mobility and stasis, the legality versus illegality binary, and human rights law seriously. However, the vast majority of refugee studies treats the figure of the refugee as nothing more than an exposed, helpless wanderer. Kifle's statement is emblematic here, essentializing as it does the refugee experience through the figure of the refugee as a vulnerable being. In other words, especially with the adaptation of Giorgio Agamben's (1998) notion of *homo sacer* to that of the refugee, the field of refugee studies has all too often foregrounded the apparent 'vulnerability' of the refugee and the notion of mobility as 'forced' (Diken, 2004; Rajaram & Grundy-Warr, 2004). It has also idealized and romanticized the experience of 'exile and diaspora' (Malkki, 1995b, p. 515).

The contemporary image of the refugee has thus become an object of knowledge-making within various discursive domains—political, social, bureaucratic, and legal—in the decades since the UNHCR was founded in 1950 (Malkki, 1995a). The question of 'who a refugee is' begins 'from the first procedure of status determination to the structural determinants of life chances' through the 1951 Geneva Convention and the 1967 Additional Protocol (Zetter, 1991, pp. 39–40). The contemporary refugee represents *in-between-ness* as both 'an insider and an outsider, existing at the borders and between sovereigns' (Haddad, 2008, p. 8). This in-between-ness results from 'the politico-ethical collision between *the raison d'état* of the nation-state, *the raison de système* of the international system, *the raison d'humanité* of the humanitarian discourse and *the raison de justice* of the global justice system' (Haddad, 2008, p. 12, italics in the original). Becoming a refugee or holding the identity/status of refugee is not the consequence of 'a breakdown in the system of separate states'; rather, it is an 'inevitable if unanticipated part of international society' (Haddad, 2008, p. 8). In a similar vein, Hannah Arendt connects the condition of homelessness, statelessness—and, eventually, the condition of rightlessness—to the rise of totalitarian tendencies among nation-states, and the totalitarian state's denationalization weapon (Arendt, 1973, p. 269).

From this perspective, the 'holy trinity' of *nation-state, territory*, and *citizen–subject* in the contemporary world system makes refugees and the condition of statelessness inevitable (Arendt, 1973, p. 282; Malkki, 1992). Indeed, this trinity produces the conditions for unwanted individuals to be readily deported/removed—leading not only to the loss of the original home, but more importantly the impossibility of finding a new one (Arendt, 1973, p. 293). As Malkki

(1992, p. 24) observes, the refugee identity compels us 'to rethink the question of roots in relation—if not the soul—to identity, and the forms of its territorialisation' within the tripartite regime of nation-state–territory–citizenship. However, it should be noted that refugees are not the product of the contemporary socio-politico-economic world system, nor are they simply a result of the politics of citizenship. Therefore, it is important to approach all essentialist notions in refugee studies critically and to move beyond politically loaded binaries/labels as well as 'categorical fetishism' in the domain of asylum (Crawley & Skleparis, 2018).

Transnationalism and refugee mobility

In the context of refugee movements, the mobility of individuals is highly politicized. It has become an issue of inclusion and exclusion, of being admitted or rejected, and of status—namely, of *legality* and *illegality*. Scholars examining the phenomenon through a critical lens have generally adopted two different perspectives. The first approach examines the immigration and asylum policies of states[1] and the role of the UNHCR in providing protection.[2] This perspective explores the escape of refugees within the frame of a 'technical and operational "solution"' (Nyers, 2006, p. xiv).

The second approach focuses on the precarious experiences of refugees and asylum seekers in the country of asylum, drawing on Agamben's notion of *homo sacer* (Fitzpatrick, 2001; Edkins & Pin-Fat, 2005; Hanafi & Long, 2010). There is no doubt that exclusionary governmental strategies and the securitization of borders have imposed limitations on asylum seekers and refugees. However, this representation of refugees—and, moreover, the term 'refugee crisis'—serve to reduce individuals taking asylum journeys to vulnerable drifters. Both tendencies reflect a state-centric view, whereby the state is a machine that has power to *include* and *exclude* individuals by throwing some of them into *bare life* living conditions. Especially with the emergence of forced migration studies, the figure of the refugee has been placed 'within the larger context of forced migration' (Adelman, 2001, p. 7). Both approaches—along with the shift to the forced migration conceptualization—largely ignore the *agency of migrants*. After all, migrants are constantly making choices, negotiating certain encounters and interactions, and selecting autonomously from among various potential paths, routes and border crossings (Nyers, 2006, 2008; Walters, 2008; Owens, 2009).

The transnationalism literature offers a distinct perspective in exploring the economic, political, and cultural cross-border activities of migrants.[3] Transnationalism is a broader notion that refers to the 'everyday practices of migrants engaged in various activities'—cultural and social engagement, involvement in political activities, and financial activities in both the home and host country (Vertovec, 2001; Faist, 2010, p. 11). The transnationalism notion in migration studies is a crucial tool to organize and contemplate the perceptions on migration and cross-border related activities involving (in)direct relationships (Faist, 2010; Pitkanen, Icduygu & Sert, 2012; Quayson & Daswani, 2013).

24 The asylum journey

In the present research, the lens of transnationalism is significant at least for two reasons. First, transnationalism poses a conceptual challenge to methodological nationalism. That is, it stands opposed to the conventional perspective on the nation-state as the 'natural' container of human populations, and the current international system as 'the [natural] order of things' (Malkki, 1992, p. 25) and the only way to make sense of 'the social and political form of the modern world' (Quayson & Daswani, 2013, p. 17). Thus, transnationalism suggests a 'dialectical relation between integrity and discontinuity, spatialized as a form of deteriorialization' (Wimmer & Schiller, 2002, p. 302; see also Faist, 2010). Second, transnationalism attempts to explore the 'permeability, transcendence, or irrelevance' (Quayson & Daswani, 2013, p. 5) of borders. It thus stands opposed to the heavy stress on borders in migration studies. In line with the transnationalism lens, the present study examines not only the crossing of national borders, but also the simultaneity and discontinuity in relationships, knowledge and tactics in space and time in the context of asylum journeys towards Canada via Turkey.

The autonomy of migration in refugee journeys

Another viewpoint that has emerged in debates in the migration literature that I find insightful for exploring migrant journeys is the *autonomy of migration* perspective. The term was first used in relation to US–Mexico border crossings to describe 'the movements of peoples into the U.S. independent of state authorization and regulation' (Rodriguez, 1996, p. 23). It emphasizes 'the relations, encounters, and negotiations' among migrants, with institutions and between states that structure the actual process of human mobility (Ashutosh & Mountz, 2012, p. 340).

The concept of autonomy of migration poses a challenge to the conventional thinking on borders, which sees them through 'the lens of centralized and coordinated state powers' (Casas-Cortes, Cobarrubias & Pickles, 2015, p. 894). The autonomy of migration perspective instead 'offers a distinct way for thinking about border control mechanisms and goals of managing mobility' (ibid., p. 894). In so doing, it offers a more 'autonomous gaze' for migration studies that allows for critical interrogation of how 'border architectures, institutions and policies interact with and react to the turbulence of migrant mobilities' (ibid., p. 894). The autonomous gaze in migration studies is a critical intervention that moves the field beyond the binary conceptualizations of *forced* versus *voluntary* migrant/migration. While the latter has generally cast unforced/voluntary migrants as economically motivated in choosing to move, refugees—through their very vulnerability, passivity, and lack of agency and autonomy in their home country—are 'forcibly' political in nature (Hein, 1993). Critical migration scholars have questioned the shift from refugee studies to forced migration studies on account of the latter's potential 'failure to take account of the specificity of the refugee's circumstances' (Hathaway, 2007, p. 349). Chimni (2009, p. 11) argues that this shift in perspective from refugee to forced migration 'must be viewed against the backdrop of the history and relationship of colonialism and humanitarianism'.

It is crucial to note that the notion of *compulsion* that is embedded in the way forced migration studies conceives of the figure of the refugee has normative implications as well. Namely, in the way the field configures and shapes modes of political imagination in approaching human mobility and migration. Political imagination as a meta-narrative 'refers to a set of assumptions or rules that are more often than not unspoken and tacit' (Walters, 2002, p. 381). The political imagination conditioned by the emphasis on compulsion (embedded, as mentioned, in the very categories 'migrant' and 'migration') simultaneously produces a set of binaries—forced/involuntary and unforced/voluntary—in imagining the migration phenomenon itself. In forced migration studies, the effect of this political imagination serves 'governmental and agency agendas' that increasingly reduce all 'irregular' human mobility to the idea of *being driven to move compulsorily* (Hathaway, 2007, p. 350, italics added). The political imagination here assumes that mobility exists on a spectrum: at one pole, sits voluntary or unforced migration and migrants; at the other, the involuntary or forced migrant. This distinction shaping our political imagination assumes that asylum seekers and refugees are 'involuntary' in their act of mobility since they are 'forced' to flee due to the fear of persecution and external forces in the home country settings. It further essentializes and naturalizes a strict and clear distinction between unforced/voluntary and forced/involuntary.

What is significant here is that by reducing the journey in this way, mobility can be governed, controlled, bureaucratized, and il/legalized along with domestic asylum and migration policies. Thus, the migratory system has been able to differentiate the movement of refugees from that of other mobile bodies—tourists, economic migrants, expatriates, and so on—who are deemed fully agential beings in command of their choices. In so doing, individuals are readily placed into a hierarchy based on the genuineness of their pain and vulnerability. More importantly, the construction of a binary—'forced' versus 'voluntary' migrants, with 'refugee claimants' automatically categorized as the former—is significant in concealing the rationale for the regulation of migration and justifying the *voluntary repatriation* projects of states and NGOs.

In this political imaginary, the general assumption for determining the admission and/or rejection of an asylum applicant is also binary. Any person that seeks asylum 'must' have been 'forced' to leave and should be able to demonstrate a well-founded fear of persecution—or worse—if the person stays. Otherwise, he/she is nothing but a voluntary migrant (most likely seeking work) and has thus arrived to further her economic interests. Turton's critical point on these categories of 'economic' versus 'political' migrants or 'free' versus 'forced' migration bears repeating. He notes that famine is a political as well as an economic phenomenon, since there is no longer any clear boundary between economy and politics (Turton, 2003). Whether forced or voluntary, any transnational journey of individuals requires that those on the move consider a range of detailed calculations, (counter-)strategies, and tactics before, during, and after the journey.

In other words, the adjective *forced* in the notion of forced migration ignores the agency of individuals, who invariably have access to human, social and physical capital of one kind or another, not to mention the possibility of using human smugglers to navigate 'illegal' routes, albeit it at staggering cost. Koser's findings underline the extraordinary profitability of the human smuggling business since today the cost of such a 'ticket' to Canada will set the asylum seeker back approximately US$20,000—including flights, passport, and visa (Koser, 2008; Papadopoulou, 2008). Even though the financial exploitation of asylum travellers attracts serious attention from the media, NGO reports, and policymakers, the political imagination leads us to consider asylum travellers as victims of human smugglers instead of questioning border regimes themselves as the root cause of the human smuggling business.[4]

My point is not to disregard the social, political, and other contingent factors leading individuals to seek asylum abroad. However, as illustrated by the fieldwork conducted for this book—and the narratives provided by the respondents interviewed for it—the essentialization and naturalization of the categories of 'forced' and 'involuntary' in the current political imagination undermines the agency of asylum travellers and the autonomy of the asylum journey. The political imagination with the 'forced' and 'voluntary' distinctions does largely ignore the calculated-ness and autonomy in the act of border crossings since no political imagination derives generally from actual empirical observation or sociological analysis of what and who is 'unforced' and 'forced' (Turton, 2003).

The *autonomy of migration* lens also works 'to move beyond the binary geopolitical divisions of North and South, West and East' (Hyndman, 1997, p. 150). This critical intervention is useful if we are to avoid the simplistic tendency of seeing refugee movement only as mobility from economically 'undeveloped' countries to the 'developed' West. Rather, the autonomy of migration lens in the transnationalism literature seeks to 'emphasize the practices, institutions, and discourses that shape [these] movements across international borders' (Ashutosh & Mountz, 2012, p. 348). As this book also stresses, the autonomy of migration perspective also permits us to go beyond the picture of refugee mobility as a linear movement from refugee-producing country to refugee-receiving or welcoming country. A more nuanced, multi-directional approach sees 'the border no longer as a solid line but as highly differentiated' zones experienced and practiced by migrants along with the multiple actors including state and its border bureaucracy as well as non-state actors, technologies, and discourses (Tsianos & Karakayali, 2010, p. 378). In addition, the autonomy of migration perspective is in line with the notion of *migration infrastructure* which acknowledges that migration is formed by multi-dimensional processes, mechanisms, and actors (Xiang & Lindquist,

2014). The autonomy of migration as a micro lens is thus, at least in part, in line with the 'journey as method' approach, which is a methodology for exploring migrant journeys and the condition of 'mobistasis'—or periodic immobility through the journey—as it pertains to asylum seeing in Turkey for resettlement to Canada (Yıldız & Sert, 2019).

Asylum journeys and the 'journey as method' approach

As touched upon in the introduction, in exploring refugee journeys I adapt Mezzadra and Neilson's (2013) *border as method* notion by framing it *journey as method approach*. And to briefly recall the discussion in that chapter, the journey as method approach invokes Paul Gilroy's (1993, p. 4) metaphor of ship making the journey across the Atlantic—i.e., 'as a living, micro-cultural, micro-political system in motion'. This method is a challenge to the field to go beyond thinking of migration as a mere practice of crossing a border, of moving linearly from point A to point B. Rather we must see the asylum journey for what it is—a series of *interactions, negotiations* and *practices* embedded in the odyssey itself. In addition, recent studies—including Ruben Andersson's (2014) ethnographic journey across borders and Shahram Khosravi's (2010) personal asylum journey—have offered crucial contributions that show how it is possible for robust scholarship on human mobility to move beyond blurred and arbitrary (not to mention politically loaded) notions of 'forced', 'voluntary' and 'transit' migration. Indeed, these two works have underscored the importance of studying the 'in situ' phases of the migrant journey—or what Coutin (2005) calls 'being en route'. Moreover, as mentioned also in the introductory chapter, they illustrate the existence of multiple border crossings and the varying points of access to routes and transport vehicles that line up with Walters' (2015) notion of the 'viapolitics' that inheres in all migration.

In general, refugee mobility has been explored in the field from a highly state-centric perspective—treating mobility as a straightforward and linear movement, i.e., from refugee-producing to a refugee-receiving country. As Clifford (1992, pp. 99–100) noted nearly three decades ago, while the *being there* aspect of the asylum journey has been prevalent in the literature, the *getting there* phase—Coutin's (2005) 'being en route'—has been sorely neglected. However, analysis of the *getting there* phase is crucial, in that it allows us to see how travellers/migrants are able to access on routes. A clear focus on the journey itself also allows us to distinguish 'who has the security and privilege to move about in relatively unconstrained ways' (Clifford, 1992, p. 107)—and, indeed, who does not. Doing so makes it possible to contemplate how the constrained spaces turn easily into spaces of death both on land and at sea. This tragic truth has been witnessed in refugee deaths on the Mediterranean Sea in capsized boats, which—as Vicki Squire (2016) points out—illustrates how the securitization of migration is justified through the death of migrants by policymakers.[5]

Focusing on journey from a *journey as method* approach along with the viapolitics aspect offers a critical intervention to the 'transit' migrant/migration conceptualization in migration studies. The 'transit' notion in the literature presents Turkey as a *transit* space to arrive at the countries of destination or resettlement. The terms transit and transit migrant have been problematized in a 'multi-sited ethnographic' study—the Transit Migration project—between 2002 and 2004, conducted in Serbia, Greece, and Turkey in the European context (Papadopoulos, Stephenson, & Tsianos, 2008; Tsianos & Karakayali, 2010; Hess, 2012). The common usage of the notion also coincides with the EU efforts to externalize the migration phenomenon towards the 'transit' countries (Oelgemoller 2011, 2017; Collyer, Düvell & de Haas 2012). Accordingly, individuals on the move as 'transit migrants are defined as aliens who stay in the country for some period of time while seeking to migrate permanently to another country' (Düvell, 2012, p. 417). Based on the given definition, the temporality and intention of a migrant to cross the country are crucial signifiers of the notion. However, they are ambiguous as Wissing, Düvell and Eerdewijk (2013) claimed. Under the 'transit' conception, the refugee figure seeking asylum in Turkey for resettlement to Canada may transform into the *transit migrant* category. This category may function as a 'political-scientific discourse' within which this discourse serves as a strategic anonymity (Hess, 2012, p. 429). In addition, the transit notion has been initially used at the European Union level to refer to a migration 'problem' to be tackled by associating the phenomenon with human smuggling sector and irregular dimension (Düvell, 2012).

For migrants en route to Europe, transit conception treats Turkey as a transit count and passage. This may shape our political imagination to consider asylum travellers under the 'transit' migrant categorization. However, treating Turkey as a transit country in the literature suggests a non-space or a type of 'immobility and truncated forms of transnationalism' (Ashutosh & Mountz, 2012, p. 336). To put it differently, the concept largely ignores experiences and practices of asylum travellers, the distinct forms of knowledge production among individuals, and the calculations as well as tactics employed by them en route to the country of resettlement during the asylum journey. Therefore, it serves to *freeze space* and to *immobilize* relations and interactions generated within the established asylum habitus. It needs to be emphasized that not all 'transit' travellers continue their journey to Europe via Turkey or arrive successfully their country of resettlement. In this sense, I share the criticism offered by migration scholars cited above. More importantly, it is important to see how Turkey as a 'transit' space stands more than a 'transit' country en route to Canada. Rather, Turkey where asylum travellers encounter asylum regulations and UNHCR to be recognized refugee and where they form local and transnational knowledge networks designates both a space of mobility and immobility. The *journey as method* approach is therefore a critical intervention by enabling scholars to understand the 'microphysics of roads' by expanding the horizon of politics of migration from a state and border centred analysis to more molecular based routes and more varied components during journeys as recent studies have underlined (Walters, 2015, p. 98). In addition, this approach serves to grasp the journey's molecular components as transportation means including animals, gateways, cities, multiple borders and crossings, and networks, as well as local and global solidarity networks.[6]

Concepts and theoretical toolkit

According to Sartori (1970, p. 1040), concepts are 'things' which 'are conceived and meaningfully perceived'. They are also, 'central elements of propositions, and—depending on how they are named—provide in and by themselves guidelines for interpretation and observation' (ibid., p. 64). In this sense, concepts are containers of a named proposition as structuring parameters in a given research. The aim of this section is to clarify concepts and theoretical framework that I utilize throughout the book.

Strategies and tactics during the asylum journey

The asylum journey involves not only mobility but also immobility, in which a series of interactions, negotiations, and encounters occur between asylum and migration regulations of states and the journey practices of travellers. In this sense, for analytical purposes, the practices of asylum travellers must be differentiated from the migration and asylum-related bureaucratic regulations.

To this end, I benefit from Michel de Certeau's (1988) categorical distinction between *strategy* and *tactic*. In *The Practice of Everyday Life*, de Certeau follows nomadic-sedentarist metaphor in which he calls spatial organization with urban planning and mapping *strategy* and the acts of pedestrians *tactics*. Distinguished this way, 'a strategy [is] the calculation (or manipulation) of power relationships that becomes possible as soon as a subject with will and power can be isolated' (ibid., p. 35). Strategies function to produce 'the proper', which serves as 'the abstract model' to 'produce, tabulate and impose' conformity (ibid., pp. 29 and 36). Following de Certeau's conceptualization, regulations and asylum/migration bureaucracies that tabulate and adjust the speed of asylum journeys are conceptualized as *strategies*. The specific strategies referred to in this book are mainly Turkey's exclusionary geographical limitation, the UNHCR's filtration process in refugee status determination, and Canada's refugee resettlement programme.

On the other hand, tactics—the acts of pedestrians or travellers—oppose the spatialization of domination that is produced and tabulated by strategies. Accordingly, a tactic uses space to 'divert through calculated action determined by the absence of proper locus' (ibid., p. 36) and to 'manipulate events in order to turn them into "opportunities"' (ibid., p. xi). Thus, a tactic does not delimit itself and 'no delimitation of an exteriority provides it with the condition necessary for autonomy' (ibid., pp. 36–37). In other words, if a strategy is the possession of the *strong* to regulate and control, a tactic in the spatial context 'is an art of the weak' who devise 'clever tricks, *knowing how to get away with things*' (ibid., p. 37, emphasis added).[7]

In a similar vein, the asylum journey involves not only abstract models and regulations as bureaucratic strategies of governance, but also tactics—the practices and acts of asylum travellers which occur in accordance with (and in opposition to) strategies. I include all the acts and practices of refugees within this notion of tactics. These practices consist of travellers' access to knowledge about the asylum journey (including what they pick up en route); their access to documents and official channels (and even to human smugglers). Practices also include the various vehicles that travellers board and the hardships they encounter along the way, their arrival at, and crossing of, borders, their experiences in the country of asylum, and in the third country of resettlement.

Moreover, the use of tactics—as I highlight throughout the book—does not necessarily mean that asylum travellers are inevitably countering or opposing the strategies they encounter. These tactics also included *negotiation* (with the authorities and with other actors) and *collaboration* in various kin-based and other networks. This conceptualization of tactics is in line with the autonomy of migration perspective, which reflects the myriad relationships, practices, techniques, and technologies that make up the migration experience. It highlights the heterogeneous 'practices of subjectivation through which migrants challenge these devices [of control they encounter] on a daily basis, giving rise to relations and practices that facilitate their mobility as well as often unstable ways of staying in place' (Mezzadra, Neilson, Scheel & Riedner, 2015, p. 62).

Adopting the tactics versus strategies distinction is important to foreground the generic practices and experiences of asylum travellers when they encounter migration and asylum regulations through the asylum odyssey. In addition, this categorical and analytical distinction allows me to avoid essentialist language, which grants only the state and its governing mechanisms the status of *structure* and *agent*. Thus, the tactics versus strategies distinction underlines the multi-dimensional processes and mechanisms—and the multiple actors—that make up the 'migration infrastructure' experienced by asylum travellers during their transnational odyssey.

The three phases of the asylum journey

The asylum journey towards Canada via Turkey involves (at least) several border crossings and encounters with numerous bureaucratic regulations. To unpack this latter category a little more, the person looking to claim asylum must first of all depart from the country of origin—doing so with a genuine fear of persecution. Second, the individual is expected to find a safe country (in this case, Turkey) and locate the UNHCR office there. Where that state, like Turkey, does not issue refugee status under the Convention to non-European applicants, the individual will need to legalize her stay in some administrative way. Finally, the person will need to be recognized by the UNHCR and resettled to a safe third country.

For analytical purposes, I disaggregate the asylum journey into three phases, in accordance with the bureaucratic requirements of seeking asylum— 1) fleeing the country of origin; 2) seeking asylum and 3) resettlement. To this end and as mentioned in the introduction, I adapt Arnold van Gennep's (1960) conceptualization of 'rites of passage'—namely, the 'passage from one situation to another or from one cosmic or social world to another' (p. 10). What is significant in van Gennep's tripartite structure is that 'liminality represents anti-structure as opposed to the structure of the social world—a structure which is first dissolved in rites of separation and later reconstituted in rites of reaggregation' (Garwood, 2011, p. 264).

Against this background, the book divides the asylum odyssey into three phases. The journey begins with *the rite of separation* from 'home' country to the country of asylum. That part of the journey spent in the country of asylum (in this book, Turkey) is the *liminal/transition phase*. Finally, the journey ends with *the rite of incorporation* or the *reaggregation phase* in the country of resettlement (in our case, Canada). The term *incorporation* refers to a situation in which

> the ritual subject [...] is in a relatively stable state once more and, by virtue of this, has rights and obligations vis-à-vis others of a clearly defined and 'structural' type; he [sic] is expected to behave in accordance with certain customary norms and ethical standards binding on incumbents of social position in a system of such positions.
> (Turner, 1977, p. 95)

The term incorporation in this present book is not used as a substitute for the notion of *integration*; rather, it is presented as the final bureaucratic phase of the asylum journey as it pertains to refugee resettlement to Canada via Turkey. I eschew using the word integration, which is a 'nebulous term' and 'a state-directed policy goal' (Brunner, Hyndman & Mountz, 2014, p. 83–84). As Li (2003, p. 316) suggests, in policy documents the term integration 'upholds the normative expectation of conformity as the desirable outcome of immigrant integration'. This understanding foregrounds the newcomers' contributions to the host community. In addition, there may be inconsistency between the use of integration discourse in immigration policy documents, and the actual experiences of refugees. Integration as a process starts 'with the arrival and ends based on newcomers' position in the society' (Phillimore & Goodson, 2008, p. 309). The process of a refugee's identification of herself/himself with 'the Canadian experience' does not necessarily begin in Canada. This phase begins mostly in Turkey when an asylum traveller is admitted as an eligible candidate for resettlement to Canada.

To disaggregate the asylum odyssey into these three phases is not to say that all travellers taking the journey have an identical experience. Moreover,

32   The asylum journey

in doing so I do not seek to generalize refugee journeys as linear experiences. Rather, it is to present a representation of the journey in accordance with the standard bureaucratic procedures surrounding asylum. This analytical division also reflects Brigden and Mainwaring's (2016) metaphor of the *matryoshka* or Russian doll for the journey of migrants.[8] In a similar vein and as mentioned already, journeys within the asylum odyssey from home country to Canada via Turkey are non-linear, multi-layered, and heterogeneous experiences that involve not only mobility and multiple border crossings, but also mobistasis—immobility and pauses during the ongoing asylum journey. The intention in disassembling the asylum journey into three phases is to unpack the experiences and practices of asylum travellers in each step. The reason for dividing the asylum journey into phases is to line it up with the formal, bureaucratic dimensions of seeking asylum in Turkey for resettlement to Canada. Bureaucratic formalities and processes are important since they exert leverage on the direction of the journey, the evaluation of the applicant, and any transformation in the applicant's status.

The transnational governance of the asylum journey

The UNHCR, Turkey, and Canada regulate the three phases of the asylum journey bureaucratically at the national and transnational levels. The book defines these three entities as the designators of *strategies*. All three retain the power of admission and rejection, and exercise this power cooperatively. The cooperative relation among three constitute what this book defines as *transnational refugee governance*. This concept of transnational refugee governance captures the multiple patterns of interaction, coordination, and negotiation between the UNHCR, Turkey and Canada.

Moreover, the concept of transnational refugee governance foregrounds how the abstract model that emerges out of the process of entering Turkey to seek asylum for resettlement to Canada as a UNHCR-referred refugee. This model conditions the bureaucratic steps that the asylum traveller learns—or is instructed—to follow from beginning to end in order for the odyssey to be successful. Put differently, the notion highlights the multiple interactions and negotiations that comprise the governance of refugee journeys—not only among asylum travellers as individuals but also between them and the various bureaucratic mechanisms they encounter, and also between Turkey, the UNHCR and Canada. In other words, coordination and negotiation between Turkey, the UNHCR and Canada structures the asylum experience by assigning both an assembled and a transnational character to the journey.

The bureaucratic procedures under this system of transnational refugee governance begin with the separation from the country of origin and arrival in Turkey as the country of asylum. It bears repeating that asylum travellers face Turkey's geographical limitation imposed on non-European asylum applicants in accordance with the 1951 Convention. Travellers then apply for asylum at the UNHCR Office in Ankara, which processes their refugee status determination. Once UNHCR Turkey recognizes travellers as refugees, the files are forwarded to Canada (and, indeed, other resettlement countries such as USA and Australia). The third bureaucratic phase begins with Canada's resettlement programme, whereby some successfully recognized travellers are invited to interview at the Canadian embassy in Ankara—followed by a medical examination—to be admitted as UNHCR-referred refugees for resettlement in Canada.

The coordination of asylum journeys at the transnational level involves a politics of inclusion and exclusion for asylum travellers. This functions as *differential inclusion*—reflecting thus 'how inclusion in a sphere, society or realm can involve various degrees of subordination, rule, discrimination, racism, disenfranchisement, exploitation and segmentation' (De Genova, Mezzadra & Pickles, 2015, p. 79). In this asylum journey towards Canada via Turkey, differential inclusion consists of Turkey's *exclusionary inclusion* and Canada's *selective inclusion*. This resembles George Bataille's (1991, p. 199) definition of sovereignty, which 'is to enjoy the present time without having anything else in view but this present time'. According to Bataille, what distinguishes the 'the domain of sovereignty' is its 'life beyond utility' through '*the enjoyment of possibilities*' (Bataille, 1991, p. 198, emphasis added). Thus, transnational refugee governance with its differential inclusion incorporates governmental strategies as *the enjoyment of possibilities*. In other words, strategies have the ability to make the traveller an object of inquiry and the mobility a *thing* to be controlled, observed and monitored and the mobile person a *thing* to be excluded or included through transnational negotiation and its frame of utility.

As touched on in the foregoing discussion, there are two types of inclusion reflected in the functioning of differential inclusion. The first is Turkey's geographical limitation of non-European asylum applicants as a way of *exclusionary inclusion* (see Chapter 2 for detailed explanation). Geographical limitation excludes non-European asylum travellers by temporarily and spatially including them into Turkey's geography, social, economic, and legal life. The differential inclusion continues with the UNHCR's status determination, whereby asylum applicants are filtered and moved on as a refugee or rejected as a failed asylum seeker.

The aspect of second differential inclusion is Canada's refugee resettlement programme. This functions as a form of *selective inclusion*. Thus, UNHCR-recognized refugees are 'recruited' for resettlement based on their personal abilities and potential self-sufficiency in Canada. In this way, as will be detailed further in Chapter 4, Canada's refugee resettlement programme via Turkey functions as a humanitarian version of immigration labour recruitment.

The asylum journey is adjusted at the transnational governance level. This adjustment, which is in line with de Certeau's notion of strategy functions to create an abstract model for asylum travellers in terms of what bureaucratic steps to follow to be recognized as a refugee and to be resettled to Canada after seeking asylum in Turkey. In addition, this abstract model leads to the

34 *The asylum journey*

formation of an asylum version of habitus, in Bourdieuian sense of the term, among asylum travellers en route to Canada via Turkey.

Along with tactics and strategy, Bourdieu's concept of habitus underscores the book's theoretical foundation. In developing the idea, Bourdieu sought to move beyond dichotomies such as individual and society, subjective and objective, and micro and macro. Habitus, therefore, reflects both 'objective structure and individual activity' (Swartz, 1998, p. 96). Accordingly, habitus is 'systems of durable, transposable *dispositions*, structured structures predisposed to function as structuring structure' (Bourdieu, 1977, p. 72, emphasis in the original). Adopting Bourdieu's notion, I refer throughout the book to the asylum habitus associated with the journey towards Canada via Turkey to underline the institutionalization and routinization of the odyssey, not only in terms of objective structures, but also the practices of asylum travellers.

The asylum habitus, thus, refers to the historical formation and formulation of the journey and the journey's perpetuation through time and space. Historically speaking, Turkey received the first mass refugee flows from Iran after the Islamic Revolution in 1979. Turkey has continued to attract asylum travellers from Iran since this time. Another neighbouring country, Iraq, started to produce asylum travellers from the early 1990s. During the 1990s, Turkey also received refugees from Afghanistan, Pakistan, Ethiopia, Eritrea, Somalia, Sudan, the Democratic Republic of Congo, and so on. In addition, Turkey currently hosts more than 3.5 million Syrian refugees who began to arrive following the outbreak of civil war in Syria in 2011.

Due to Turkey's geographical limitation on non-European asylum travellers, individuals who are granted refugee status by the UNHCR in Turkey must wait for resettlement to Canada or other resettlement countries. Regarding resettlement to Canada, the country has operated its humanitarian programme since the early 1980s through the collaboration with the UNHCR and various countries of asylum. In other words, the historical, political, and contingent factors that pertain to the geography of conflict in the Middle East have paved the way for transnational refugee governance through differential inclusion and strategies. These, in turn, have structured a type of asylum habitus among travellers.

This notion of asylum habitus offers a unique perspective on the mobility of refugees. In other words, asylum habitus—understood in Bordieusian terms as a 'structured structure' (Bourdieu, 1977, p. 72)—emerges through the various practices, improvisations and tactics of travellers. It perpetuates itself through the production, reproduction and diffusion of knowledge about routes and regulations (and other matters) among asylum travellers. Consistent with Bourdieu's general notion of habitus as 'an acquired system of generative schemes', *asylum habitus* is then formed by asylum travellers who obtain information (and misinformation) and use tactics as 'a system of cognitive and motivation' in their respective points of reference (Bourdieu, 1990, pp. 53–55). The asylum habitus conceptualization is in line with the autonomy of migration approach, which sees 'migration as a social movement in the literal sense of the words, not as a mere response to economic and social malaise [and] as a creative force within these [social, cultural and economic] structures' (Papadopoulos, Stephenson and Tsianos, 2008, p. 202).

Viewing the asylum habitus in such a way, however, does not preclude the significance of governance strategies that seek to map, control, regulate and adjust the volume and speed of the journey. Indeed, the asylum habitus reflects these strategies, insofar as it is transnationally and bureaucratically organized by the UNHCR and the collaboration between Turkey and Canada. Moreover, it is actualized and re-actualized through the tactics and practices of asylum travellers en route. In addition, the asylum habitus conceptualization moves the discussion beyond the notion that mobility is 'forced' by foregrounding the calculated and structured reasoning of asylum travellers in the course of their odyssey.

Moreover, with the asylum habitus conceptualization the journey gains a 'relative autonomy with respect to external determinations of the immediate present' (Bourdieu, 1990, p. 56). In other words, the asylum habitus is 'a present past that tends to perpetuate itself into the future by reactivation in similarly structured practices' (ibid., p. 54). The past–present interaction among asylum travellers also *perpetuates* transnational knowledge networks. It exists through the adoption—by travellers just starting out—of the successful tactics practiced by asylum travellers in the past. Successful tactics and failed practices thus provide useful feedback for present and future travellers as they plan and prepare to begin the odyssey. In this way, the asylum journey is cast as 'part of ongoing connections, relations and articulations' (Featherstone, 2008, p. 44).

In a similar vein, failed tactics or asylum practices en route to Canada via Turkey are significant for present and future travellers since tactics en route can be situational and travellers need to be flexible when they encounter—and seek to negotiate—state-imposed strategies and mechanisms. More importantly, to view the process through the lens of asylum habitus is to think of routes and crossings—and asylum and resettlement spaces—as 'produced and practiced, simultaneously physical, mental and social' relations, negotiations and encounters (Merriman, 2012, p. 37).

Figure 1.1 offers a useful summary of the concepts introduced in this section and allows us to contemplate the political imagination of refugee movements away from the classic sedentarist–nomadic approach to the asylum habitus conceptualization. The schema illustrates a general map of the political imagination of migration based on the categorical and analytical distinction of sedentarist and nomadic thinking. To put it differently, if asylum regulations aim to control and order the rules of the journey and to accelerate and decelerate its speed, asylum travellers devise tactics that seek to navigate—and indeed overcome—those strategies. In this sense, the conceptual framework presented aims to foreground both the repressive/exclusionary and productive/effective aspects of power in the context of asylum

36 The asylum journey

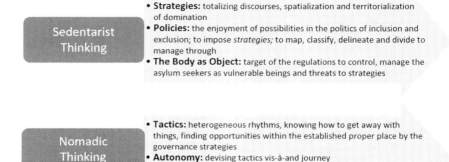

Figure 1.1 Mobility's political imagination under sedentarist and nomadic thinkings

politics. This two-sided Foucauldian notion of power in the asylum journey is replete with a combination of encounters and negotiations constituting the journey as a transnational and multi-layered process beginning with the first encounter with a travel agency to final resettlement in Canada.

Conclusion

This chapter has laid out the general debate raised by the autonomy of migration approach in migration studies and the literature related to refugee journeys. I have highlighted the turn in refugee studies from 'forced migration' to the study of 'transnationalism'. In addition, the chapter has detailed the four, key conceptual, analytical and theoretical frameworks—namely, tactics and strategy, the three phases of the asylum journey, asylum habitus, and mobistasis— that the reader will encounter in her own journey through the book.

In the light of these conceptual frameworks, this book seeks to fill the analytical and empirical gaps that exist in our understanding of asylum/refugee mobility by tracing the journeys and routes of travellers through the extended asylum odyssey. The critical use of the conceptual and theoretical notions deconstructs the legal and bureaucratic binaries such as legality and illegality of the journey as well as travellers taken this legalized and/or illegalized journey by moving beyond the state-centric conceptions in the field of mobility.

Notes

1 For a more detailed discussion of contemporary asylum and migration policies, see Adelman, 1991; Gibney & Hansen, 2003; Gibney, 2004; Squire, 2009; Mountz, 2010; Abass & Ippolito, 2014; Hamlin, 2014.

The asylum journey 37

2 See Loescher's works on the role of the UNHCR (Loescher 1994, 1996, 2001a, 2001b; Loescher, Betts & Milner, 2012).
3 For more discussion, see Portes, Guarnizo & Landolt, 1999; Cheran, 2006; Baubock & Faist, 2010; Dahinden, 2010.
4 The UNHCR report titled *Global Trends: Forced Displacement in 2017* presents recent numbers on global forced displacement. Available at www.unhcr.org/5b27be547.pdf
5 The IOM's missing migrants project and Amnesty International's campaign to stop deaths en route are two examples that highlight the significance of routes and pathways in the global human migratory system. For information on the IOM's Missing Migrants project, http://missingmigrants.iom.int/ And for more details on AI's campaign on securing the routes, www.amnesty.org/en/latest/campaigns/2015/10/eight-solutions-world-refugee-crisis/
6 There are many local and global migrant solidarity networks. For example, Migrants Solidarity Network (GDA) in Turkey (http://gocmendayanisma.org/); the No One is Illegal (NOII) movement in Canada (www.nooneisillegal.org/); and the global mobility network called the No Borders Movement (http://movement-noborders.blogspot.ca/).
7 Here it is useful to note that I do not follow de Certeau's distinction between the 'weak' and the 'strong'.
8 The *Matryoshka* or Russian doll is a set of nested wooden figurines of varying sizes. See https://en.oxforddictionaries.com/definition/russian_doll

2 Asylum and resettlement policies as an 'abstract model' for the asylum journey

As highlighted in the previous chapter, in the context of refugee movement strategies and tactics are not only opposed, but are also in constant negotiation with one other. In other words, strategies and tactics are *relational*. Strategies provide abstract models both for regulators in establishing the rules and protocols associated with mobility and for the mobile individuals who are expected—at least by the regulators—to obey. In this vein, asylum and resettlement related documents function as an abstract model for states and NGOs, on the one hand, and asylum applicants, on the other.

The aim of this chapter is to demonstrate how transnational refugee mobility towards Canada via Turkey is negotiated at the transnational level through an interaction between Turkey's geographical limitation and Canada's resettlement programme, coordinated by the UNHCR. This three-way nexus underpins a distinct type of transnational refugee governance in which the bureaucratic conditions that structure transnational asylum journeys are created and strategies of inclusion and exclusion are deployed.

Viewing the label 'asylum seeker' through a critical lens, the present chapter focuses on three key elements that structure transnational refugee mobility towards Canada via Turkey. The first is the international legal regime underpinning the global refugee system itself—namely, the 1951 Geneva Convention and the 1967 Additional Protocol. These two significant documents map the norms constituting and regulating the designation of persons as refugees, the conditions that must exist for an applicant to be granted the status of 'asylum seeker', and what procedures the UNHCR and countries of asylum resettlement follow in seeking to manage and control the process. The second focus is Turkey—specifically, the geographical limitation it imposes on asylum travellers from non-European countries of origin and its role as the country of asylum. The third point of emphasis is Canada's resettlement programme abroad, specifically that which operates in Turkey to resettle asylum travellers who have been granted refugee status by UNHCR Turkey.

The stacked-Venn diagram below (see Figure 2.1) provides a helpful summary of the bureaucratic processes and transnational negotiation that take place through the asylum journey nexus of home country–Turkey–Canada.

Asylum and resettlement policies 39

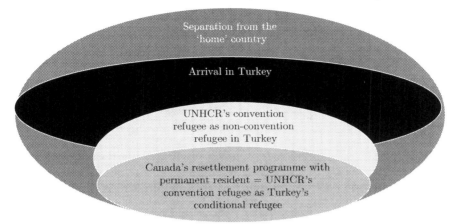

Figure 2.1 The stacked-Venn diagramme illustrating the relational and processual asylum journey en route to Canada via Turkey

The diagram underlines the relational and processual aspects that non-European asylum travellers encounter and interact with in their quest to realize resettlement in Canada by seeking asylum in Turkey. It lays out, on the one hand, all of the relational and processual aspects of the exclusionary and inclusionary strategies in asylum governance—as well as the hierarchical pattern these assume. On the other, it highlights the negotiation of each aspect with the others during the process of asylum and resettlement.

The movement begins with the 'separation' of individuals from the 'home' country—including everything involved in the decision to leave—in this schema marked out in dark-grey (the outer oval). This part of the diagram demonstrates travellers intending to seek improved living conditions. The arrival phase—marked in black—covers persons arriving in Turkey either legally or illegally. At this stage, prospective asylum applicants from non-European countries of origin encounter Turkey's system of asylum governance, including its geographical limitation. This limitation, which means non-European asylum applicants cannot remain indefinitely in Turkey or settle permanently there, is what structures the later phases of the transnational refugee mobility—namely from Turkey onwards to Canada. The pale grey stage addresses the encounter with the UNHCR's Turkey office as applicants seek asylum and wait for determination of their refugee status. For asylum travellers who successfully gain refugee status, the resettlement stage of the journey to Canada—shown in mid-grey (bottom oval) in the diagram—can begin. The use of shading in the diagram is a deliberate attempt to underline not only shifts in time and space throughout the journey, but also the transfiguration and reconfiguration of social, political, and legal identities and/or interpellations during the process of transition and/or arrival from one phase to another.

To put it simply, the traveller located in the light blue part carries the label 'citizen (or resident) of Country A'. Then, once the traveller arrives in Turkey either legally or illegally and seeks asylum, the UNHCR process metamorphosizes the traveller into an 'asylum applicant', mapped in black in the diagram. If the UNHCR recognizes the person as a refugee, the traveller takes on that label/attribution. However, Turkey only recognizes the same person as a 'conditional' or 'non-convention refugee' who is awaiting resettlement in Canada in accordance with Turkey's refugee regulation and geographical limitation (see the section on Turkey's asylum governance in this chapter). After several years, the traveller departs from Turkey to Canada thus taking on the label of 'new immigrant' with permanent residency status. In short, the diagram above provides an illustrative summary of the multi-dimensionality of the process and the multi-layered intersectionality of refugee policy in the mobility from 'home' country to Turkey (as the country of asylum) and from Turkey to Canada (as the country of resettlement).

The UNHCR's formation and role in defining refugees

The UNHCR was formed in 1950 based on the normative frame of the Universal Declaration of Human Rights (UDHR). Its role initially was to coordinate and manage the ongoing humanitarian crises caused by the Second World War, which had generated millions of refugees in Europe (Loescher, 1996). The UNHCR was regarded—especially at the time of its founding—with some scepticism by particularly the United States, and so ratification of the 1951 Geneva Convention was negotiated such that there would be no threat to national sovereignty or any additional financial burden imposed on the signatory parties (Loescher, 2001a). The 1950 Statute of the UNHCR lays down two core mandates and the scope of the organization. First, it seeks 'to ensure refugees' access to protection' by coordinating access with signatory states; second, it is tasked with providing 'durable solutions' for individuals in need of help both in the country of asylum and the country of resettlement (Loescher, Betts & Milner, 2012, pp. 1, 2).

The 1951 Geneva Convention relating to the Status of Refugees is the centrepiece of the global refugee regime, prescribing fundamental norms on the protection of refugees. The Convention defines precisely the designation of a refugee person and what conditions must obtain for an individual to be accorded the designation of refugee. The 1951 Convention's definition of refugee was *geographically* restricted to the European continent and referred *temporally* to the period prior to 1951. The 1967 Additional Protocol to the Convention was negotiated from 1965 as an attempt by the UNHCR to remove these temporal and geographical limitations as its mandate was increasingly undermined by the original 1951 limitations.

Refugee protection during this initial period functioned principally as a weapon against communism—an ideological tool for the Western liberal democracies to assert the apparent superiority of Western values over those of the communist countries during the Cold War (Loescher, 1996). The 1960s—a period of escalation in the ideological polarization and confrontation between the Soviet Union and the United States—heightened US interest in the UNHCR. Hathaway (1991) aptly describes Cold War refugee governance as a period of humanitarian protection prioritized by Western democracies in line with pro-Western values in terms of admission numbers and a high percentage of resettlement. Loescher (1996), for instance, provides a useful account regarding the anti-communist American refugee policy during the Cold War. Under the Reagan administration between 1981 and 1989, the United States admitted more than 700,000 refugees; 96 per cent of these individuals were from communist countries, the intention being to *embarrass* the communist bloc (Loescher, 1996, p. 21). During this period, resettlement countries like the United States and Canada functioned not so much as countries of generalized refugee resettlement, but more like welcoming destinations for political asylum for individuals feeling communist rule.

Since the 1980s, global governance of refugee mobility has had to adjust to changed circumstances—namely, the increased number and character of refugee-producing countries and the skyrocketing number of individuals fleeing them. While the global population of refugees was under three million in the early 1970s, by the 1990s this number had shot up to almost 20 million (Watson, 2009). Two developments from the 1970s onward—the conflicts in Indochina[1] and a series of rolling crises in the Middle East—triggered a huge increase in the number of individuals in need of protection and a diversification in refugee-sending countries. This shifted what had been a post-Second World War European problem into a truly global one, at the same time transforming asylum seeking itself into a broader 'political and legal issue involving sovereignty and rights' (Fassin, 2013, p. 42). This transformation underlines that the asylum process is 'a right of states, not of individuals whose only right is to request and to enjoy asylum once [and if] it is granted' (Schuster, 2003, p. 1).

The increase and diversification of numbers extended the UNHCR's role to finding a permanent place of resettlement for persons in need and to convincing unwilling traditional Western resettlement countries with declining rates of admission and resettlement to do more.[2] Even though the UNHCR highlights the importance of resettlement as an expression of international solidarity and as a responsibility-sharing mechanism, its *Resettlement Handbook* underlines that resettlement is not a legal obligation and 'no country is obliged to resettle refugees' (UNHCR, 2011b, p. 5). This has created ongoing difficulties in finding permanent safe countries for refugees to settle in.

Moreover, consolidation of the 'asylum seeker'[3] label has coincided with a period of an increasing numbers of individuals in need of the UNHCR and an unwillingness among states to facilitate resettlement. At the bureaucratic level, the label[4] limits the target population without having any particular legal basis in international law, in the process greatly expanding the administrative discretion of states while minimizing their humanitarian obligations. It has thus served a political purpose, designed to provide a basis for limiting the number of successful applicants by establishing and then justifying a long and complex bureaucratic process of refugee status determination under the UNHCR system. This contrasts the contemporary period with the much less bureaucratic approach of the Cold War, in which refugees were generally admitted immediately and their legal status determined relatively quickly (Fassin, 2013). In other words, it has become part of the strategic governance of individuals seeking asylum since the label 'recognizes both a process of identification and a mark of identity; [it] implies something independently applied' (Zetter, 2007, p. 173). As such, it has underpinned a system that hierarchically categorizes asylum applicants as either 'genuine' refugees or 'bogus' asylum seekers. The consolidation of the use of the bureaucratic asylum seeker label has further affected the image of individuals seeking asylum. Since the term does not guarantee an applicant's permanent status, the distinction between genuine and bogus refugees, has provided governments with a rationale to deport those deemed 'fake' or 'bogus'.

Approaching this from a Foucauldian perspective, the asylum seeker label has a spatial task in differentiating 'genuine' from 'bogus' applicants and constructing a body of difference in the process of refugee status determination. The aim here is to 'tame and govern the undesirable consequences' of the skyrocketing number of asylum applicants (Rose, 1993, p. 285). More importantly, it has functioned to discipline and divide by labelling and scaling the total sum of the refugee population by seeking 'to maintain a distance between the knowledges and allegiances of experts and [the] calculations' of signatory states (ibid., p. 285). Here, discipline is a technique for organizing, regulating, and normalizing not only rules and norms, but also behaviours of individuals.

The construction of the asylum seeker label as a bureaucratic strategy has thus made it possible to effectively eliminate and limit the number of 'genuine' convention refugees. It has done so by qualifying the term refugee itself with a number of bureaucratic labels that bolster state discretion and expand the means to govern and discipline individuals, i.e., 'convention refugee', 'non-convention refugee', 'bogus' and/or 'genuine' asylum seeker, and so on. This regime thus exercises disciplinary power, since both the UNHCR and signatory states are accorded the authority to establish the criteria for delineating who will be recognized as a 'convention refugee'. This is made possible through 'the victimization of refugees' in which the existing refugee regime 'is only able to provide support to people if they obey and behave as demanded by the protection regime' (De Genova, Mezzadra & Pickles, 2015, p. 71). This aspect of the label reflects what Didier Fassin (2013) has articulated as *truth making* and *truth telling* in asylum seeking in France. Fassin has demonstrated how the bureaucratized asylum governance system there approaches asylum seekers with increased suspicion, and assumes they are 'bogus' until proven otherwise. In other words, the truth telling and truth making in the process of status determination justifies the asylum seeker label since the genuine-ness or otherwise of the applicant has *yet to be determined*. The label therefore forms part of the filtration process in the global system of asylum governance, which provides immediate refugee status to only a *few* applicants, forces the *many* to wait as *asylum seekers*, and rejects *multitudes* as 'bogus economic migrants'.

In the 1990s, asylum journeys were increasingly impaired by increased security measures and control practices at borders. Especially at the USA–Mexico and EU borders, states entered a phase of aggressive combat against the phenomenon of undocumented/illegal/irregular migration. Measures against 'illegal' migration and human smugglers saw the harmonization of global definitions of asylum into domestic asylum and national migration regulations (Sassen, 1999).[5] In the context of the EU mobility regime, the 1997 Treaty of Amsterdam sought to enhance internal freedom, mobility, and justice by taking measures at the edge of the European migratory system with enhanced external border controls, asylum, immigration, and the prevention of crime—i.e., the phenomenon of illegal migration (Bourbeau, 2011; Provine & Sanchez, 2011).

The harmonization of global asylum regulations into the domestic asylum and migration policies reflects what Walters (2004) has described as 'domopolitics'. For Walters, domopolitics 'implies a reconfiguring of relations between citizenship, state and territory' at the national level with the putative aim of enhancing the wellbeing of society by enhanced domestication of migration and asylum regulations (Walters, 2004, p. 241). In other words, domestic asylum and migration politics has gradually reconfigured the 'normative conditions of refugee status determination, a process mirrored by harmonization of asylum and immigration policy at the supranational level' (Zetter, 2007, p. 181). The further integration of global refugee governance into domestic immigration regimes in the 2000s has legitimized more and more preventive immigration politics and bureaucracy—ostensibly for the sake of domestic security or national wellbeing (Watson, 2009).

The relation and difference between the terms 'asylum seeker' and 'refugee'—as well as deployment of the notion of 'illegal' migration—thus functions as a new modality in the domain of asylum governance. This new modality resembles what Canguilhem (1991) has discussed as the distinction between the 'normal', as opposed to the 'abnormal'. If 'the normal'—or, in our frame of discussion, 'the genuine'—is a refugee subject under the 1951 Convention, an asylum seeker arriving by sea or land now has to wait to be identified as either normal or abnormal. In the case of a negative outcome, the person is deemed to be abnormal or pathological for the 'harmonious' equilibrium of the state, due to his or her apparent *abuse* of the refugee system. Once, during the Cold War as discussed above, an individual pleading for refuge at a point of entry would likely be granted refugee status more or less immediately. Now, individuals appearing at the border are interpellated very differently—as mere *applicants* who must wait for hearings conducted by global and domestic authorities to be completed.

Turkey's asylum governance and geographical limitation

The UNHCR's global codes on refugees have increased cooperation between the Commission and the Convention's signatory states, including Turkey. This section of the chapter provides further details of that cooperation, with a focus on developments in Turkey. It begins with a brief historical survey of Turkey's asylum governance and the country's ratification of the 1951 Geneva Convention, which marked a turning point in immigration policy. Second, it details Turkey's governance strategy of geographical limitation on non-European asylum applicants—what I call throughout the book *exclusionary inclusion*. This term simultaneously highlights the inclusion of asylum travellers into Turkey's territorial space in accordance with the global refugee regime *and* the exclusionary aspect of Turkey's asylum governance. In other words, the steady removal of non-European asylum applicants from Turkish territory through the UNHCR's resettlement programme in collaboration with resettlement countries like the United States, Canada, and Australia.

The early 1950s saw a significant reconfiguration of the governmental rationality of Turkey's asylum and refugee policy, with the ratification of the 1951 Geneva Convention and its related protocols. Turkey took this step to gain legitimacy in the international arena under the conditions of Cold War ideological bipolarity. By ratifying, Turkey extended and revised the limited definition of refugee under the previous immigration regime, contained mostly within the country's 1934 Law of Settlement[6] (Sert & Yıldız, 2016). The legal definition of who could be accepted into Turkey as a refugee or an immigrant was very limited at that time, the former being defined as 'a person who belongs to Turkish culture and arrives in the country to seek asylum as a result of exigency and has no intention to settle in Turkey permanently'. Under this regime, any refugee with the intention to permanently settle in Turkey was required to apply to the governor of his or her respective place of temporary residency with a final decision to be made by the Minister of Interior (MoI) and the Council of Ministers (Article 3).

The 1934 Law of Settlement formed part of the larger strategy to create an ethnically and culturally homogenous nation-state by regulating the movement of individuals towards the new Republic, founded in 1923 (Kirişci, 2000). The early Turkish immigration regime thus crafted a *national refugee* category[7] for the resettlement of individuals deemed in need of protection based on their *affinity with Turkish culture* but who were otherwise residing outside Turkey's borders after the collapse of the Ottoman Empire. In other words, a national refugee was a person from one of ethnic groups speaking a Turkic-language fleeing the Balkan countries, Central Asia and/or the Soviet Union, or any Muslim inhabitant of a territory of the former Ottoman Empire, including Albanians, Bosnian Muslims, Pomaks and Tatars (Kirişci, 1991, 1996b). The underlying rationale emerged from the broader early Republican project of constructing an ethnically and culturally 'pure' Turkish nation-state, since the founders perceived the heterogeneous and multi-cultural structure of the Ottoman Empire as the main reason for its collapse (Kirişci, 2000).

Ratification of the 1951 Geneva Convention along with the cooperation with the UNHCR by opening the Ankara office in 1960 was thus a significant milestone in the evolution of Turkey's asylum governance. For the first time, the country standardized its refugee definition in accordance with international norms and regulations by recognizing the role of the UNHCR in designating refugee status to individuals. However, as mentioned in previous chapters, the definition of the term 'refugee' as laid out in the original Convention document was limited in terms of geography, referring then to any person escaping from European countries due to events prior to 1951 (Goodwin-Gill, 2008). From the mid-1960s, the UNHCR sought to revise this definition to remove these limits of time and geography. This culminated in the 1967 Additional Protocol to the Convention. The Protocol, however, left the decision to remove the limitations to signatory states. While Turkey ratified the Protocol, and removed the time limitation, it—along with Monaco, Congo and Madagascar—maintained the geographical limitation (Kirişci, 2007). By retaining this latter restriction, Turkey was simply exercising its 'sovereign right' to decide, as laid out in the 1967 document.[8]

In its current form, Turkey's Law on Foreigners and International Protection (LFIP)[9] defines a refugee as follows:

> A person who as a result of events occurring in European countries and owing to a well-founded fear of being executed for reasons of race, religion, nationality, membership of a particular social group or political opinion, is outside the country of his/her citizenship and is unable or, owing to such fear, is unwilling to avail himself or herself of the protection of that country; or who, not having a nationality and being outside the country of his/her former residence as a result of such events, is unable or, owing to return to it, shall be granted refugee status upon completion of the refugee status determination process [sic].
>
> (LFIP, Article 61)[10]

For individuals fleeing a non-European country of origin, Turkey's asylum governance uses the label *conditional refugee*. A conditional refugee is defined as follows:

> A person who as a result of events occurring outside European countries and owing to a well-founded fear of being persecuted for reasons of race, religion, nationality, membership of a particular social group. [...] Conditional refugees shall be allowed to reside in Turkey temporarily until they are resettled to a third country.
>
> (LFIP, Article 62)

The Protocol has thus offered states valuable discretionary power to determine their boundaries of exclusion and inclusion during humanitarian mobility of refugees. The upshot under Turkish law is that a person from a European state

46 *Asylum and resettlement policies*

seeking political asylum can be granted refugee status in Turkey (and resettled permanently on that basis), while someone from outside Europe pursuing asylum cannot be recognized as such. This is the governance posture that I term *exclusionary inclusion*. Geographically, exclusionary inclusion illustrates how Turkey's asylum politics excludes asylum applicants from non-European countries by explicitly rendering their inclusion in Turkey temporary. Those non-European asylum applicants that are successfully admitted as a refugee by the UNHCR, are labelled as non-convention or conditional refugees. This distinction between convention and non-convention refugees, according to Turkey's asylum governance, is not a restriction against basic rights of individuals. Rather, it is a right that Turkey has pursued based on the options made available by the 1967 Additional Protocol, which bridges humanitarian mobility to Turkey, then to Canada by creating a *transnational refugee structure*. [11]

Turkey's decision to maintain the geographical limitation did not have any significant impact until the early 1980s. In the 1970s, few claimants for refugee status were received at all, and none from outside Europe. Beginning in the 1980s, a series of crises—notably in the Middle East—saw a new era in the management of 'unwanted' or 'undesirable' refugee flows begin. Through into the 1990s, the country saw a sharp increase in the number seeking safe haven due to instability and wars in the Middle East and the Balkans. Exclusionary inclusion via the geographical limitation began to take effect as Turkey sought effective strategic means to govern flows of individuals fleeing Iran, Iraq, Afghanistan, Bulgaria and, later, Bosnia.

The first major political crisis of the new era occurred in neighbouring Iran in 1979 with Khomeini's revolution, which saw more than one million Iranian nationals flee to Turkey (Kirişci, 1996a). Between 1980 and 1988, the Iraq–Iran war ravaged the region and produced a considerable number of people fleeing to Turkey. Events in the Balkans were also important for the Turkish migratory system. When, in 1989, Todor Zhivkov's Bulgaria adopted a policy of assimilation and exclusion— mainly targeting ethnic Turks and Muslims—these Bulgarian nationals sought safe haven in Turkey. The wars produced by the breakup of Yugoslavia in the early 1990s and in Bosnia in 1992 resulted in another massive displacement of people. Turkey's response to this mobility from the Balkans is significant—especially in its showcasing of how the 1934 Law of Settlement functioned.

Another significant migratory flow towards Turkey occurred due to Saddam Hussein's authoritarian regime in Iraq—specifically his use of chemical weapons against Iraqi Kurds in the early 1990s. More than one million Kurdish people fled to neighbouring countries as a result. To manage the flow of refugees, Turkey created a buffer zone for thousands of Kurdish people at the border between Iraq and Turkey, who were housed there in tent cities. Turkey's buffer zone strategy aimed to keep Iraqi nationals stationary at the south-eastern border, the intention being that they would be returned to their homes in Iraq once the conflict was resolved (Kirişci, 1996a). Then, in 2003, the US invasion of Iraq saw more human rights violations there and fresh waves of Iraqis seeking asylum in Turkey. Considering the countries of origin and routes taken by potential asylum seekers, Turkey—located at the crossroads between the Middle East and Europe—is a geographically strategic space for individuals making the asylum journey and remains attractive given its proximity to European countries along with resettlement opportunities to safe countries.

With hundreds of thousands of Iraqis entering, Turkey updated its outdated 1934 Law of Settlement. It introduced the 1994 Regulations on the Procedures and the Principles Related to Mass Inflows and Foreigners Arriving in Turkey or Requesting Residence Permits with the Intention of Seeking Asylum from a Third Country.[12] The 1994 Asylum Regulation[13] has further restricted the mobility of asylum travellers or conditional refugees within the country by consolidating the satellite city regulation. In the early 2000s, while the number of satellite cities was around 30 out of 81 provinces, today the number has reached 62, with the arrival of Syrian nationals on a scale requiring significant expansion of the space needed to house them. This can be read as the de facto removal of the satellite city regulation for Syrian newcomers. In accordance with the satellite city regulation, conditional refugees and asylum seekers are resettled in designated cities by the MoI. Furthermore, asylum seekers and conditional refugees are obliged to provide a signature once a week, or sometimes twice a week, in person at the local police station. If they wish to leave their assigned city, they must request permission from officials beforehand, and if granted permission by the local police they leave on a defined temporary basis. If an asylum seeker leaves his or her satellite, according to Articles 17 and 25 of the Aliens Law (No. 5683), he or she may face a symbolic financial penalty.

This mandatory and temporally uncertain stay means the satellite city functions as open camps. The satellite city—as an urban settlement rather than an enclosed camp—is 'both the emblem of—and the social condition created by—the coupling of war with humanitarian action'. In no way a traditional encampment, both entry to and exit from it are restricted, and any restriction which involves keeping life 'at a distance from the ordinary social and political world' has to be regulated by bureaucratic mechanisms (Agier, 2002, pp. 317–318). Thus, Turkey's asylum governance restricts both the temporality of the stay of an asylum traveller in the country based on geographical origin, but also the mobility within the country itself. Turkey's geographically exclusionary asylum governance foists 'protracted uncertainty' on non-European asylum applicants by imposing 'indefinite knowledge, limited knowledge, and unpredictable legal status' on them (Biehl, 2015, p. 57). Moreover, this uncertainty in waiting and status determination in Turkey is mainly a result of the UNHCR's global refugee protection regime. UNHCR Turkey is the responsible bureaucratic apparatus for dealing with the affairs of non-European asylum applicants. In other words, the collaboration between Turkey and the UNHCR allows Turkey to decline responsibility for the uncertain and unpredictable waiting these people face.

48 Asylum and resettlement policies

Turkey's geographical limitation functions, then, as a kind of geographical racism that fragments the population based on country of origin. Moreover, it ranks the different groups so fragmented, creating hierarchical partitions within the concerned population and subdividing the subjects to control them in accordance with the politics of asylum inclusion and exclusion. This is in line with Foucault's discussion on the modern state's racism and biopower in which 'racism is inscribed as the basic mechanism of power', with race forming the 'break between what must live and what must die' (Foucault, 2003, pp. 254–255). To be more precise, an asylum applicant is included *temporarily* with the risk that she will later be excluded *permanently*. If, however, individuals are convention refugees (i.e., a European national) they are under permanent protection in Turkey and can settle wherever they want, based on the principle of free residence.

Thus, a hierarchical, racial categorization is bureaucratically created for refugees, in which geographically divided 'difference is represented' and 'otherness is produced' based on the 'continent of origin' (Goldberg & Solomos, 2002, p. 3). It should also be noted that Turkey's asylum governance does not *explicitly* marginalize individuals regarding country of origin. The point is to highlight that the distinction of non-European asylum applicant in the first place produces effective 'racisms without [explicit] racism' by signalling 'exclusionary or debilitating racist expressions where the targeted group is not identified through the use of explicit racial language' (Goldberg, 2008, p. 1714). This system concomitantly creates a geographically racialized bureaucratic order and a governance rationale of elimination based on the distinction between 'Europe and its Others' (Pieters, 2002, p. 17).

In terms of demography, Turkey has historically drawn most of its asylum applicant population from Afghanistan, Iran, Iraq—and recently Syria—as the table below details.

Table 2.1 presents both the number of asylum seekers and of refugees that have arrived in Turkey from Afghanistan, Iran, Iraq, and Syria (the main sending countries)—as well as from Somalia, the most common country of origin among African refugees in Turkey. If Syrian nationals are excluded from the data, asylum seekers and refugees from Iraq and Afghanistan are the largest group, followed by arrivals from Iran. The table is appealing to trace the increasing rate of asylum seekers and the declining rate of individuals who are granted refugee status by the UNHCR. It also illustrates that the UNHCR recognizes almost each Syrian as de facto refugee considering the lower number of Syrian applicants.

The numbers are cumulative with new applications added to those from previous years. The reason for the increasing number of Afghani asylum seekers accumulating in recent years is the unwillingness of resettlement countries to settle them. This means refugees from Afghanistan are more likely to stay in Turkey with less chance of resettlement to a third country. Moreover, the massive arrival of Syrians since 2011 has meant that other refugee groups have become statistically irrelevant: more than 95 per cent of refugees in

Table 2.1 Turkey's asylum seekers and refugees based on the country of origin (2010–2017)

Origin		2010	2011	2012	2013	2014	2015	2016	2017
Afghanistan	Asylum seeker	1,956	2,395	14,587	22,330	33,108	90,150	118,116	157,810
	Refugee	1,491	2,613	3,517	3,926	4,188	3,846	3,423	5,603
Iran	Asylum seeker	2,706	2,613	3,663	6,249	11,441	18,735	24,626	25,615
	Refugee	1,911	2,993	3,040	3,321	3,388	5,262	6,966	8,308
Iraq	Asylum seeker	600	3,678	3,431	19,065	54,520	94,455	99,678	115,657
	Refugee	5,277	7,071	9,478	13,467	17,542	24,135	30,398	37,319
Somalia	Asylum seeker	335	646	389	879	1,020	1,598	1,224	2,145
	Refugees	932	1,105	1,669	2,153	2,389	2,364	2,239	2,219
Syria	Asylum seeker	65	205	200	110	250	297	180	163
	Refugee	9	19	248,466	585,601	1,557,899	2,503,549	2,823,987	3,424,237

Source: Data extracted from UNHCR Population Statistics, http://popstats.unhcr.org/en/persons_of_concern (accessed July 2018)

50 *Asylum and resettlement policies*

Turkey are currently from Syria. Syrians are recognized by the UNHCR as refugees de facto; therefore, there is an immense difference between asylum seeker and refugee numbers. Another critical point regarding Syrians is that even though the UNHCR's data and documents admit arrivals from Syria as refugees de facto, Turkey—as in the case of Iraqi Kurds in the early 1990s—constructed refugee camps near to the Syrian border and labelled Syrian arrivals as 'guests' to be later returned once the conflict is resolved. The label 'guest', which has been recently changed to 'holder of temporary protection', illustrates the willingness of Turkey to exclude Syrians since the term connotes no legal, political, and social category at the national level. Most Syrians are currently living in Istanbul or are dispersed across the country, and the current discourse in Turkey is more on the permanent integration of Syrians. There is also subsidiary protection introduced by the LFIP which is a different category from temporary protection. Accordingly, subsidiary protection involves someone as follows:

> A foreigner or a stateless person, who can neither be qualified as a refugee nor as a conditional refugee, shall nevertheless be granted temporary protection upon status determination because if returned to the country of origin or country of [former] habitual residence would: (a) be sentenced to death or face the execution of the death penalty; (b) face torture or inhuman or degrading treatment or punishment; (c) face serious threat to himself or herself by reason of indiscriminate violence in situations of international or nationwide armed conflict.
>
> (LFIP, Article 63)

Article 91 on temporary protection addresses Syrians arriving in Turkey and can be interpreted as Turkey's strategy to differentiate the UNHCR's de facto Syrian refugees from others. According to UNHCR data, through to 31 May 2018 more than forty-eight thousand Syrians have been resettled to more than thirty different resettlement countries. Table 2.2 illustrates the total resettlement numbers to five main countries since 2011.[14] In September 2018, UNHCR has handed over the registration of non-Syrian asylum applicants and their refugee status determination process to the DGMM's provincial

Table 2.2 Numbers on resettlement of Syrians via Turkey between 2011 and 2018

United States	13,326
Germany	6,823
Canada	5,737
Netherlands	4,616
France	4,612
Total	35,114

Source: *UNHCR Resettlement Data Finder,* http://rsq.unhcr.org/en/rsq.unhcr.org/en/#H0ch (accessed 10 July, 2018).

branches. As of 10 September 2018, individuals who apply for international protection in Turkey should register the Provincial Directorates of Migration Management including referral processes. This change does not mean the abolishment of Turkey's geographical limitation. Further research can be conducted on how this change will influence the established asylum habitus en route to resettlement countries by seeking asylum in Turkey.

In a nutshell, Turkey's exclusionary inclusion policy in asylum governance has produced three remarkable results. First, it has created a blurred refugee definition by constructing the conditional refugee label for non-European asylum travellers and a 'temporary protection' category for Syrians individuals. Thus, the geographical limitation has provided Turkey with a flexible means to govern the non-European asylum seeker population by sometimes labelling them as 'guests'. Guests are transformed into holders of temporary protection with the governmental strategy to exclude mainly non-European newcomers.

Second, it has created a two-tiered system of asylum governance in which the UNHCR is more actively involved and cooperates with Turkey in the refugee status determination process and resettlement of successful cases to a third country. Thus, the problems of conditional refugees and asylum seekers faced in Turkey are not the main concern of Turkey's asylum bureaucracy but are the responsibility of the UNHCR. Third, it has transformed Turkey from a country of asylum to a transit or transition space en route to countries of resettlement like the USA, Canada, and recently European countries. The geographical limitation functions therefore as a 'legal' and appropriate way to remove conditional/non-convention refugees—a 'kind' and politically correct version of deportation to resettlement countries.

Canada's refugee resettlement programme and selective inclusion

As laid out in the previous section, Turkey's geographically exclusionary asylum governance has transformed Turkey from a country of asylum to a transition space en route to third countries through the cooperation with the UNHCR and resettlement countries.[15] Canada is one of the traditional resettlement countries and has operated resettlement of UNHCR-recognized refugees from the Middle East since the 1980s. In this, it has actively collaborated with the UNHCR, the IOM and other state parties like Turkey, Egypt, Jordan, and Lebanon in selecting those best fitted for resettlement among the UNHCR-recognized refugees (Hyndman & McLean, 2006).

Accordingly, this section focuses on UNHCR resettlement to Canada. By drawing upon the resettlement figures and Canada's asylum and resettlement programme, the section argues that Canada's resettlement governance abroad functions as a system of what I call *selective inclusion*. It does so by choosing UNHCR-recognized refugees based on their family or personal networks, and their personal abilities and attributes and potential for self-sufficiency.

52 Asylum and resettlement policies

Canada's asylum system is based on two types of refugee programmes: resettlement for overseas refugees and an inland asylum application process. Canada ratified both the 1951 Convention and the 1967 Additional Protocol in 1969, one year after the United States' ratification (Macklin, 2009). It is still the world's second largest country of resettlement with its 'bureaucratic centralization and high levels of agency insulation from both politics and judicial review' (Hamlin, 2014, p. 11). This means it offers more comprehensive protection 'in all potential venues' within the process of refugee status determination and resettlement processes (ibid., p. 176).

Until the passing of the 1976 *Immigration Act*, amended by the *Immigration and Refugee Protection Act of 2002* (IRPA),[16] Canada implemented its own asylum and refugee resettlement programme, and did not have domestic legislation in the asylum domain. The Department of Citizenship and Immigration Canada (CIC) administers the resettlement programme, which has been effective since 1978, with the collaboration of the UNHCR and the country of asylum (UNHCR, 2013). Canada's *Immigration Act 1976* was one of the most welcoming pieces of legislation, and the Act successfully incorporated the UNHCR convention standards into Canada's immigration law. The Act created two categories of refugee—convention refugees and humanitarian refugees. The latter was developed 'to admit people from overseas who did not meet the Convention's specific definition' (Adelman, 1991, p. 173), based on the UNHCR's definition of a refugee as someone in 'fear of well-founded persecution'. Canada's welcoming and more liberal asylum policy continued until the end of 1980s, and the Canadian people were awarded the UNHCR's Nansen Award in 1986 for their generous and humanitarian asylum and refugee admission policy (Macklin, 2009).

In contrast to Turkey—which constructs a distinct hierarchical and geographical categorization of refugees in its official definition—Canada's domestic regulation adopts the 1951 Convention definition of a refugee. For inland asylum applications, the Immigration and Refugee Board (IRB) was established as an 'independent tribunal' in 1989 (Macklin, 2009, p. 82). The Board conducts hearings and determines who is a Convention refugee (or a person with similar circumstance in need of protection) for the purposes of resettlement. The country resettles between seven and ten thousand UNHCR-recognized refugees annually from among the fifteen to twenty thousand submitted refugees by the UNHCR after the selection process conducted by visa officers overseas (see Table 2.3 below).

However, the increasing number of boat people in the late 1980s prompted a significant transformation in Canada's welcoming asylum system. A deterrence policy in refugee resettlement emerged with the introduction of the *Refugee Reform Bill* of 1988 (known as C-55) and the *Refugee Deterrents and Detention Bill* of 1988 (C-84) (Hamlin, 2014). These two pieces of legislation not only introduced a stricter policy of deterrence in refugee status determination to reduce the number of asylum seekers but established a more comprehensive schema for selecting UNHCR-recognized refugees

Table 2.3 Canada's resettlement numbers through 31 May, 2018

Year	UNHCR submission	Departures to Canada	Via Turkey
2014	15,032	7,233	1,949
2015	22,886	10,236	1,125
2016	19,790	21,865	2,911
2017	4,118	8,912	1,196
2018	4,258	1,894	187

Source: Data extracted from UNHCR Resettlement Data Finder, http://rsq.unhcr.org/en/rsq.unhcr.org/en/#Sh8j (accessed 10 July 2018).

for resettlement. It also provided for more 'discretionary detention for asylum seekers' in line with heightened security and risk concerns (Hamlin, 2014, p. 48). The enactment of IRPA in 2002—notably bills C-31 and C-11—were a 'direct response to September 11' (Macklin, 2002, p. 21). Moreover, the entire amendment—especially C-31 and C-11—was very controversial and the subject of much debate, in a way that the original 1976 legislation simply had not been.

In the early 1990s, Canada aimed to secure its land border by reducing the number of illegal entries generally and arrivals of asylum applicants from the United States in particular. The country's approach to curbing those entering after an unsuccessful attempt in safe third country (i.e. the United States) was modelled on Europe's 1990 Dublin Convention (Macklin, 2005, 2013). This attempt was completed with the *Safe Third Country Agreement* with the United States in 2005, which sought 'to deflect asylum seekers who pass through the United States en route to Canada' (Hoerder & Macklin, 2006, p. 812) and 'to make it impossible for prospective asylum seekers to travel to Canada' to claim asylum inland (Macklin, 2009, p. 106). Thus, Canada has successfully secured its only land border against entries from the United States, where 'around 30–40 per cent of asylum seekers [had entered] Canada' previously (ibid., p. 107). In other words, if a person already travelled through the United States as the first country of arrival, his or her status should be determined there. Thus, an asylum seeker arriving via land—in practice, most often from Mexico—cannot enter Canada from the United States with the intention of seeking asylum. Canada can send such an asylum seeker back to the USA since: 1) the asylum seeker arrived there first; and 2) it is a 'safe country'—defined as a 'non-refugee producing [country where] refugees can enjoy asylum without danger' (Kjaergaard, 1994, p. 651). The 2005 *Safe Third Country Agreement* has resulted in a significant drop in entry numbers via land from the United States (Macklin, 2009).

In addition, IRPA has mandated interdiction at sea and in the air to reduce 'illegal' entries, with severe penalties for any marine and air companies who violate the law. This proves how travel agencies are expected to perform the task of border controls and checks. Furthermore, Canada requires an entry visa from most of the major refugee-producing countries. In other words, an

54 Asylum and resettlement policies

individual from such a country must first obtain a valid Canadian visa before landing in Canada and requesting asylum. Since such a visa will almost certainly never be granted to anyone deemed likely to seek asylum in the first place, this can be interpreted as creating a de facto condition of 'inadmissibility' to Canada for potential asylum seekers from those countries (Macklin, 2009).

As opposed to Turkey's geographical limitation, Canada's asylum governance implements a 'designated countries of origin' approach.[17] These are mainly European and Western countries that are considered safe and respectful of human rights. Whereas Turkey implements a geographical limitation over individuals who arrive from places known as traditionally refugee-producing countries, Canada controls asylum-related mobility from the designated countries to prevent abuse of the refugee regime. For example, if a person from Germany arrives in Turkey and seeks asylum there, he or she can be granted refugee status. If the same person arrives in Canada and seeks asylum, he or she cannot be recognized as a refugee since Germany is a designated country of origin. Or, if a person from Iran arrives in Turkey and seeks asylum, he or she cannot be recognized as a convention refugee since Iran is a non-European country. If the same person arrives in Canada and seeks asylum, he or she *can* be granted refugee status since Iran is not one of the designated countries.

Regarding resettlement, immigration, and family reunification, Canada's Refugee and Humanitarian Resettlement Program operates based on three categories: government-assisted refugees, privately sponsored refugees, and blended visa office-referred refugees under the administration of CIC, which allocates a target number by consulting provincial governments to determine the number of refugees for resettlement (UNHCR, 2014). Based on numbers or quotas provided to it, CIC prepares an Annual Report and proposes a total number for resettlement to Canada's parliament every November. With the consultation of provincial governments, the federal government allocates a quota for resettlement numbers and sends the allocated numbers to the visa offices abroad. Visa officers conduct interviews with refugees abroad to select who will be resettled. Then, target numbers are shared with resettlement partners, the UNHCR and the IOM (UNHCR, 2014). Accordingly, government-assisted refugees are those UNHCR-referred refugees who are granted financial, social, and cultural support from the federal/provincial governments—such as monthly financial assistance, language courses, help in finding accommodation, and so on—during their first year in Canada. This is not the case for the inland refugee claimants, who can access only limited assistance—such as help finding accommodation and financial support—until the completion of refugee status determination (Murdie, 2008).

The second category is privately sponsored refugees who are supported by organizations or private individuals for up to one year (UNHCR, 2014). These individuals can be persons in refugee-like situations. This means that they do not necessarily have to be UNHCR-recognized convention refugees.

The category of 'blended visa office-referred refugees', which was launched in 2013, are UNHCR-referred refugees who have been matched with private sponsorship and are thus supported jointly by the government and private parties (UNHCR, 2014).

IRPA regulates the principles for immigration, asylum seeking, and resettlement to Canada. Those resettlement objectives delineate ideational principles to help persons in need of resettlement by fulfilling Canada's humanitarian duties and to support family reunification by collaborating with international organizations and NGOs, other federal departments, and provincial governments. At the same time, immigration objectives are under the framework of integration discourse and the social, cultural and political benefits that immigrants can provide. The discourse underpins the public health and safety in the case of admission and successful integration of prospective immigrants.[18] Note that once resettled, they are no longer refugees, but immigrants with permanent residency status. This means that Canada's immigration and resettlement is a venue of intersection where the selection fits into the integration discourse of economic immigrants and family reunification with concerns about the security and health of society. While Turkey's exclusionary asylum governance denies the social, political, and economic integration of the asylum applicants, Canada resettles some of Turkey's geographically excluded asylum applicants by selecting refugees in line with economic immigration and integration discourse.

To be considered for resettlement to Canada, an individual refugee or a family should: 1) meet the UNHCR criteria as the recognized refugee; 2) be eligible as a stateless non-refugee and/or; 3) be a non-refugee dependent family member (UNHCR, 2011b). What, then, are the basic requirements that a potential refugee should meet to be considered for resettlement? Resettlement of government-assisted refugees from Turkey is subject to 'highly selective and state-managed' scrutiny (Hyndman & McLean, 2006, p. 346). After arriving and seeking asylum in Turkey, resettlement refugees must *first* convince the UNHCR to grant them refugee status. Then, the UNHCR submits the cases of the recognized refugees to the Embassy of Canada in Ankara. Visa officers in the Embassy call potential resettlement refugees for interview. During the interview, visa officers consider such criteria as the interviewees' personal abilities—including their ability to speak French and/or English—their education and profession, familial ties in Canada and their potential for self-sufficiency during the first three to five years after being resettled there (UNHCR, 2013, p. 4).

Today, refugee resettlement via Turkey is heavily weighted towards family reunification. In other words, the existence of familial ties is a principal catalyst for resettlement of UNHCR-recognized refugees in Canada. Interviews with Iranian and Iraqi resettled refugees that I conducted both in Turkey and Canada suggest that a resettlement refugee is more likely to have a social, cultural, financial sponsorship or social capital/network in resettlement sites (D'Addario, Hiebert & Sherrell, 2007). Moreover, they have at least one family member with the experience of having applied for asylum in Turkey and being resettled to Canada in the past. Therefore, established social networks and social capital are a crucial in the resettlement process (Lamba & Krahn, 2003). This is also the case for other resettlement countries, like Australia, and has emerged as a reality for resettlement of Syrians.

In Table 2.4, I chose four countries of origin in terms of highest number of asylum applicants and refugees in Turkey (see Table 2.1). Canada resettles mostly Iranian, Iraqi (and more recently Syrian) refugees via Turkey, but also a small number of Afghanis. As both tables suggest, the historically structured asylum habitus is at work here. Iranian and Iraqi refugees have been resettling in Canada since the 1980s. This is the basis for the established asylum habitus that has emerged since, whereby networks and circulation of knowledge among travellers has solidified over time and Canada becomes the 'natural' destination for new asylum travellers commencing the odyssey via Turkey.

Table 2.4 Resettlement to Canada via Turkey through UNHCR's collaboration through 31 May 2018

Country of origin	Year	Number of refugees
Afghanistan	2014	15
	2015	20
	2016	0
	2017	15
	2018	0
Iran	2014	1,019
	2015	352
	2016	193
	2017	121
	2018	43
Iraq	2014	892
	2015	687
	2016	279
	2017	327
	2018	35
Syria	2014	4
	2015	52
	2016	2,438
	2017	742
	2018	101

Source: Data extracted from UNHCR Resettlement Data Finder, http://rsq.unhcr.org/en/rsq.unhcr.org/en/#4VMg (accessed 10 July, 2018).

For the resettlement of Syrians, the first flights arrived in Canada early December 2015 from other countries in the region, like Lebanon and Jordan. Canada completed the resettlement of 25,000 Syrian refugees from Jordan at the end of February 2016[19] and resettled over 8,200 Syrian refugees from Lebanon.[20] Canada began to resettle Syrian refugees from Turkey in early 2016. According to an IOM press releases, the first group of 284 Syrian refugees arrived in Canada from Turkey in January 2016.[21]

Considering the selection criteria that visa officers take into account, Canada's refugee resettlement programme functions more as a process of 'selective migration'. Here, the country applies a 'human capital model' for the selection of permanent immigrants (Koslowski, 2013, p. 26). To be more specific, factors including education, personal qualifications, language ability (English or French), and personal support networks are prioritized by visa officers. While the statutory wording is such that these criteria 'may' be considered by Canada's visa officers abroad, in practice they form the bedrock of selection. The annual approval of thousands of refugees from Turkey according to 'best fit' criteria thus demonstrates how the 'humanitarian' refugee resettlement programme turns into a means of human capital recruitment. In sum, the discretionary power provided to visa officers means that they function like border security forces and labour recruitment agencies.

It should be highlighted that in the course of my fieldwork in Turkey, an IOM staff member[22] stated to me that Canada's refugee resettlement programme is still 'more welcoming' to refugees in comparison with Australia and United States. Indeed, Hamlin's (2014) comparative study on the politics of asylum in United States, Canada and Australia suggests as much. Hamlin found that Canada is more welcoming in its resettlement programme—with the incorporation of UNHCR guidelines into Canada's IRPA—and that its Supreme Court is less involved in the asylum process and policies compared to Australia's High Court.

Nevertheless, it is clear that Canadian asylum and resettlement governance has become more integrated within the country's broader immigration system over time. This is manifest in the language in the Act, which emphasizes the *value of integration*, such that implicitly or otherwise, fitness is prioritized over, need. For instance, the Act emphasizes how refugees—like other kinds of migrants—impact Canada's social, cultural, and economic structure. In sum, this channel of migration has increasingly been expected to comport with the discourse of 'regular' immigrants established patterns of integration into Canadian society—namely, that they be ready to integrate from day one.

Once a refugee's resettlement is successfully completed, the conditional refugee (the label attributed by Turkey's governance regime) takes on a new attribution—*new immigrant with permanent residency status*. The metamorphosis of the individual at this point reflects a broader fact about the key differences that underly the Turkish and the Canadian systems—the system of *exclusionary inclusion* set against that of *selective inclusion*. The first difference arises from Turkey's geography: while Canada is isolated from global humanitarian crises, Turkey's geopolitical position makes it a 'natural' point of entry for massive flows of people fleeing difficulty. The second relates to the first: while Turkey has generally faced a 'blanket' problem in the context of rolling political crises in neighbouring countries, Canada has historically been a primary resettlement site for the UNHCR as it seeks to find a home for referred refugees collecting in crisis zones. These differences are complementary and make the UNHCR's guidelines a 'natural' bridge between the two systems. In other words, the asylum journey has become a transnational one whereby Turkey's exclusionary inclusion produces a 'pool' of potential cases that have the opportunity for selective resettlement to Canada via the UNHCR and the IOM.

In a nutshell, Turkey—as the primary space of mobistasis—temporarily hosts non-European asylum travellers who must be eventually resettled elsewhere. UNHCR Turkey conducts interviews of asylum travellers to determine their status. The Embassy of Canada decides the eligibility of persons for resettlement. Those deemed eligible must then clear a medical examination before arriving in Canada. Finally, the IOM organizes the cultural orientation programme in Istanbul and distributes flight tickets and other bureaucratic documents to those who are to be resettled.

More importantly, for resettlement countries like Canada, Turkey has become a kind of 'refugee bazaar'—a 'marketplace' of people from which permanent immigrants can be selected. Geographical limitation produces this 'pool' of 'human capital', with non-European asylum travellers mainly from Iran and Iraq settled into a structured asylum habitus, while resettlement to Canada is becoming more and more selective. In other words, Turkey as the asylum space functions to select the 'best fitting' refugees for resettlement to Canada and eliminates 'misfit applicants' who are submitted to the Embassy of Canada by the UNHCR. This 'selective concern' has been prevalent 'in the interest of domestic economic development' in Canadian refugee and resettlement governance since the 1980s, even though Canada has continued to collaborate with its Western allies in fulfilling its international human rights law on refugees (Hathaway, 1988, p. 676).

In addition, it is line with the UNHCR's discourses on resettlement—which emphasize 'no legal obligation', 'burden sharing' and 'prevention of fraud'. For instance, the UNHCR's *Resettlement Handbook* states that 'resettlement activities are particularly vulnerable to fraud because of the benefits they offer' (UNHCR, 2011b, p. 69, 115).[23] In this sense, while Canada shares the burden of Turkey by resettling refugees, the country needs to be selective due to the apparent vulnerability of the programme to fraud and needs to select the resettlement refugees in accordance with the 'integration' discourse. In a nutshell, Canada's resettlement governance via Turkey functions as an immigrant recruitment programme based on *quality* rather need. The *humanitarian needs* of Turkey's conditional or non-European refugees are met by Canada's refugee resettlement programme, if—and only if—refugees can convince (through devised and improvised tactics) all the bureaucratic mechanisms that they are *worthy*. In the end, Canada aims to maximize the utility and benefit that it can extract from its own 'humanitarian' refugee resettlement programme.

Conclusion

Policies in the governance of asylum and refugee mobility are significant since they map and tabulate abstract codes and guidelines along with their respective interpellations. The chapter has documented how the asylum and refugee regulations of Turkey and Canada serve to frame and map transnational refugee journeys to Canada via initial asylum seeking in Turkey. The chapter has highlighted how an official and bureaucratic structure to fully regulate asylum journeys to Canada via Turkey have been facilitated by state-to-state cooperation between the two countries.

Turkey—by choosing to maintain geographical limitation—excludes non-European asylum travellers as refugees and allows them only temporary stay in Turkey until they are resettled to a third country by the UNHCR. More importantly, geographical limitation as a strategy of *exclusionary inclusion* has historically formed a pathway in Turkey for largely Iranian and Iraqi asylum travellers to move to the United States and Canada. Turkey's geographical limitation has thus turned the country into a transition space for asylum travellers in which the restriction itself makes Turkey an attractive site for seeking asylum en route to Canada.

In contrast to Turkey's exclusionary inclusion, Canada's resettlement programme is one of *selective inclusion*—based on a 'best fit' selection of individuals for resettlement. The chapter has demonstrated how visa officers in the Embassy of Canada in Ankara thus act simultaneously as border guards *and* labour recruitment agents by prioritizing the personal attributes of the applicants in the process of admission.

This transnational structure of refugee mobility has been in operation since the early 1980s. Since this time, a structured asylum habitus among asylum travellers has consolidated, a development that will be further discussed in later chapters. Moreover, it has transformed Canada's refugee resettlement programme into a family reunification one through the selective inclusion. By selective inclusion, the country can integrate its humanitarian resettlement programme more in line with the 'regular system' based on the personal qualities of potential newcomers. Furthermore, it has taken on the benefit of a 'triple filtration' process of highly bureaucratized governance that starts with Turkey's asylum bureaucracy, moves to the delineation process of 'genuine vs bogus' by the UNHCR, and concludes with induction and medical checks by the IOM.

Notes

1 The increasing numbers of persons waiting for resettlement and the phenomenon of 'boat people' that emerged in the 1970s proves that few countries have been willing to take on resettlement responsibility. The so-called 'boat people' came predominantly from Vietnam as an outcome of the war there starting in the late 1970s and continuing to the 1990s. This is, according to the UNHCR, related to economic and social factors associated with the journeys of 'boat people' (UNHCR, 2011b, pp. 48–49).

60 *Asylum and resettlement policies*

2 For more information, see the UNHCR *Resettlement Handbook* (2011, pp. 3 and 36), which lays out the three main functions of resettlement.
3 For an archaeological discussion of the concept of asylum, see Didier Fassin's (2013) ethnographic work. His article begins with Ancient Greek and Roman usage, when the term asylum was coined. At that time, it connoted sacredness and hospitality. For a further discussion of the etymological trajectories of the term asylum and its relation to sanctuary, see Jennifer Bagelman's (2016) work on sanctuary.
4 James Hathaway, in his opening speech, stated clearly that 'asylum seeker' is a political term, constructed to limit the boundaries of protection and assistance to individuals seeking asylum until refugee status—a distinct legal category, unlike asylum—has been determined (UNHCR Turkey Third Academic Seminar, Keynote Speech. *Turkey's Experience with Urban Refugees: Modalities and Future Prospective,* May 15–16, 2012).
5 For instance, at the EU level. In the UK, this has been achieved in successive statutes—namely, the *Asylum and Immigration Appeal Act 1993*, the *Asylum and Immigration Act 1996*, and the *Immigration and Asylum Act 1999*.
6 Law No. 2510 of 1934 regarding immigration and refugee movement into the country. This statute—also known as the Law of Settlement—remained the only law regarding the asylum and refugee system in Turkey until the 1990s.
7 This category was devised after the Turkish War of Independence, following the partition of the Ottoman Empire at the end of the First World War. Population exchanges between Greece and the new Turkish Republic in 1922 and 1923 resulted in some two million Greek Orthodox and Muslim Turkish nationals being forced to move residence (Oran, 2004). Based on the 1934 Law of Settlement, although Muslim Bosnians, Circassians, Pomaks, and Tatars were admitted for resettlement in Turkey, non-Muslim Gagauz Turks, and Shi'a Azeris were not considered as national refugees or accepted immigrants (Kirişci, 2000).
8 The 1951 Convention and 1967 Additional Protocol are available at www.unhcr.org/protect/PROTECTION/3b66c2aa10.pdf (accessed 10 July, 2016).
9 Official Gazette No. 28615, Law 6458 April 11, 2013.
10 The *Law on Foreigners and International Protection* (LFIP) was published in the Official Gazette in April 2013 and has been translated into ten foreign languages including English, Russian, Italian, Bulgarian, German, Spanish, French, Greek, Persian, and Arabic. The documents can be accessed at www.goc.gov.tr/icerik6/the-law-on-foreigners-and-international-protection-in-10-languages_914_1017_1405_icerik The English-language version of the LFIP is available at www.goc.gov.tr/files/files/YUKK_I%cc%87NGI%cc%87LI%cc%87ZCE_BASKI(1)(1).pdf. (accessed 10 October, 2016).
11 Under the section defining 'conditional refugee', the law provides further explanation on the grounds for adopting the term as a right of states in international law. The law stipulates: 'Turkey signed the 1951 Convention with a "geographical restriction" which has been stipulated in Article 1 of the Convention'. Available at www.goc.gov.tr/icerik6/conditional-refugee_917_1063_5783_icerik (accessed 10 October, 2016).
12 The 1994 Asylum Regulation was revised in 2006 and was replaced with the LFIP in 2013.
13 Since the early 2000s, Turkey has facilitated cooperation in the domain of asylum and immigration with European countries, EU agents, and EU border agencies in an attempt to harmonize its migration law in line with the EU *Acquis Communautaire* (see Kaya, 2009 on Turkey's harmonization of its asylum and migration legislation).
14 For further resettlement statistics on the Syrians under temporary protection, see www.goc.gov.tr/icerik6/temporary-protection_915_1024_4748_icerik For statistics on international protection, see www.goc.gov.tr/icerik6/international-protection_915_1024_4747_icerik

Asylum and resettlement policies 61

15 As of 2018, there are twenty-seven resettlement countries worldwide (see www.unhcr.org/information-on-unhcr-resettlement.html). The rise in the number of resettlement countries since 1980 can be regarded as the UNHCR's success to convince more countries in finding permanent and durable solutions and spaces to refugees; however, the number of admitted and resettled refugees has not increased due to the constructed labels and bureaucratic categories.
16 IRPA was amended again in December 2014.
17 For the list of countries, visit www.canada.ca/en/immigration-refugees-citizenship/services/refugees/claim-protection-inside-canada/apply/designated-countries-policy.html (accessed September, 2018). As of 15 February 2013, Mexico has been added to the list of designated countries.
18 For the detailed content of IRPA, including the objectives of the Act, see http://laws-lois.justice.gc.ca/eng/acts/I-2.5/index.html (accessed September, 2018).
19 Available at www.iom.int/news/canada-iom-complete-resettlement-25000-syrian-refugees (accessed July 12, 2016).
20 Available at www.iom.int/news/resettlement-syrians-lebanon-canada-passes-8000 (accessed July 12, 2016).
21 Available at www.iom.int/news/first-syrian-refugees-fly-turkey-canada (accessed July 12, 2016).
22 Interview held in Istanbul, July 2014.
23 For a detailed explanation of the resettlement and fraud, see Chapter 4 of the *UNHCR Resettlement Handbook*.

3 The separation phase of the asylum journey

Brigden and Mainwaring (2016, p. 409) have aptly adopted the metaphor of the Russian doll (*matryoshka*)—namely 'a nested series of journeys within journeys'—to describe the asylum odyssey. The image of the *matryoshka* perfectly captures the various elements of the governance regime—including asylum regulations—employed by states and other actors as well as the tactics and practices asylum travellers adopt in negotiating these en route. This is no less true for the asylum journey to Canada via Turkey, which involves a number of distinct phases for asylum travellers along the way.

The next three chapters in the book (Chapter 3, 4, and 5) are dedicated to the empirical analysis of each of these phases, in turn. More concretely—drawing on Arnold van Gennep's (1960, pp. 10–11) notion of 'rites of passage'—they address, respectively, the *separation phase* (en route to Turkey), the *liminal phase* (in Turkey) and the *incorporation phase* (arrival in Canada). These phases, however, imply no normative teleology and should not be seen in strictly linear terms. As the metaphor of the *matryoshka* suggests, they are *relational* (as parts of a loosely structured whole) and *nested*. And each phase also involves multiple journeys for each asylum traveller. In a sense, the odyssey of every traveller is its own *matryoshka*—once unpacked, we see a distinct set of individual experiences and engagements between travellers and the bureaucratic regulations and strategies of asylum governance they encounter along the way.

The present chapter takes up the first phase of the journey, the separation phase, which is the part of the odyssey in which the traveller is planning the move and preparing for what is to come. By bringing their narratives and experiences into a structured empirical analysis in this chapter, the presentation of the separation phase underlines the first step in the asylum traveller's mobility: the decision to move from the 'home' country and to set out. What will follow will be a multi-journey odyssey that takes travellers first to the country of asylum and then onward, hopefully to the country of resettlement. Along the way, they will engage in a multitude of practices within a structured asylum habitus, in which the production and diffusion of information and misinformation—and the further diffusion of the knowledge so produced—will be central.

Asylum seeking as tactic

> I have a role model [referring to her mother], who went to university, became a nurse and is an independent woman [...] As a role model, she differs from what the Iranian tradition expects of us [women]. I did not want to be a part of [that]. I wanted to finish my education, to become an independent woman. So I left my country to finish my education and I did it without encouragement from anyone.[1]

This statement by Janice—a Baha'i Iranian asylum traveller—underscores her motivation to leave her home country. And her stated motivation differs somewhat from the conventional wisdom concerning the refugee experience, which essentializes the fear, vulnerability and repression faced in the home country. Janice decided to take the asylum journey to continue her university education—Baha'is are banned from entering public universities in Iran. Her asylum journey, however, can be seen as a certain kind of personal strategy of investing effort to reach self-autonomy and independence rather an imposed strategy in Iran following the Islamic Revolution, which is when the ban on Baha'i education came into effect.

To begin with, seeking asylum is a response to strategies which rationalize a *proper* space of exclusion, discrimination, and inequality of certain groups in their home countries. This includes Baha'is and/or Lesbian–Gay–Bi–Trans–Queer (LGBTQ) individuals in Iran, and Christian and/or LGBTQ individuals in Iraq. It also extends to ethnic, gender, or belief-related fear of persecution in Afghanistan, Sudan, Somalia and Syria. The asylum journey is a necessity for an LGBTQ individual's survival, since this is one of the most marginalized groups in Iran. It is a 'right to escape [as] a privileged way to subjectivity, a road to freedom and independence' (Mezzadra, 2004, p. 267). The experience of Janice highlights that an asylum journey is more than the politics of exclusion and inclusion—it is for many also a 'formative and transformative experience' that offers new opportunities, like access to education (BenEzer & Zetter, 2014, p. 297). More to the point, travellers retain the agency to navigate the state's discriminatory strategies, which seek 'to produce, tabulate and impose' conformity. Here, the strategy and tactics of 'calculated action determined by the absence of a proper locus' come in to play. In other words, travellers navigate by '*knowing how to get away with things*' (de Certeau, 1988, pp. xix, 36, 37, italics added).

For instance, Ingrid—an asylum traveller from Iran—described how she launched her asylum journey when I asked her about what kind of discrimination she had faced in Iran. She summarized this as follows: 'we [the Baha'i] were not allowed to enter university or even take the university entrance exam [...]. Actually, we lived under all manner of conditions like this [discriminatory and exclusionary policies]'.[2] The statement provides a clue on how discrimination in Iran has become so ingrained in everyday life that it forms the motive to start out on the 'journey of hope', as one respondent memorably described it to me.

The separation phase of this journey of hope is the first bureaucratic step of the asylum odyssey. It includes preparation, as well as the deliberate and calculated tactics and planning required for the 'pre-crossings' stage (Soto, 2016). This planning involves accessing valid travel documents, visiting travel agencies and packing (or, if the travel is being arranged through human smugglers, *not* packing). This is a phase of *rehearsing*, a fact that is inseparable from the formation of a structured asylum habitus among past, present and future travellers. Travellers drill how they will navigate the various hardships they can expect along the way and the multiple dimensions of migration infrastructure they will encounter: border controls and the immigration bureaucracies of the countries en route. It is also the first phase of improvisation and rehearsal of tactics in the quest for a better life in the country of asylum and resettlement.

The role of *information* here is central. In other words, prospective asylum travellers obtain information—and, indeed, *mis*information—from experienced travellers about the odyssey. This can consist of knowledge about how to trace routes, which transport to use, where to stay in Turkey, and the best place to nominate for resettlement through the UNHCR. It may also include what to say (and *not* to say) during interviews with Turkish authorities, the UNHCR, and Canadian visa officers.

Within this asylum habitus, the transfer of (mis)information is situated in a complex of network relations. This information/misinformation network is—as Brigden (2013) notes—a form of 'mobile knowledge' that constitutes, in Featherstone's terms, 'forms of agency' (2008, p. 8). It has a beginning in time and in space, such as when a prospective traveller from Iran or Iraq begins to calculate steps and obtain information on Canada and Turkey during the separation phase. More specifically, it is part of a 'multi-dimensional geography [in which] time and space' (and, indeed, space–time) become 'both locational and experiential' through the perpetuation of practices and relations en route (Merriman, 2012, p. 34). Space, then, is not a 'passive locus of social relations'. Rather, it is an assemblage of 'produced and practiced, simultaneously physical, mental and social relations, negotiations and routinized practices, as well as repudiations of certain governance strategies (ibid., p. 37). Spatially situated and habituated practices generate transnational and translocal dissemination of knowledge, which creates 'new kinds of solidarity' among travellers (Featherstone, 2008, p. 116).

In a nutshell, the asylum habitus of travellers—and the networked solidarity among them—is informed by the (re-)production of knowledge about the journey among travellers—past, present, and future. This 'mobile knowledge' is central to asylum travellers' agency and knowledge about what my respondents call 'the United Nations in Turkey'—where the UNHCR office is located, and the number of interviews they are obliged to go through for resettlement. Each aspect of this knowledge is gleaned from the combined experience of travellers who have taken this journey before. In this sense, the produced and obtained knowledge by travellers constitute a certain kind of power/knowledge, which provides a productive and effective way to support the initial step in the journey.

'*Ben Turkce bilmiyor*': Pre-travel preparation

The phrase '*Ben Turkce bilmiyor*'—memorized by one of the Iranian travellers I interviewed—is, when stated this way, grammatically incorrect. It can, nevertheless be understood, and translates as 'I don't speak Turkish'. Stella's mistake, however, may be—unconsciously or otherwise—deliberate, in the sense that she may have intended to make it clear to both local people and the Turkish authorities that she *really* does not know Turkish. Or, at least, to indicate a very poor grasp of it. This was the only Turkish sentence that she and her family learned before crossing the border to Turkey. Stella learned this sentence—and learned to *memorize it*—from other asylum travellers. These might have been friends and/or relatives who had already experienced the journey—including a period of mobistasis in Turkey—and had been finally resettled in Canada. This underlines the importance of established knowledge networks within the structured asylum habitus. Memorizing this sentence can be regarded as a tactical move for Stella, for specific encounters with the Turkish local community upon arrival in Turkey. This small practice of memorization calls attention to a bigger question: the extent to which the pre-journey stage—the entire odyssey really—is rationally calculated and deliberate or a hurried escape from a repressive country of origin. Whether unconscious or deliberate, rational or hasty, this micro-practice signifies the presence of some calculated tactics in this initial period.

The asylum travellers I conducted interviews with in Turkey and Canada were mostly Iranian and Iraqi. As mentioned in the last chapter, nationals from Iran first began taking the asylum odyssey via Turkey to countries of resettlement—mostly the United States, Canada, and Australia—in the 1980s; for the Iraqis, this dates to the 1990s. In any event, for both nationalities the asylum journey has now become a 'routinized path', a consolidated asylum habitus. This routinization of the path of asylum via Turkey makes the separation phase a rather more calculated and organized one than it would have been in the early 1980s. Importantly, this established habitus provides present and future asylum travellers with a 'strategy-generating' principle within a 'structure of consciousness [to] enable agents to cope with unforeseen and ever-changing situations by rendering a panoply of things to say or not to say, things to do or not to do' when en route (Shields, 1991, p. 34). Furthermore, today's prospective travellers have been exposed to the habitus, in one way or another, *from birth*—namely, 'early childhood experiences in a family of a particular social class' through improvised and adjusted temporal and spatial practices shared through the family (ibid.). For instance, Ashley, an asylum traveller from Iran, reported such in habituated knowledge when stating: 'we [refugees] in general call Turkey the "second country" that leads to the "third country", like the United States, Canada or Australia'.[3]

For Melissa from Iran, the established asylum habitus meant her separation phase was fairly straightforward. Her two aunts—one lives in the United States, the other in Canada—had undertaken the odyssey via a 'second country' years before. One aunt left Iran after the revolution, passing through Pakistan without valid documents, and was resettled in the United States.[4] Her other aunt took an entirely different path, via Turkey in 2002 on the train with a valid passport, and was resettled in Canada.[5] Similar to Melissa's information gathering, Margaret from Iraq and Kim from Iran were aware of the asylum journey during the separation phase since their uncles and aunts were living in Canada, where they had been resettled via Turkey. Kim's sister had arrived in Turkey six months before Kim and was resettled in Canada just three months before Kim arrived there to join her.

Similarly, Stella from Iran—whom we met before—has many relatives in Canada including her two uncles and her aunt. One uncle left Iran in 1996 without valid documents, arrived in Pakistan where he sought asylum, and waited for ten months there. He was later resettled to Canada. Stella also mentioned family members in Germany but quickly added that 'Germany does not accept refugees and there is more support for refugees in Canada'.[6] Here, once again, we see the role of information in decision-making in the separation phase—in this case, the knowledge that Germany is not as welcoming to refugees as Canada and that the latter is a better bet than the former. Sarah has an uncle who was resettled to Canada via Turkey around twelve years ago; furthermore, she had two uncles living in Turkey before she began her asylum journey. Baharan from Iran has an uncle living in Canada who arrived there almost 35 years ago not as a refugee but to study and work in Canada. These brief examples offer clear insight about the range of connections, relations, and information obtained before the journey that shape it—even before the potential traveller has set off.

The separation phase is also process obtaining knowledge about migration infrastructure— the 'systematically interlinked technologies, institutions and actors' that structure the migration experience (Xiang & Lindquist, 2014, p. 122). Travellers must organize a visa and passport, arrange transport (either through the state-run 'legal' travel agency or 'illegal' human smuggling one), and prepare luggage. This is last thing travellers do in 'getting ready' for the journey. Thus, the separation phase is not only the stage and process of obtaining informal knowledge from previous or present asylum travellers, but also an encounter with the state and its border bureaucracy. This bureaucratic encounter is heavily weighted with *documentation*. At this point in the separation phase travellers know they must ensure a range of crucial documents—visas, passport and travel tickets—are all in order.

Indeed, the 'legality' or 'illegality' of travel documents plays a central role in how the journey itself is labelled. A set of binary attributions—namely, irregular/illegal/undocumented versus regular/legal/documented—are deployed in states' immigration and border regulations, as well as by organizations such as the IOM and the UNHCR, all of which depend on the traveller's documentation. Having access to a valid/legal passport also differentiates Iranian asylum travellers by gender and age, as well as political opinion and sexual orientation. This differentiation introduces different modes of tactics regarding spatial practices and experiences devised en route.

For instance, male citizens in Iran who reach the age of 18 must complete mandatory military service—if a male citizen has not yet completed his service, he is unlikely to be issued a valid passport. Ali from Iran noted how difficult is to obtain a passport in Iran before the age of 18 as the authorities fear boys will flee the country to avoid conscription.[7] A man who has already served in the military, in contrast, can easily obtain a passport. In a nutshell, access to travel documents for young Iranians in the separation phase is *sharply bifurcated by age and gender*—and this has a direct impact on how men and women travel and the routes they take. Boys or men who cannot obtain a valid passport must find 'forged' travel documents or have to begin the journey without documents, using 'illegal' travel agencies.

Political prisoners and homosexual individuals in Iran have similar problems gaining access to a passport. For asylum travellers without a passport, the 'getting ready' phase—like preparing luggage—is much more straightforward for asylum travellers with one. In the former case, the documentation dimension is basically nil. For instance, Ramon, who is gay, did not want to serve in the military—as a gay man he is deemed abnormal and marginal in his home country's politics. Therefore, his only option was to find an 'illegal' travel agency to flee. Similar to Ramon's separation practice, Barry—having been raped and sexually and verbally abused by the Iranian police on several occasions—decided to embark to Turkey without a passport since he had not completed military service. He paid US$700 for his travel and passed himself off as Afghan as a tactical move, since he was the only Iranian among other 60 'illegal travellers' on board the smugglers' transport.[8] In Barry's preparation stage, a backpack had to suffice for his border crossing to Turkey—that was the only luggage his human smuggling travel agency would allow. John, another gay asylum traveller, obtained knowledge on human smuggling networks from a friend who had been resettled to Sweden via Turkey in 2003, and John crossed the Iranian border without valid documents with the hope of joining his friend in Europe.

Regarding the relationship between sexuality and mobility/citizenship/border crossing, seeking asylum is motivated by state policy—namely, its wish to reinforce a hetero–national ideal by condemning homosexuality as a sin. Individuals who embark on the asylum odyssey on account of sexual orientation highlights how the hetero–normative discourse of the state creates a venue of exclusion in domestic politics by forming a transnational queer mobility (White, 2013). On top of this, families in conservative Iranian society create significant difficulties for LGBTQ individuals fleeing the home country. The travel taken by Amir as a gay asylum traveller was through an illegal travel agency—he also had no passport since he had refused to serve in the military. Like Amir, Andrew—who had already been in Turkey several times

68 *The separation phase of the asylum journey*

to look for work—mentioned that life began to change when he was in the military. Andrew—both gay and Christian—described his experience in his 'home' country where he was imprisoned for 18 months. He stated that other soldiers asked him why he did not attend prayers in the mosque. He was then was caught attending an 'underground' church.[9] He said: 'it was Friday around 3:30 pm'.[10] He was then accused of having sexual intercourse with another man, and he was again imprisoned and tortured. He was kicked out of the military and issued with a 'red ID card'—a document in Iran that identifies to all that the bearer is a homosexual. Crucially, this 'special' ID marks the state's official categorization of Andrew's homosexuality—an identity marker that will follow him everywhere as a kind of 'civil death'. As Andrew told me, the red ID meant he would never have an opportunity to find work, nor gain societal and political approval in Iran. Even though he had a valid passport to start the asylum journey, he travelled via 'illegal' travel agents since his father withheld his passport as a way to exert control over his son and to prevent him leaving the country. Like Andrew, Patrick has a father that sought to control his movement, going to court to assert before a judge his son's sexual orientation. Patrick denied his father's statement but was detained. The court decided to send him to a doctor to determine whether he was gay or not. At the hospital, Patrick found a way to escape, and contacted human smugglers to begin his journey of hope.

Obtaining documents for the journey requires less effort for female travellers and applying for a passport is a less suspicious act than it is for Baha'i, homosexual and young male individuals, as well as some family members who had experienced thus during the 1980s and 1990s. This does not mean that access to valid travel documents has always been strict. For instance, the degree of access to passports for Baha'i individuals in Iran has changed over time and become easier than the 1980s and 1990s. Some Baha'i respondents mentioned the difficulty in obtaining a passport. Azadeh from Iran stated that 'Baha'is were not allowed to have a passport ten years ago [...] The only option [then] was to go underground to Turkey; but now we don't need a visa for to go there.'[11] 'Underground' here refers to travelling via human smuggling travel agencies. The visa-free access has become a facilitator, with far less effort needed to complete travel documents. There are two possible reasons of this change. First, the Iranian state might have shifted its perspective towards Baha'i individuals. Second, the state may have sought to make it easier for Baha'i citizens to obtain travel documents to push them to flee the country. However, the current attitude of Iran towards its Baha'i citizens remains discriminatory especially in the higher education domain, which also makes it difficult to find work.

Contrasting the calculation and planning required in the separation phase within the structured asylum habitus, Ahoo referred to her decision to begin the journey as 'an accident', stating that

One day my cousin with his wife came to my home [...] He was talking with his wife's mother, and they were going to America, and he said, 'one moment' and then to me 'You have problems here. Do you want to go to America?' I said, 'I will not leave my country.' And he said, 'They are in Kayseri [a Turkish city], they have a house, furniture, everything.' I again said, 'No.'[12]

Two weeks later, she called her father to tell him she had decided to head to Turkey after all, having become more conscious about resettlement abroad. She and her daughter already had a valid passport. Four weeks after the conversation with her cousin, she bought train tickets knowing that Iranians do not need a visa for Turkey. Whether it is contingent or an accident, Ahoo had enough time to calculate and legitimize her account of separation, checking possible transportation means, preparing the luggage and passports, and paying for train tickets. She was ready to take the train and practice the liminal phase in Turkey with the hope of reaching the resettlement and incorporation phase to Canada. Ahoo's experience of planning and preparation thanks to the structured asylum habitus is a privilege that most asylum travellers from the African continent, and Syrian travellers who have no time to plan, do not generally enjoy.

Planning and preparation underline that asylum journeys are not always forced—as is typically pictured in the political imaginary of asylum seeking. Natasha's journey signifies the dimensions of *autonomy* in the asylum journey—which stands in stark contrast to the supposed vulnerability and passivity of refugees. Natasha—25 years old—faced resistance from her father to leave Iran; she told him: 'you are putting obstacles between me and my future'. She recalled that initially her father was intransigent: 'there was no point to discuss it because his argument to keep me in Iran would never change and neither would my argument to leave'. However, in an act of agential autonomy, Natasha suggested to her father that he approach a third party—unknown to either him or her—who would hear both sides and suggest a way to resolve the disagreement. They went to a counsellor—not a traditional, conservative one, according to Natasha, but one open to different views. After listening to father and daughter, the counsellor advised: 'I think you should give your daughter permission to advance her future and her life'.[13] Two weeks later, Natasha's father asked her to apply for a passport which took a couple of weeks to arrive. Three months later, her father purchased her flight to Turkey, where she sought asylum.

Travellers from the African continent do not enjoy the benefits of visa-free entry to Turkey like Iranians. However, the separation phase nevertheless bears similarities in terms of the role of 'mobile knowledge'. Like Iraqis and Iranians, they use social media tools and smart phone apps like Facebook and WhatsApp to communicate with successful travellers in Turkey or Europe. For many travellers from Africa, Istanbul is a central part of the process—a crucial hub en route to Europe and a space in which mobistasis is facilitated by the 'settled life' of the city (Schapendonk, 2016, p. 235). African travellers come from a diverse array of places and countries, including ones located in the Horn of Africa—Somalia, Ethiopia, and Eritrea—but also West and Central African countries like Nigeria, the Democratic Republic of Congo, Senegal, and Ghana.

Drawing on the strict formal immigration categories and documents of states, these individuals would be considered 'economic migrants'. Their journey is mostly regarded as an 'illegal' and economically motivated due to the use of 'illegal' travel agents to make the journey towards Europe (Brewer & Yukseker, 2006). The arrival country is based more on contingencies in which the asylum habitus for travellers from Africa may differ from that of the Iranian and Iraqi travellers. Especially, human smuggler's changing navigation en route to the 'destination'—typically, Europe—may influence the direction of the journey. Therefore, different situational and flexible tactics must be employed along the way, seeking asylum is one tactic mainly learned en route.

For instance, Sophie from Ethiopia informed me she was a member of a political organization in her 'home' country, and her life was in danger. She started to gather information and knowledge about opportunities abroad through Facebook. During the separation phase, she decided to follow the same route that her contact person—her friend's boyfriend—had travelled to get to Europe several months before. At the time of the interview, her network was in Greece, but she did not know where he was when she was getting ready for her journey. Accordingly, Sophie's network first arrived in Turkey, and then passed to Greece via Turkey in a small boat. She stated that 'Turkey is a possible country to pass to another country [...] from Greece to Germany, Italy, or London'.[14] Sophie's reasoning resembles the Iranian asylum traveller's imagination of Turkey as the second country for resettlement to a third country. However, it significantly differs regarding the journey's mode. The journey Sophie and her network arriving in European countries via Turkey took is 'illegal' whereas it is a legal journey through asylum seeking and resettlement via the UNHCR for Iranian and Iraqi travellers, as well as Syrians more recently.

Sophie went to a legal travel agency in her 'home' country Ethiopia by arranging her documents and flight ticket, as well as a 15-day 'invitation letter' for her visit to Turkey. While we were interviewing, she calculated around US $5,000 the amount that she paid to the travel agency for Turkish visa, flight ticket to Istanbul, and 15 days 'invitation letter' from a friend in Turkey. What is tactical in Sophie's separation phase is that first, she found a connection to be an example to experience the routes as in the case of many asylum travellers. More importantly, in her case, an invitation letter with a contact information from an African individual living in Istanbul is the most valuable tactic for her journey to get a valid visa and a flight ticket to Turkey. She along with her 'legal' documents and a 15-day visit to Turkey, knew the visit would be longer than 15 days since her intention was to continue onward to Europe and not to go back.

In the case of travellers from Africa, the decision to initiate the journey is not always based on the UNHCR's 'well-founded fear of persecution'. It can be due to the desire to find a job and better opportunities abroad by crossing multiple borders in which state discourse on journeys with economic reasons is rather negative by seeing 'undocumented/illegal' migration as economically motivated. This discourse impairing most African travellers legitimizes the intervention of the multiple state and non-state institutions or bureaucracies in the 'economically' motivated 'illegal' journey by deconstructing the notion that 'any place could be home' (Tete, 2012, p. 106). By deciding to travel to Saudi Arabia with her passport via plane, Sonia from Eritrea initiated her journey of hope with the motivation to support her family by noting the limited opportunities in home country to provide the necessities of life for her kids. She knew friends that had gone to Saudi Arabia to work as baby sitters and domestic workers. However, her experiences as a Christian in Saudi Arabia led her to decide to travel towards Syria and then to Turkey—in both cases using 'illegal' travel agents—with the hope of crossing to Greece.

In Jamal's case, this involved making quite a few trips back and forth across borders home and then again back towards his 'destination', Italy. He first escaped from the conflict in Sudan to Libya. In Libya he began to work and saved some money before going back to his home country to arrange his illegal journey with his two friends towards Italy from Libya via boat. This indeed tells us that his motivation was not to seek asylum in the beginning, but to sail towards Italy. Jalal's deliberate decision to travel led him to save money and to contact human smugglers as a travel agency for the journey of hope. Jamal was also constrained because citizens cannot easily apply for a passport from the Sudanese state, forcing him to turn to human smugglers. Even with a valid passport, he would have had next to no chance of obtaining a visa for Italy due to his country of origin. Jalal sailed with the hope of reaching Italy. The captain told travellers to jump into the water and swim to land. However, when Jamal along with his friends arrived at the land, they realized that they were not in Italy, but the journey had ended up in Izmir, Turkey.[15]

In the case of Syrians, the decision is more an escape from the country towards neighbouring countries like Turkey, Lebanon and Jordan due to the violence of the Bashar al-Assad regime. Therefore, the decision to take the journey has been rather hasty—in contrast to the separation phase practiced by travellers who can draw on the structured asylum habitus of friends and family networks who have already completed the journey. The asylum journey of Syrians to resettlement countries via Turkey began in earnest in 2015. Therefore, the journey has not yet fully become routinized due to the lack of translocal knowledge networks and massive flows as in the case of Iranians and Iraqis who have consolidated a structured asylum habitus since the 1980s and the 1990s. Indeed, considering the early arrivals along with the construction of camps at the Turkish–Syrian borders, the initial intention of Syrians was not to stay in Turkey but to wait out the conflict in hope of a resolution. The separation phase of the Syrians' journey of hope since 2015 has thus been focused on making the financial arrangements to find travel agents to cross the border.

Nevertheless, Syrians exhibit recognizable practices and encounters during the separation phase. Most families deliberately focus on preparing female members—daughters, wife(s), old grandmothers—children, and sons who are of military age first. The elderly and women are rightly seen as the most vulnerable and should flee the country first. Military age sons are also vulnerable to being called up for military service by Assad's regime. Michael from Syria recalled how, in 2013, the family sent his grandmother, aunts, mother, sisters, and children to Turkey—they had to pay US$100 per person to police at the border. Male members of the family stayed to ride out the conflict, hoping it would soon end. Almost two weeks later, with the help of his uncle working in Saudi Arabia Michael and his brother along with other five male members of family began their journey towards Turkey.[16] Syrian families sending their sons of military service age gather information about where to arrive in Turkey. They transfer money to the old to support them or receive money from the young working in Turkey to facilitate the journey for those who have yet to depart Syria.

After the completion of the getting ready phase for the travel, the next step is the physical travel and access to the means of transportation, which can be the train for many Iranian asylum seekers, a flight, or a bus for Iraqi asylum travellers, or walking through 'illegal' travel agents, if an individual does not have a passport.

Vehicle matters: transportational momentum

Massey's (2005, p. 117) question, 'What is it to travel'? addresses a crucial aspect of space and the way it is produced by (and within) social relations in terms of time and space:

> So take the train […] But this time you are not just travelling through space or across it. Since space is the product of social relations you are also helping […] to *alter* space, to participate in its continuing production.
>
> (Massey, 2005, p. 118, emphasis in the original).

To observe the production of social relations across space as Massey suggests, I took the train from Kayseri (Turkey) to Iran's capital Tehran in 2015—returning from Tehran to Ankara ten days later. Transportational momentum matters since which vehicle one decides to take has a major impact on whether the journey will be deemed 'legal' or 'illegal'. Walters' (2015) notion of 'viapolitics' captures the political nature of the vehicle—not merely as a carrier, but also as a micro political image that plays a crucial role in how fluid labels like documented/regular/legal or undocumented/irregular/illegal migrant and migration are actually assigned. In other words, it is not only the routes chosen that matter for viapolitics, but also the actual modes of transport, which act as sites of mediation and contestation en route (Walters, 2015).

As mentioned, Iranian travellers with a valid passport have visa-free entry to Turkey. What is crucial about this is that it allows Iranians to purchase tickets (plane or train) in advance legally, as prospective tourists, even if they have no plan to return to Iran. This proves that the 'tourist' label can turn into an 'asylum applicant' label fairly easily. Amanda, an Iranian traveller, noted that almost 'ninety per cent of Iranians take the train' to arrive in Turkey to seek asylum and she further noted that 'the train is the most common way'.[17] At this point, the question arises: why not fly? Is the plane only something the elite can partake in? The nexus here, however, is not socio-economic nor necessarily about saving money. It is, just as much, a calculated decision based on diffused knowledge about the logistics of the journey and the requirements of engaging the various bureaucracies. Nevertheless, cost is an issue. For instance, Janice told me how she was lucky to find a cheap flight ticket and explained the reason:

> many Iranian singers and performers are not allowed to give concerts in Iran, and they generally sing and perform in Turkey. At the time, I was looking for both train and flight tickets to Turkey, and because a series of planned concerts in Turkey had been cancelled, there were seats available, and the price was comparable to the train.[18]

For Janice, taking plane was just a matter of contingency—a happy coincidence thanks to a cancelled concert planned for Turkey.

It is certainly the case that the train is cheaper than flying. In March 2015, the train ticket from Tehran to Ankara was around CAD$90 and plus €10 at the Turkish border for entry,[19] whereas the flight ticket for an adult ranges from US$321–1,483.[20] Considering Ingrid's journey with her two brothers and her parents, the train is the most reasonably-priced transportation means for a family of five.[21] However, the train schedule is a significant limitation—it travels every Wednesday from Tehran to Ankara and the journey entails around 70 hours on board.

But cost is just one factor. A second dimension is luggage, which is also far easier to transport by train. Naturally, the limit by air is two pieces of luggage each with the possibility of another piece at extra cost. Train passengers, in contrast, can bring all kinds of items—including furnishings for their prospective apartments, enough basic foodstuffs for a couple of months during their stay in Turkey and until they find a proper market for their basic needs. For instance, Maria travelling via train brought basic stuff including rice and oil—and even says she saw some travellers bringing furniture for the apartment.[22] Another traveller brought seven suitcases—impossible via plane. Some respondents who travelled alone told me that their parents visited them in Turkey, arriving via train, spending around a week in Turkey, and then returning to Iran.

74 *The separation phase of the asylum journey*

Third, the train is much more conducive to the kinds of 'mobile knowledge' and the consolidation of networks that constitutes the asylum habitus. Flying involves a great deal more formality compared to the train—from check-in to going through customs at the other end. It is also faster, with no expectation that passengers will speak to one another. Every passenger on board is expected to remain in his or her seat from the moment of departure to the moment of arrival, which precludes the exchange of information and the possibility of informal conversation with other travellers. Thus, flying mitigates against the transmission of 'mobile knowledge' or the consolidation of networks. This—ironically enough—is just like the journey of human smuggling, where each traveller is instructed to keep quiet, and to keep communication to a minimum on board (Kaytaz, 2016).

The train journey, however, lasts around 70 hours—more informal, it allows for the ready development of 'intimate social bonds' among travellers (Vogt, 2016, p. 376). Indeed, the journey is so long that people end up by necessity talking and getting to know one another. The train thus constitutes a distinct travel experience in terms of production of social relations with other travellers on board about what to expect—how to conduct themselves— in Turkey and even Canada. For instance, Cher recalled how she met with a family en route to Turkey while taking the train. One became a friend, who was later resettled in Toronto. They still communicate via Facebook, and call each other via Viber, or other smart phone apps.[23]

The fourth reason is strategic, and concerns the arrival city in Turkey. The selection of destination city is related to travellers' social networks and familial ties. When flying, the departure and arrival cities are fixed: flights from Tehran are either to Ankara or Istanbul only, with no stops in-between. As opposed to the flight, travelling via the train from Tehran to Ankara involves multiple destination cities like Tehran, Tabriz and Razi in Iran and Van, Kayseri and Ankara in Turkey.

Figure 3.1 depicts Razi train station—the last stop at the Iranian border. Border forces perform the checks and controls of passports and luggage along with some passengers. For instance, we waited around seven hours for the 'security' check of all luggage and passports during my journey to Tehran. One border agent collected everyone's passports and then himself checked each one singlehandedly. What interested me during the control process was that the border guards manually emptied the carrier and reloaded it without opening any of the luggage. The reason for waiting an extra one or two hours was that border forces approached one of the travellers with suspicion since he seemed drunk and different than the 'normal', i.e., 'heteronormative' norms. After taking him into a separate room, police checked his backpack. Then, the collected passports were return one by one to passengers. In the meantime, the 'suspicious' traveller was able to get into the train to continue his journey; however, he got off the train before his destination due to the presence of police waiting for him at Tehran station.

Figure 3.1 Razi train station, the Iranian-Turkish border
Courtesy of the author. June 2015

Map 3.1 was drawn by Kim and illustrates her journey from Shiraz to the destination city Kayseri.

Kim's journey began in Shiraz, heading by bus to Tehran; from Tehran, she travelled to Kayseri via train. Kim has drawn the Iran–Iraq border in red, to signify the 'bloody' Iran–Iraq war that raged through the 1980s. The circle on the map that Kim has drawn is the Van Lake where the Iranian train carries the passengers up until this point. From the Van Port, travellers take the ferry to arrive at the Tatvan train station where the Turkish train continues the journey. Kim described her feeling of great relief when they were crossing the Van Lake by depicting her practice as the journey of hope. She and other passengers celebrated the arrival in Turkey by singing and drinking—something not possible either on a plane or on the Iranian train. I also observed similar practices during my journey, whereby some female travellers removed their headscarves and donned t-shirts upon boarding the ferry and Turkish train. One passenger played his guitar in the restaurant section of the Turkish train, while almost all travellers were drinking beer and wine, which are prohibited in Iran.

However, taking the train is not available for most asylum travellers. Iraqi, Somalian and Syrian travellers, as well as persons who do not hold 'legal' travel documents, do not have this option. For Iraqi asylum travellers, transportation is more likely to be via bus or car if they have legal travel

76 *The separation phase of the asylum journey*

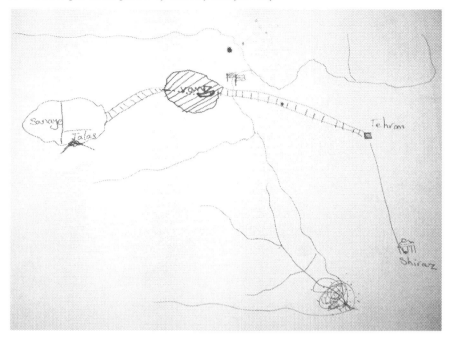

Map 3.1 The mapped asylum journey of an Iranian traveller
Courtesy of the author. Interview, June 2014. Istanbul, Turkey

documents. Otherwise, they must cross the border via human smugglers, which is a widespread part of everyday reality in the region. Smugglers transport travellers on foot, by van or truck—and even on animals like donkeys or horses. For instance, when I was in Tehran, a barista at the coffeehouse showed me a video on his phone that his cousin had recorded of the journey of 'illegal' travellers with human smugglers via pack-animals.

Map 3.2 depicts the journey without a passport of Barry—an 'illegal' homosexual traveller from Iran. Barry stated that after arriving at the border they stopped in a village to arrange the next step of the travel. It took four days to arrive in Turkey by foot, interspersed with periods resting and sleeping in hidden spots on both sides of the border. The same distance could be covered in around 30 minutes by bus or car.

Travelling via human smugglers is full of risks due to the geographical and climatic conditions, but also bandits (*hirsiz*), as well as presence of military in the region (Kaytaz, 2016). Securitization and bandits prompt human smugglers to find 'more innovative and riskier strategies' that make routes more dangerous (Stone-Cadena, 2016, p. 345). By using the most clandestine routes and by navigating the safest possible routes, human smugglers function as safeguards for 'illegal' migrants and/or their passengers (Vogt, 2016). The routes are concealed even as this 'clandestinity [is] a hidden, yet known'

The separation phase of the asylum journey 77

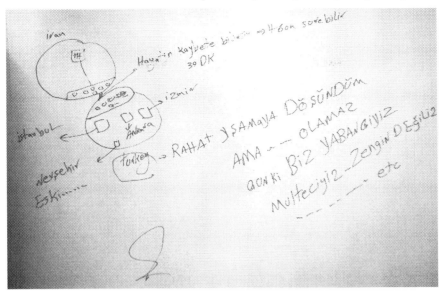

Map 3.2 An Iranian asylum traveller drawing the border crossing via 'illegal' routes
Courtesy of the author. Interview, June 2014. Istanbul, Turkey

phenomenon by states and border securities (Coutin, 2005, p. 195). To return to Barry's journey, it took place in December, which is a very tough month considering the cold weather. He recalled: 'I was lucky to be alive, managing to arrive in a Turkish village' close to the border. In his mapping, he not only drew small houses in villages on both sides of the border as little squares, but also located his satellite city (Nevsehir), the UNHCR's office in Ankara, and his favourite three Turkish cities—Istanbul, Eskisehir, and Izmir. He expressed his feelings as a 'refugee' in Turkey as he practiced the liminal/transition phase: 'I thought to live comfortably [...] but it cannot happen. Because we are aliens, refugees [...] we are not rich, etc'.[24]

Simon also travelled via human smugglers since Like Barry, his passport was kept by his father to prevent his potential escape from Iran. By being aware of the possibility of travelling via human smugglers to Turkey, Simon stated:

> My friends [one year before his journey] told me if we pay US$5,000, a car drives us to the mountains. We start walking around 30 minutes at the Turkish border. Then another vehicle arrives to take us to cross to Greece. But around fifty percent of them die at the Greek border [...] I did not try because I was scared.[25]

Instead, Simon paid US$3,500 to human smugglers and an extra US$100 to the Iranian police at the border. During his journey, he was given a donkey to cross to Turkey. Upon arriving at a border city along with around 20 other travellers from Sri Lanka, Afghanistan, and Iran, they stayed a couple of nights in a small, derelict shed. They were then divided into groups of two by human smugglers to be sent to Ankara where UNHCR Turkey is. He also informed me that two Sri Lankans, one Afghan and some Iranian travellers were sent back to their countries of origin. The price of the journey grows every year due to the 'increasing involvement of non-migrant actors and the growing number of government regulations [which leads] to higher migration costs' (Xiang & Lindquist, 2014, p. 123).

Paying around US$10,000 to human smugglers, Ahmed undertook the journey from Iran to Turkey on foot. He could not travel legally because of the risks—he is a member of a political organization. Regarding access to valid documents, he stated that it 'all depends on time and government [...] Some people travel secret ways because they do not have passport'.[26] When they arrived at the Iranian side of the border, a person took them to Turkey where they stayed in a cabin for a couple of days. During his travel, Ahmed broke his leg when he fell of his mule but was required to get back on to finish the long, four-hour journey. Eventually, he arrived in Turkey—still with a broken leg.

Travelling via human smugglers almost invariably entails using animals like horses, donkeys, or mules as carriers of clandestine migrants across borders. This use of animals to cross the hurdled mountains on the Turkish–Iraqi and Turkish–Iranian borders is a rather unexplored theme in migration studies that needs further investigation and exploration. What is most interesting in the border crossing via mule or donkey is that the asylum traveller is not merely a passenger in this case, but also the *pilot and navigator*—often left to traverse the journey alone. The traveller is responsible for his/her own border-crossing route, which is a tactical move by human smugglers to keep distance and avoid capture or being tracked by border technologies and security forces.

Moreover, it must be noted that the selection of the means of transport is not related to the socio-economic status of the asylum traveller—he or she has the means to pay many thousands of dollars for this journey. The interviews with of asylum travellers suggest that the journey via animals is *the most expensive* in comparison with the journey via plane and train. This aspect of the journey reveals the paradox in which the economy of mobility is inverted. In other words, the most 'primitive' means of mobility—i.e., via animals (donkey, mule, and horse) and by foot—becomes the most expensive way of arriving in Turkey.

Travelling to Turkey is not always a one-way trip. Some respondents from Iran stated that they travelled to Turkey with their valid passport before seeking asylum. The rationale of these 'tourist' visits can be sometimes to see friends or relatives who have been practicing the liminal phase in Turkey, or sometimes to look for seasonal work in Turkey. Andrew—whom we met earlier—worked in Turkey through a company from 1997 to 1999. He later returned Turkey to practice his asylum journey in 2012 due to his sexual orientation.

The separation phase of the asylum journey 79

The map drawn by Patrick is one of the most striking examples that demonstrates the non-linearity of the journey with multiple crossings. In 2009, Patrick arrived in Turkey via bus and applied for asylum due to a fear of persecution related to his sexual orientation. However, his refugee status was rejected by UNHCR Turkey. He had to return Iran after a while since he could not afford to stay in Turkey as a 'bogus/rejected' asylum applicant. After spending several months in Iran, his fear from persecution increased along with his father's pressure on him. As illustrated in Map 3.3, Patrick travelled to Georgia via bus with 'forged' travel documents. He applied for asylum there and his refugee status was recognized by UNHCR Georgia where he spent around eight months in a refugee camp. Patrick asked UNHCR Georgia about the possibility of resettlement to Canada, following his conversation with a human rights activist based in Toronto. He stated that 'They [UNHCR] told me Georgia does not work like Turkey or Malaysia. So I decided to go back to Turkey'.[27] Then in 2012, he travelled to Turkey via bus from Georgia en route to his resettlement country, Canada. Patrick's asylum journey is significant to navigate the multiple routes and underline how tactics devised by himself on the routes are flexible and situational based on the knowledge that he obtained in practicing the routes. The information he obtained highlights the transformative power of 'mobile knowledge', which provided him with useful information to resume his asylum journey to Canada via Turkey.

The multitude of routes is mostly prevalent for asylum travellers from the African continent. It is directly related to their difficulty accessing 'legal' travel documents. In other words, for travellers from Eritrea, Ethiopia, Somalia, or Sudan, the travel is based less on routinized routes towards the resettlement

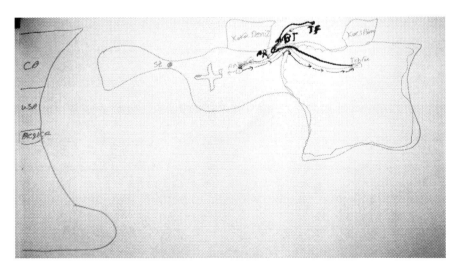

Map 3.3 Multitude of routes en route to Canada via Turkey
Courtesy of the author. Interview, June 2014. Istanbul, Turkey

80 *The separation phase of the asylum journey*

country via Turkey, than it is for asylum travellers from Iran and Iraq. The spatial and temporal organization of the journey from 'home' to 'there', as well as the tactics en route, involve more multiplicities, multiple routes and border crossings, and multiple trajectories in which the journey follows not only the act of asylum seeking, but also the act of crossing to Europe and mobistasis in Istanbul. One image of the African asylum traveller's odyssey is provided by Sonia's mapping of her journey. In it, she details her negative experiences en route and the hardships that she faced in her travel with human smugglers.

Sonia's map, with its multiple border crossings and periods of mobistasis, reveals how borders—whose aim is to filter the migrants and adjust the volume and speed of mobility—are transient and porous. She began her journey from Ethiopia to Saudi Arabia for work. After working in Saudi Arabia several years, in 2005 she arranged 'illegal' travel through smugglers to cross to Syria. Sonia paid US$1,000 and travelled via small truck with thirty others. After arriving at a drop off, they started walking for seven days. She worked in Syria for a couple of years and decided to initiate another journey after saving some money. This time destination was from Syria to Greece via Turkey and she paid US$500 to human smugglers in which travel to Turkey via walking lasted five days.[28] On her map Sonia expressed her feelings about the journey. At the right corner of her list, she first wrote 'human trafficking is bad', a statement which reveals Paul Gilroy's (1993) expression of *double-consciousness* of a traveller during the journey by simultaneously being aware of the 'illegality' and 'legitimacy' of her journey. Second, she underlined the fear of rape on the route in which as a tactical move, she covered her face like a Muslim woman to protect herself. She also noted that not only female travellers, but also male travellers can face sexual assaults and rape by human smugglers. Third, hunger was the hardship during

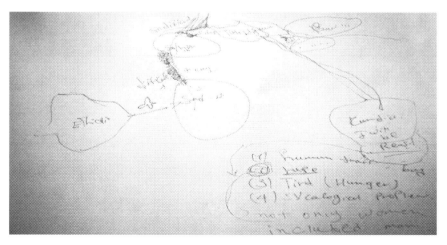

Map 3.4 An Eritrean asylum traveller's mapping of her journey
Courtesy of the author. Interview, May 2014. Istanbul, Turkey

both seven days walk from Saudi Arabia to Syria and five days walk from Syria to Turkey. Fourth, she listed the psychological problems and traumas associated with the journey with human smugglers.

Conclusion

As suggested at the start of this chapter, the odyssey of every asylum traveller is like a *matryoshka* doll—a set of nested journeys one within the other. The purpose of this chapter has been to 'unpack' this odyssey to reveal the distinct set of individual experiences and engagements between travellers and the bureaucratic regulations and strategies of asylum governance they encounter along the way.

Being en route is part of the separation phase—the first bureaucratic step of the asylum journey. It is mostly calculated with rigorous planning, thanks to the structured asylum habitus in which each traveller experiences it in a unique way. The consolidated asylum habitus provides travellers with border-crossing knowledge—that underscores the significance of the production, reproduction, and diffusion of knowledge through the interaction of past, present, and future travellers.

The chapter has also highlighted how practices on the routes are not fixed. Rather, they are non-linear with an indeterminate beginning involving not only mobility, but also immobility, stoppings, and waiting while being en route—what I refer to as mobistasis. At this stage, momentum in the transport sense involves taking the bus, the train, or a plane—and even walking or travelling with the assistance of pack-animals. Yet the vehicle is more than a mere carrier—it designates the mode of the journey—whether it is legal or illegal based on access to travel documents. The chapter has accentuated that while the train is definitely cheaper, the selection of this mode of transport is not necessarily a signifier of a socio-economic status. It is related, rather, to knowledge obtained from those experienced travellers that have gone before and access to travel documents—and, more importantly, to the improvised tactics en route. Asylum travellers who successfully complete the separation phase are ready to practice the next bureaucratic phase in Turkey—the liminal/transition phase—during which they will draw again on asylum knowledge they have obtained in advance.

Notes

1 Interview, 20 January, 2015. Ottawa, Canada.
2 Interview, 19 January, 2015. Ottawa, Canada.
3 Interview, 20 January, 2015. Ottawa, Canada.
4 The year is not exact. Iranian discussants generally tend to date the journeys of their family members in general terms as either 'after the Revolution' or 'before the Revolution'.
5 Interview, 17 June, 2014. Istanbul, Turkey.
6 Interview, 7 January, 2015. Ottawa, Canada.

7 Interview, 2 March, 2015. Ottawa, Canada.
8 Interview, 16 June, 2014. Istanbul, Turkey.
9 The constitution of the Islamic Republic of Iran recognizes Islam, Christianity, Judaism, and Zoroastrianism as official religions. Article 13 of the Iranian Constitution recognizes them as People of the Book and they are granted the right to exercise religious freedom in Iran. Five of the 270 seats in parliament are reserved for each of these three religions. However, after Khomeini's Islamic Revolution in 1979 every citizen is expected to be a Shia Muslim. Being a member of any other religion causes social, political, and economic condemnation and exclusion for the individual both at the societal and state levels. Therefore, going to the church can be reason for social and political stigmatization for a person who can be monitored by the state and its forces due to being seen in a church.
10 Interview, 24 June, 2014. Istanbul, Turkey.
11 Interview, 21 January, 2015. Ottawa, Canada. As a part of its Westernization attempts in the mid-1960s, Turkey revised and lifted its visa requirements with certain countries, including Romania, Yugoslavia, Portugal, and Iran (Acikgoz, 2015)
12 A female traveller from Iran. Interview, 2 February, 2015. Ottawa, Canada.
13 Interview, 20 January, 2015. Ottawa, Canada.
14 Interview, 5 July, 2014. Istanbul, Turkey.
15 Interview, 5 June, 2014. Istanbul, Turkey.
16 Interview, 21 June, 2018. Aksaray, Turkey.
17 Interview, 7 January, 2015. Ottawa, Canada.
18 Interview, 20 January, 2015. Ottawa, Canada.
19 For my trip to Tehran on June 2015, I paid €40 for a one-way train ticket. Buying a return ticket is not an option, as tickets can only be purchased for travel inside each respective country. Iranians do not have to buy round trip train ticket for their journey to Turkey. In early August 2015, Iran and Turkey decided to suspend the direct train between Ankara and Tehran for security reasons, following an explosion on the line. The cancellation of the train schedule between Turkey and Iran is one of the ethical concerns that I have felt even though the reason is not related to this research. www.anadoluhaber.org/tahran-ankara-tren-seferleri-durduruldu (accessed 25 August, 2015).
20 www.iranrail.net; https://online.turkishairlines.com/internet-booking/availabilityInt.tk (accessed 4 March, 2015)
21 Interview, 19 January, 2015. Ottawa, Canada.
22 Interview, 23 June, 2014. Istanbul, Turkey.
23 Interview, 2 February, 2015. Ottawa, Canada.
24 Interview, 16 June, 2014. Istanbul, Turkey.
25 Interview, 22 June, 2014. Istanbul, Turkey.
26 Interview, 25 February, 2015. Ottawa, Canada.
27 Interview, 16 June, 2014. Istanbul, Turkey. The UNHCR in Malaysia operates with government agencies and non-governmental organizations in dealing with asylum seekers and refugees in Malaysia. They stay temporarily since Malaysia is not a state party to the 1951 Convention and its Protocol Relating to the Status of Refugees. Malaysia works with UNHCR in temporary stay of individuals seeking asylum. For more information, see www.unhcr.org.my/About_Us-@-UNHCR_in_Malaysia.aspx
28 Interview, 26 May, 2014. Istanbul, Turkey.

4 Practicing liminal space in the 'journey of hope'

How does Turkey's geographical limitation influence the 'journey of hope' after the separation phase is complete? This chapter explores this question, focusing closely on the asylum journey's second phase. It provides much-needed insight into the experiences and practices of asylum travellers during their stay in Turkey. In so doing, it examines three main points: 1) arrival in Turkey; 2) seeking asylum and changing labels at the bureaucratic level or metamorphosis in bureaucratic categorization; and 3) the experience of mobistasis—stasis within mobility.

The second, *liminal* phase of the journey—drawing on the notion coined by van Gennep (1960)—begins when the asylum traveller arrives in Turkey. *Liminality* here describes the change from one status to another and the spatial and temporal in-betweenness experienced by travellers in this phase, which demands that they participate in procedures/interviews arranged by the UNHCR, the Turkish asylum system and Canada's resettlement programme. In other words, the 'liminal entities' within this phase 'are neither here nor there; they are betwixt and between the positions assigned and arrayed by law, custom, convention, and ceremonial' (Turner, 1977, p. 95).

Moreover, this is a phase of the intersection and intense interaction among a discrete set of refugee governance strategies—the UNHCR's global refugee protection regime, Turkey's geographically exclusionary system of asylum governance and Canada's selective inclusionary resettlement programme. Travellers also experience a kind of bureaucratic metamorphosis in this phase—from undocumented/documented migrant to asylum seeker/refugee. They also experience a period of stasis—interim spatial and temporal immobility—within the ongoing asylum journey, an experience that I call mobistasis. Mobistasis refers to a state of immobility within mobility by underlining an episodic passage of stillness, and perpetual becoming in the course of asylum journeys. The temporal and spatial experience in Turkey with mobility and immobility is a challenge to transit migration conceptualization. In other words, this liminal phase is where asylum travellers who intend to resettle to Canada find themselves indefinitely paused, immobile within Turkey's geographically exclusionary asylum governance regime and their envisioned commencement of the incorporation phase in Canada.

84 *Practicing liminal space in the 'journey of hope'*

Arrival and liminality in Turkey

The liminal phase begins when travellers successfully take the means of transport to Turkey. My respondent Kim from Iran, whom we met in the previous chapter, referred to her journey as the 'journey of hope', a hope she began to feel precisely as she crossed Lake Van in Turkey. It was at this very point that she realized she would face 'no more discrimination' in her life and that she could look forward to being resettled in Canada following the several months of waiting in Turkey.[1] As stated earlier, Turkey has been a space of liminality within the structured asylum habitus among Iranian and Iraqi travellers since the 1980s. Since 2011, the asylum habitus for Syrians fleeing the violent conflict to neighbouring countries has assumed a similar form.

The Turkey route was not the only one that Iranian travellers without access to a passport took in the early 1980s. They also travelled in the other direction, toward Pakistan. Some of my respondents' family members were resettled to Canada via Pakistan. Khosravi (2010) shares why the Iran–Pakistan border was the ideal choice for those serving out their eighteen-month mandatory military service in the early 1990s. Soldiers at the Iran–Pakistan border could even purchase an apartment on the Pakistani side after bribing border officials, setting up a clear pathway for escape. The selection of Pakistan was closely related to the path beaten by human smugglers as well.

After the early 1990s, travelling to Turkey became the safest and most common route both for travellers and for human smugglers. The change from Pakistan to Turkey is a signifier of how information is central in the shifting of routes over time and the improvisation of tactics devised en route by travellers and travel agents. According to Joseph, the shift from Pakistan to Turkey emerged out of an underlying logic for asylum travellers 'to follow the safest route'—in this case to Turkey instead of Pakistan.[2] In addition, the lack of a visa obligation to enter Turkey from Iran has become an important factor facilitating the encounter with the UNHCR.

The selection of Turkey is also related to the operation of the UNHCR and resettlement to a third country thanks to Turkey's geographical limitation, as well as information obtained within the structured habitus from experienced travellers. For instance, Ashley stated that the 'UN Office [sic][3] in Turkey is very popular and well-known among Iranian people'. She also mentioned other UN offices in neighbouring countries without naming any of them.[4] This information is also prevalent among Iraqi asylum travellers.

Cultural proximity between Turkey and Iran is another reason Iranian travellers choose Turkey for the liminal phase. For instance, Janice noted that 'instead of going and seeking asylum in one of the Arab countries, we go to Turkey. I know stereotypes can be bad, but Iranian people don't like Arab people and culture'.[5] One respondent explained that this stereotype among Iranians against Arab countries had emerged as a result of the Arabic courses they have been forced to take at school since the Islamic Revolution. Janice further noted that Ankara is her favourite place in Turkey since it reminds her of her home city, Tehran. Sarah briefly summarized the similarity of culture and tradition between Turkey and Iran by adding there is 'more freedom in Turkey'.[6]

At the bureaucratic level, once asylum travellers arrive in Turkey, they are expected to register at a governorate. However, most travellers register at the UNHCR first, and then are settled to their designated satellite cities. This choice over the order of registration reflects information obtained by travellers beginning at the separation phase. For travellers who already have their contacts and networks in Turkey, the most obvious choice after arrival is to spend several days or weeks with friends or relatives who are already settled in one of the satellite cities. For Iranian travellers, this is most likely to be Kayseri or Eskisehir. This is not incidental—Kayseri, a designated satellite city, is the site of one of the main train stations on the Tehran–Ankara railway and has emerged as a hub for Iranian asylum travellers for that reason. I experienced this for myself on the train from Tehran to Ankara during my field research. We arrived in Kayseri around 4 a.m., and almost all the passengers disembarked at Kayseri station where volunteers with Farsi signboards were waiting to assist and guide passengers. Something similar obtains in Eskisehir, another designated satellite city, two hours from Ankara, that is also mostly populated by Iranian asylum travellers. Those destined for Eskisehir stay on the train all the way to the terminus in Ankara. Then they carry on by local bus or train to Eskisehir where they are met by friends or relatives. For Iraqi and African travellers, the main destination city is more likely to be Istanbul where the translocal networks and communities of asylum travellers from those places have been consolidated.

Spending several days or weeks in arrival cities forms part of established logistical and tactical practice. For example, a traveller can get settled, drop his or her luggage off and have a place to lodge without needing to search or pay for accommodation. For instance, Amelia had a cousin who arrived in Turkey a year before her arrival to Turkey. Her cousin who currently lives in Canada helped Amelia to find furniture and a room to lodge. Beyond this logistical aspect, taking time to register has a tactical purpose, allowing the traveller to obtain exact knowledge about the liminal phase. They can be *informally* up-to-date on where exactly is the UNHCR office in Ankara is and what their fellow travellers have said to the UNHCR in order to be recognized as refugee. It is a stage to learn asylum bureaucracies or how to get away with things when they encounter UNHCR's refugee status determination, Turkey's asylum governance, and Canada's resettlement programme. After spending some time with friends or relatives and getting exact knowledge about the liminal space, some of the travellers are ready for their first, brief encounter with the UNHCR during which the main interview for refugee status determination will be scheduled. Some travellers continue to stay with friends/relatives and share the cost of the rent, which is a financial contribution from both parties. This explains why most travellers mostly from Iran and Iraq bring sufficient money to pay for the journey and living costs. Thus, they also complete the liminal phase's first stage of finding accommodation and obtaining exact knowledge on UNHCR to be ready for change from one status to another.

Metamorphosis and seeking asylum as a tactic

The liminal phase involves both physical in-betweenness in terms of spatiality and metaphysical mobility, i.e., transformation and/or metamorphosis of statuses. It further highlights the transformative dimension of the journey at the identity and status level. This metamorphosis resembles the Kafkaesque notion of the term in which, Gregory Samsa one day wakes up and finds himself *transformed into an insect* in his bed with his same human mind (Kafka, 2009). For asylum travellers, the formal metamorphosis occurs when they encounter the UNHCR's refugee status determination. In other words, the bureaucratic process transforms a traveller's previously attributed bureaucratic and legal labels such as legal/regular/documented and/or illegal/irregular/undocumented migrant on the routes and a citizen of one of the refugee-sending countries into asylum seeker and refugee status.

Kim described her feeling of anxiety due to metamorphosis into a refugee subject in the first night in Kayseri after her first encounter with the UNHCR.

> One day, I woke up, looked at my room and asked: 'Behrouz, my brother, where are you?' Because we were sharing our room [in Iran], but I couldn't see him [...] I realized I was alone in my room, I was alone in Turkey and I was a refugee.[7]

Interestingly, Kim asked me 'what is an asylum seeker?' when she was reviewing the consent form for our conversation. This demonstrates how the concept of asylum seeker as a political term serves to limit boundaries of protection until the determination of legal category of refugee status. Kim's experience accentuates a crisis of identity which 'only becomes an issue when it is in crisis [...] when something assumed to be fixed, coherent and stable is displaced by the experience of doubt and uncertainty' (Mercer, 1990, p. 43). The crisis of identity Kim's experience reminds us that the identity 'as a production' instead of 'an already accomplished fact' is a 'never complete, always in process, and always constituted within, not outside, representation' especially considering the arbitrariness of the legal–bureaucratic labels attributed to travellers (Hall, 1990, p. 222).

The first interview occurs when the traveller registers as an asylum applicant in person with the UNHCR at the Ankara office. Here, they lodge their formal application, briefly state the reason they are seeking asylum, and are assigned a satellite city in which they are expected to reside for the duration of the process. At that moment, the label of 'asylum seeker' is formally assigned to the traveller. Then, the UNHCR sets up an appointment for refugee status determination—which some respondents call the 'main interview'. The status determination interview will determine whether a person is a 'genuine' refugee or a 'bogus' applicant, really an economic migrant—namely, whether he or she has a legitimate 'fear of persecution' to flee the country of origin or not. While some travellers were scheduled for status determination one month after their registration (pre-interview), some were scheduled almost a year later.[8] During my interviews with them, most respondents expressed the stress they felt during interviews with the UNHCR. These interviews are 'make or break' and respondents understand that the UNHCR will grill them to differentiate the 'fake cases' from the real ones. For instance, Jamie's friend arrived in Turkey seeking asylum claiming a genuine fear of persecution on account of the Baha'i faith. After several interviews, however, his case was rejected by the UNHCR since the 'UN found that he was not a Baha'i'.[9]

After the interview, the UNHCR shares information with Turkey's Ministry of Interior (MoI) and informs asylum applicants which satellite city they have been assigned. Now they are expected to reside there and 'check in' at the local police station once a week while they wait around two years for eventual resettlement to Canada. They are later given an identity document with a foreigner identification number that is valid for one year, issued by the MoI as a residence permit. The ID, or what my respondents call their *kimlik*,[10] must be renewed every six months at a cost of 90TL (around US$15) for an adult and 45TL (around US$8) for a person under 18 years old. This residence permit, which does not include permission to work, carries a social security number for the travellers that allows them to access from some rights such as education, health services or financial assistance. More importantly, it is necessary to hold a valid permit in order to exit Turkey to the resettlement country. Each interview conducted by the UNHCR—along with the regulations that persons must follow—is, then, a distinct type of ritual, a particular experience of liminality in the journey from separation to incorporation.

During my visit in Tehran, I witnessed an episode of bureaucratic metamorphosis. As I sat in a coffeehouse, one of the baristas struck up a conversation with me and asked me where I was from. I told him I was from Turkey, which piqued his interest, and he showed me several photos that he had taken in Ankara, where he had stayed for approximately three months. I returned some days later to the same coffeehouse and the barista, Mehdi, came to sit with me to chat. He was eager to show me a document in his possession with the UNHCR banner on it. It turned out that Mehdi's story was an interesting case. He had travelled to Ankara and registered with UNHCR Turkey as an asylum applicant in March 2015. However, his status determination interview had been scheduled for over twenty months later—December 2016. Mehdi was supposed to remain in his designated city in Turkey for the duration, but he instead decided to wait out the status determination process in Iran—the country from which he had fled to the UNHCR in Ankara claiming a genuine fear of persecution.[11] I consider Mehdi's act of seeking asylum as a situational and flexible tactic with significant risks. If the UNHCR notices his border crossings, he will never obtain refugee status. If his home country realizes what he is up to, he will be imprisoned. It is important to note that he does not have to pay his weekly visits to police as he is still waiting for the initial hearing of the UNHCR to be designated as an 'asylum seeker'. Therefore, he is not yet assigned to a designated satellite city.

Some experiences and rituals of bureaucratic metamorphosis are to be expected in the liminal phase thanks to the asylum habitus. Barry's experience, for example, exemplifies the way that produced and diffused knowledge about practicing liminality can be further diffused in chance, casual, and indirect ways. In our interview, Barry told me that while living in Iran he had no knowledge about asylum seeking and did not know anyone there who had applied for asylum. He had, however, struck up an online acquaintance with someone living in Los Angeles who had never applied for asylum but who, by sheer chance, managed to 'help in the process of resettlement to the USA'. His online contact relayed to Barry that he had come across asylum travellers who had been resettled via Turkey in his neighbourhood in Los Angeles. He suggested to Barry that he would try the same thing, and travel to Turkey and seek asylum for resettlement to the United States. Simply by following an offhand suggestion from a casual online acquaintance on the other side of the world, Barry made his way to Ankara for UNHCR interviews with the hope of resettlement. Of course, liminal experiences are generally more highly consolidated and routinized for most travellers. Janice's narrative is indicative here. In our discussions, she described her own experience of seeking asylum in Turkey in precisely those terms: 'it is some kind of routine [... and] I chose to follow the routine'.[12]

Most asylum travellers arriving from Africa have rather different experiences of bureaucratic metamorphosis. For these arrivals, the tactic is not initially for permanent resettlement to a third country, but rather to stay in Turkey *legally* as part of the transformative dimension of asylum journeys. For instance, Sonia, an asylum traveller from Eritrea, travelled to Turkey with human smugglers from Syria in 2008 with the hope of moving on at some point to Europe. She paid the smugglers' fee but while in Istanbul waiting to cross to Greece, the smugglers asked for more money. Having no further funds, she decided to stay in Istanbul and developed a connection with fellow travellers from Africa there.[13] She later decided not to undertake the Turkish–Greek border crossing, which she described as 'so difficult' to make (see Map 3.4 in Chapter 3). She settled in Istanbul and found a job in a restaurant with the help of friends that she had met in Turkey. Her friends in the neighbourhood mentioned the possibility of staying 'legally' in Turkey. Accordingly, after living in Istanbul approximately one year without legal documents, she told me: 'I registered with the UN in 2009 [...] Other African people told me about UN'.[14] Through her application to the UNHCR in 2009, she has obtained the asylum seeker label which temporarily provides legality for her stay in Turkey. In 2013 she was a UNHCR recognized refugee waiting for resettlement to a third country. She stayed in Turkey until her resettlement to the USA in late 2016. This eight-year period of *remaining* directly challenges the classic notion in migration studies of 'transiting', instead signifying *mobistasis*—stasis within mobility.

In 2014, by obtaining legal travel documents and an invitation from an Ethiopian friend living in Istanbul, Sophie decided to follow a friend's 'illegal' journey to Greece via Turkey. Sophie told me that she had decided in the end not to go to Greece since 'the way [referring to crossing to Greece in a small boat] is not legal [...] Police are everywhere, and they can shoot'.[15] In the meantime, a recognized refugee from Ethiopia who lodges in the same building as her, suggested she legalize her stay in Turkey by 'registering with the UN [sic]'. Both Sonia and Sophie's narratives suggest that asylum travellers from Africa learn about seeking asylum in the liminal phase having undergone separation for other reasons. In other words, seeking asylum is both a spatial and situational tactic to remain legally in Turkey. If the resettlement occurs, they do not have to engage in a border crossing to Europe with smugglers. Thanks to diffused knowledge about the challenges at the Turkish–Greek border, Sophie—at least for now—has decided against using smugglers to cross to Europe.

The Syrians arriving in Turkey are recognized as refugees de facto by the UNHCR. They are required to register with Turkey's Directorate General of Migration Management (DGMM) to legalize their stay and to benefit from the rights afforded them under secondary protection. If they apply for asylum through the UNHCR, they wait in Turkey as asylum seekers for resettlement to third countries. However, most Syrians do not apply for asylum through the UNHCR since the process is uncertain in terms of time and seeking asylum does not guarantee resettlement to a third country. Most Syrians I interviewed in Istanbul and Aksaray stated their preference to stay rather than be resettled to a third country.[16] Most Syrians, therefore, expect to remain in Turkey under protection until the conflict is over and they can return to Syria. For them—beyond the uncertain time taken to process resettlement—religion is an important part of the equation: most Syrians staying in Turkey are Sunni Muslims. In our discussions, they noted that they feel better staying in a country where they can pray freely.

On the other hand, the distinct visibility of the Syrians means that—compared to African, Iranian, Iraqi, and Afghan travellers—local reactions are often quite negative, even hostile. Locals who have been led to expect that the Syrians' stay will be temporary and that they will soon return are not happy to see Syrians in public parks, at factories, and on the streets as if permanently settled in Turkey.[17] Syrians are mostly accused of being responsible for the increasing rate of crimes in Turkish cities by locals through social media platforms—Facebook, Twitter or Instagram. Access of Syrians to universities is mostly based on misinformation among locals. They consider that the state sponsors the university education of Syrians, which is a burden for the Turkish society and state (Erdogan, 2014). In other words, it is a vast misallocation of the state's resources that ought to be spent on Turkish citizens.

The conditions under which Syrian travellers remain expresses the notion of differential inclusion. Here, their status transforms into a kind of legal limbo (are they 'guests' or 'protected persons'?) and a form of 'negotiated citizenship' in so far as the bureaucratic metamorphosis of Syrians has undergone so many shifts as the Turkish government has adjusted its position on the question of their stay and status (Baban, Ilcan & Rygiel, 2017, p. 42). Moreover, confronted with the need to survive for an unknown duration in different cities of Turkey requires Syrian travellers to adopt new tactics. Here, they practice 'integration as a survival mechanism' through a range of transnational and translocal activities such as remittances from family members abroad, exchange of information regarding business investment, and advice about other destination countries (Şimşek, 2018, p. 1).

Metamorphosis by seeking asylum provides not only *legality*, but also *visibility* in the liminal phase. Visibility enables asylum travellers to engage in formal, legal governance mechanisms without fear of deportation. More importantly, they have chance to benefit from limited but some basic rights including health care, primary education, or requesting a work permit. This legality and visibility for asylum travellers makes Turkey not only a country of asylum, but also a temporary space of sanctuary. Article 89 of the Law on Foreigners and International Protection (LFIP) lists the assistance and services—including access to primary and secondary school education,[18] social assistance, health services, and access to the labour market—that an individual under international protection can benefit from. Regarding health and medical services, applicants and their beneficiaries, if they have financial difficulties, can benefit from general medical insurance, which is covered by the DGMM. Beneficiaries are asked to contribute to the full or partial amount of the premium of the medical insurance in accordance with their financial means. However, they must settle in one of the satellite cities to benefit from these rights.

In addition, they have free access to the asylum- and migration-related networks and organizations such as UNHCR Turkey,[19] Support to Life,[20] TOHAV,[21] the Helsinki Citizens Assembly,[22] CARITAS Turkey[23] and ASAM,[24] for social, financial, psychological and legal assistance. They can participate in migrant solidarity networks without fear of deportation. ASAM, which is the implementing partner of the UNHCR, has 46 offices in 41 provinces across Turkey. Other organizations operate mostly in Istanbul and so the services of these humanitarian organizations are not available for most refugees living in different satellite cities. In most cases, social and financial assistances in different satellite cities operate without coordination and operate on a 'first come, first served' basis.

Stasis within mobility: mobistasis in the satellite city

The liminal phase is a stage in which travellers prepare for the transition from separation to incorporation. Rituals in this phase include interviews with the UNHCR and local authorities, and, most significantly, the wait for resettlement and/or status. The completion of procedures for the next bureaucratic phase—incorporation, which begins with the approval to travel to Canada—takes around two years and sometimes more than five years. The waiting with uncertainty is part and parcel of mobistasis—that is, as introduced above, not a complete halt but a state of stasis within mobility; pausing and waiting en route to Canada via Turkey.

Travellers are subject to bureaucratic procedures in the liminal phase in their designated satellite cities. As stated previously the satellite city regulation is one of the core strategies of Turkey's asylum governance. For asylum travellers from European countries, there is no such satellite city regulation. Convention refugees[25] can settle in any city in Turkey they choose and benefit from the same rights that a Turkish citizen has.

According to Turkey's MoI, the satellite cities are unproblematic urban spaces of residence in terms of security and order. However, it is not clear regarding what makes a city unproblematic, and whose security is taken into consideration. The regulation is an example how migration bureaucracy officially adjusts the speed of mobility by temporarily housing applicants in satellite cities during the asylum journey en route to Canada. In other words, it renders Turkey as a space where mobistasis is structured and realized. As such, it makes little sense to speak of Turkey as a space of transiting—or a 'transit country'—since movement at this point is neither linear nor smooth.

Experiences in satellite cities are also conditioned by reproduced knowledge and established translocal networks. Kayseri—a key destination city for Iranians—is a case in point. For instance, Stephanie who was expecting Kayseri to be a small village before her arrival in the city, stayed more than thirty months.[26] Everyday practices in the satellite cities reflect changes in time and space but also the internal life-world of individuals themselves. Travis notes how he chose to approach his two-year stay in Turkey, as 'living my life in the present tense'—i.e., living life to the full. He contrasts this with the experience of his mother: 'if you talk to my mom, she will say more negative things about her experience in Turkey since she stayed at home all the time doing nothing'.[27]

Lena arrived in Turkey via train with the expectation that Kayseri would end up being assigned to her as satellite city and so spent the first several days there. However, when she went to Ankara for registration, the UNHCR Turkey office assigned Adana as her satellite city. She explained that this was 'because there were many refugees in Kayseri [and] the quota was full'.[28] More importantly, Lena's cousin was already in Adana where she stayed around thirteen months until her resettlement to Canada.

Like Lena, Ahoo was informed by her cousin about Kayseri when she was in Iran. She also made Kayseri her first port of call before going to Ankara to visit the UNHCR. She was hoping to settle in Kayseri to share a flat with her relatives who were about to resettle to the USA. However, UNHCR Turkey explained to her that Kayseri was 'closed for refugees' due to the accumulation of asylum travellers in the city. Ahoo was settled in Nevsehir as her satellite city and began to obtain information about the city from a friend was

92 *Practicing liminal space in the 'journey of hope'*

waiting for resettlement as an asylum seeker there. In addition, she remembered that her mother's cousin had also lived in Nevsehir before resettlement to Australia.

While Ahoo was looking for an apartment, her friend informed her that her mother's cousin's daughter was still living in Nevsehir. Ahoo had thought that they had all been resettled to Australia, but her friend explained: 'your cousin's daughter lives here [...] The rest moved to Australia, but she stayed behind and is still here'.[29] When the family had gone to the airport for resettlement, the daughter had not been able to take the plane with her parents. As she was over eighteen years old, her case was different from her parents' and she had been forced to remain and wait another two months in Turkey before she could join her parents in Australia. Consequently, Ahoo and her daughter moved in with the cousin's daughter in the flat she was renting. After the cousin's daughter eventually made the move to Australia, Ahoo kept the flat for another 20-plus months.

Ahoo's experience proves the importance of asylum habitus and social capital among past, present, and future travellers in the context of mobistasis, in which social ties are more dynamic and comprehensive rather than static. This habitus is structured not only in destination country, but during mobistasis en route. In other words, it is based mostly on temporary solidarity during mobistasis in Turkey through various practices, including: 1) the *exchange of knowledge*, 2) *sharing* an apartment and living expenses, and; 3) *participating in cultural and social activities* with civil society organizations and other travellers who have similar backgrounds. If an asylum traveller needs information on social and legal assistance from an organization located in Turkey, an experienced traveller, who has been already resettled to Canada, can advise the current traveller about which organizations to go to during his/her stay. These transnational practices—alongside social, familial and friendship networks and the translocal ties established en route—are important in 'easing the unpredictability' of the asylum odyssey to Canada via Turkey (Bagelman, 2016, p. 39).

Mobistasis for Iraqi travellers is rather short due to the US resettlement programme following the invasion in 2003. Upon arrival in Turkey, mobistasis takes place mostly in Kurtulus (Istanbul), a place they prefer over their designated satellite cities.[30] Staying in Istanbul for Christian Iraqi travellers is firstly linked to the shorter waiting process for resettlement under conditions of mobistasis. Second, it is intimately related to networked solidarity—they can more readily find accommodation and access the assistance of NGOs in Istanbul, especially church, and church-related organizations.[31] However, staying or waiting in Istanbul has a significant financial cost for them. If they do not settle in a satellite city, they cannot obtain the temporary residence permit for foreigners (*kimlik*). If they do not have temporary residence permit, they cannot benefit from certain rights or readily exit from Turkey for resettlement to a third country. According to one fieldworker I spoke to, some Iraqi travellers who chose to stay in Istanbul ending up accruing a hefty fee to the police department of foreigners for their resettlement process to start—around TL5,000 (around US$900).[32] As Istanbul is not one of the satellite cities, this fee accrues monthly as an administrative 'penalty' for those who chose to reside in Istanbul instead of staying in their designated satellite cities and acquiring the official residence permit. In this sense, the residence permit—granted to those who 'follow the rules' and wait in their allocated satellite cities—functions as 'internal borderwork' to keep asylum travellers away from certain designated areas that the authorities prefer they stay out of (Moffette, 2014, p. 266).

As mentioned, a crucial part of mobistasis for asylum travellers is the requirement to remain and wait within satellite cities, this being enforced via the required weekly or twice-weekly visit to the local police station to be checked off. This is part of a governance strategy to monitor travellers and prevent them from leaving their satellite cities, at least for any extended period. If they need to leave the designated city—even for the UNHCR interview in Ankara—they must first seek permission from the police or what refugees call the *Yabancılar Şubesi* (police department for foreigners). Sarah narrated the difficulty in obtaining the necessary permission— which is usually based on the discretion of the police—as follows:

> Sometimes they [the police] do not give permission […] I went to a UN interview in Ankara without asking permission […] I had injured my foot at one point and so had missed some signatures [check-ins]. I had a doctor's letter [to cover those absences] but when I went to the police for permission [to go to the UNHCR in Ankara], they refused. I think they were mad at me.[33]

In a lyrical rather than literal sense, I am reminded of the words of the smash-hit love song 'Every Breath You Take' from the English band 'The Police', written by Sting and released in 1983. The song famously begins, 'Every breath you take/ Every move you make/ Every bond you break/ Every step you take/ I'll be watching you.'[34] The rationale of having travellers 'sign in' then is to but a break on the speed and direction of mobility within Turkey, and to maintain regulations by keeping asylum seekers in their designated satellite city. Travis, a traveller from Iran, explained a different logic underpinning the regulation, namely: 'to control the population, so they are doing well […] because refugees are expected not to have a lot of money and a luxurious life'.[35]

In addition to monitoring through weekly police station visits, Althusser's imaginary scene of *interpellation* in describing ideology also occurs, as practiced by Elif during her period of mobistasis. According to Althusser (2014, pp. 188–196), ideology 'interpellates individuals as subjects' and it also '"acts" or "functions" in such a way as to "recruit" subjects among the individuals, or "transforms" individuals into subjects through the very precise operation'. In a similar vein, Elif experienced the Althusserian interpellation of ideology as follows:

One day in Kayseri, we were playing snowball at the public park with other refugee friends, we were a group. The police came and asked to see our *kimlik* [sic] [...] I understand their control attempts; it is for security and this is their country [... and] we are refugees, foreigners.[36]

This narrative supports how asylum travellers themselves internalize the bureaucratic process of being questioned by the police.

Under conditions of mobistasis, asylum travellers can access primary and secondary education in their satellite cities with the permission of the school principal. However, the language of instruction in most institutions is Turkish, which poses problems for most asylum travellers in following and understanding lectures. Stephanie arrived in Turkey with her family when she was 14 years old. She and her sister, along with two other refugee friends from Iran, were at the same high school in Kayseri. During her stay of around 27 months in Kayseri, the school chose not to progress Stephanie through the grades with the other classmates, leaving her where she began: in Grade 9. Even though she was not successful in progressing due to her limited Turkish language skills, she noted that her experience overall had been positive, since she had gained many new friends.[37]

Mark is from the Democratic Republic of Congo (DRC), but his native language is French. While his assigned satellite city is Yalova—where he is formally expected to settle and remain—he has taken steps to enhance his own social capital by taking classes at the French high school in Istanbul. By registering with the school, he has created an opportunity to remain de facto in Istanbul and to build a life there. Mark noted that the police had agreed he could 'sign in' at the *Yabancılar Şubesi* in Yalova once a month instead of once a week, making the whole process of domiciling in Istanbul much easier. In the meantime, he found a temporary job as a translator at one of the asylum-related organizations. Mark's case can be read as a tactical move to surmount the internal bordering of Turkey's asylum governance system by registering with the French high school—his 'anchor' in Istanbul and his principle means to enhance his social capital.

For travellers from Iraq, families are more hesitant to send their children to school due to the shorter resettlement process. Families are also keen to cut as many expenses from the family budget as possible, schooling for their kids being a major one. Education for Syrian children is more a necessity compared to other asylum travellers since most Syrians choose not to take the resettlement route.[38] This means that most Syrians stay in Turkey with no intention to resettle or to return to Syria. Turkey should therefore take solid steps to educate Syrian children, of whom almost 40 per cent remain out of school, attending (for the most) temporary education centres supported by UNICEF.[39] For the integration of Syrian children into social, cultural and economic life, Turkey should follow a more rigorous programme of comprehensive school-age education for young Syrians.

Travellers need work to survive, a challenging task since the temporary residence permit does not provide the right to work legally. An asylum traveller holding the six-month residence permit can apply for such a right, but the process is laborious. He or she must apply for permission to work with the Ministry of Labour and Social Security, while the prospective employer must lodge a separate application to the same ministry for the work permit to hire the applicant.[40] Due to these bureaucratic hassles, travellers generally struggle to find 'legal' work during their stay in Turkey. In other words, the geographical limitation imposed on non-European asylum travellers also creates *a restriction in access to the labour market*. This exemplifies the nexus between borders, labour, commodities, capital and the market within a 'regime of labour control' that forces many travellers into precarious financial conditions during mobistasis in Turkey (Papadopoulos, Stephenson & Tsianos, 2008, p. 222). Regulator exclusion from the labour market is also a reminder to asylum travellers that they are not economic migrants. And the result is that they are forced to work in illegal black-market jobs under difficult conditions without any social security as part of an adverse 'process of production, dispossession [and] exploitation' (Mezzadra & Neilson, 2013, p. 23).

The work permit issue is more challenging for travellers from Eritrea, Ethiopia, Somalia and Sudan than for asylum travellers from Iran and Iraq. The main reason is that asylum travellers from the latter two countries generally bring sufficient money to cover their expenses for several months. For instance, Samantha arrived in Turkey from Iran with just enough money to cover expenses until she found work in her satellite city, Denizli. Her qualifications—a bachelor's degree from Iran's Bahá'í Institute for Higher Education (BIHE)—meant she was able to pick up work as an English instructor at a private institution there. Samantha stated that 'refugees know that they are not allowed to work' and that asylum travellers from Iran thus generally come prepared with some money during their stay in Turkey or can access financial support from their families in Iran.[41]

For African travellers, in contrast, working 'illegally' is the norm. The kind of work African travellers most often find is what they call *çabuk çabuk* (fast, fast)[42] jobs in small clothing factories or sweatshops in which both the employer and employed are aware of the 'illegality' of the situation. The employer benefits from the pool of a cheap labour without paying any social insurance benefits for workers who are 'off the books'. Asylum travellers are manipulated as cheap labour forces by working under precarious conditions.

This is the situation for many Syrians who also provide many Turkish employers with a ready supply of cheap labour, especially in the agriculture sector. For instance, Jason for several weeks worked on a farm in Konya, earning TL20 (US$4) for each day of work in contrast to the 60TL the employer was paying Turkish workers.[43] The employer did not pay his salary and then told him to take his complaint through the official channels. This example indicates the vulnerability of travellers, especially Syrians who are stuck in Turkey, to exploitation.

There are also instances where Syrian travellers are exploited by Syrian employers. The exploitation of 'cheap' Syrian labour occurs mostly through unfair real estate brokerage, as follows. A Syrian who has already registered in the Turkish system and has access to financial means, rents a flat at around TL700. Then, he rents the flat to other Syrians who have just arrived in Turkey for around TL1,500–2,000, pocketing the difference. For shop space, the rent is much higher.[44] As stated above, most Syrian travellers are not planning to apply for asylum and move to resettlement in a third country via Turkey. The access of Syrians to work and business opportunities is greater than for asylum travellers from other non-European countries. According to a TEHAV report, since 2011 Syrians have established more than 7,000 companies in Turkey—mostly in the construction, real estate, and wholesale trade and brokerage sectors.[45]

In some cases, the work experience is shorter than short-term employment. For example, with the help of her roommates Ashley found a job in a small factory. On her fourth day at the factory, she was called in by her employer, and asked to leave because she was not 'çabuk[fast]' like her roommates. After getting paid for three days work, she was not sad about losing her job since it was not permanent. She explained that 'I was working from 8:00 to 18:00 with a 30-minute break'.[46] Sarah from Eritrea worked in a similar small factory in a different satellite city by managing to work for only few days due to 'ten hours a day and all day standing'.[47] For her it was unbearable. Sophie also spoke of her one week of 'çabuk çabuk' work experience in a clothing factory in Istanbul. At the end of her fourth day, her feet were swollen due to standing all day. She was not able to return to work and, at the end of the week, she was fired without payment. When she chased her employer up about her salary, she was paid just TL20 (US$4) for the entire week's work.[48]

Not every work experience is negative memories for asylum travellers. For instance, Jamie expressed that he had the best work experience working in a photo gallery in Turkey. He described his boss as 'the nicest person on the planet'.[49] In the state of mobistasis, he had many chances to travel within the country both for his job and personal trips from the coastal part of Turkey to Istanbul. Kim who received her master's degree in clinical psychology in India before arriving in Turkey, found a job in her satellite city working as an assistant at the psychology clinic. Mark—the French-speaking refugee from the DRC who we met earlier—found rewarding work as a translator in a refugee-related NGO in Istanbul.

Regarding engagement of travellers with the host society, some have experienced difficulties in finding affordable accommodation. During my fieldwork in Isparta, I called a landlord to enquire about renting his place. At the beginning of our conversation, he described the apartment—the number of rooms and the rental price—and the days and times that the flat was available for inspection. He then asked what I do for work—I claimed I was a refugee from Iran. The landlord then informed me that he and his wife only rent their place to Turkish citizens.[50] Most landlords demand higher rentals from foreigners, and this is especially true for travellers from Syria. For instance, if a flat is normally TL1,000, the landlord demands TL 2,000, which leads four or five families to share the same apartment.

At the same time, the 'share economy' of asylum traveller renting also facilitates a counter-strategy of *getting away with things*. As an example, an asylum traveller from Afghanistan was asked by the *Yabancılar Şubesi* to declare an address to obtain his residency permit in Yalova. Although he was living in Istanbul at the time, he rented an entire place in the satellite city but then sublet all of the rooms to other asylum travellers, while retaining his room in a shared apartment in Istanbul. Subletting his apartment in the satellite city allowed him to both retain his 'official address' in Yalova—crucial for his stability in the liminality stage—and created extra income to support himself by renting other rooms to other travellers, while also helping others find accommodation in Yalova.

On the down side, the impact of the Syrians on the housing market produces resentment among local people towards Syrians, who are held responsible for rising rents and other prices in general. The bias against other travellers seems to be directed at Syrians at the societal level. During my field trip and conversation with locals in Aksaray, they generally had positive things to say about Iraqi, Iranian, and Afghan travellers—the complaints and the biased language was directed primarily against the Syrians. Thus, the Syrians were demonized by local people indirectly by comparing them with Iraqi, Iranian and Afghan travellers, who were in turn openly praised: 'Afghans are hardworking and earnest [...] never begging on the streets', or 'Iraqis are better and quiet, as well as harmless', or 'Iranians are like us, never seeking any economic assistance from Turkey'.[51] In other words, local people express their uneasiness about the existence of Syrians by praising travellers from other countries. Yet it is interesting that—before the mass arrival of Syrians—local people were directing similar complaints at Iraqi and Afghan travellers. I argue that local people want to rationalize their misgivings while retaining their own core identity as 'hospitable Turks'. In other words, locals are keen to reflect the image that 'Turkish society is welcoming, not a discriminatory society'. They can justify the rationale that 'if locals have problems with Syrians, it is not about Turkish society. It must, rather, reflect the wrongdoing of Syrians'.

In addition, renting a place with relatively more expensive price fuels biases towards travellers. The general assumption among locals is that if they can afford to rent this or that place, they are not 'genuine' refugees. For instance, a local person criticized some attitudes of Syrians such as drinking coffee by claiming that they are not real refugees since they are laughing and drinking coffee on the streets while there is a war in their country. This negative image is closely linked to the general assumption which sees a refugee as a vulnerable person who should 'look sad and depressed'. In line with this image of vulnerability, Melissa stated that 'Turkish people think that refugees should not have any money. Thus, [since they have some resources] local people assume refugees get money from the Turkish government'.[52] This image of refugees approaches Aristotle's distinction of *zoē* (bare life including breathing and eating) and *bios* (a way of good life including biological and political) regarding who deserves what kind of life, as well as Agamben's (1998, p. 8) *homo sacer* notion, as a bare subject 'who may be killed and yet not sacrificed'.[53]

LGBTQ travellers are especially subject to discriminatory practices and hate speech in satellite cities. Most LGBTQ individuals living in satellite cities are marginalized both by local inhabitants of satellite city and the police. A local respondent in Isparta described a gay asylum traveller as neither a man nor a woman.[54] The respondent's description reflects what most Turkish people think: being gay, lesbian or transgender degenerate the moral codes of society. To note, not every satellite city exhibits such discriminatory discourse against LGBTQ asylum travellers. However, if they stay out of metropolitan areas, they are more likely to experience negative conditions. For instance, John lived in the satellite city of Kastamonu for a year, and he told me that he was beaten and stabbed due to his sexual orientation and outlook. John later applied to move to another satellite city. He was settled in Kirsehir, another conservative city —and very unwelcoming for a homosexual individual. He was beaten there and one of his teeth was broken. He moved to another satellite city, Denizli, where he stayed for 15 months.[55] Similarly, Simon was first settled in Kastamonu where he had problems and suffered sexual discrimination. He applied to be transferred to another satellite city and was settled in Denizli where he lived for 17 months.

Melissa underlined the stereotypical attitudes in Denizli not only from Turkish people, but also among refugees themselves—especially against LGBTQ and Afghan asylum travellers. She narrated an incident she witnessed in Denizli. Some Iranian travellers had organized an Iranian night at a bar and some asylum seekers from Afghanistan saw the fliers and attended. However, some of the Iranian refugees grew aggressive toward the Afghani bar-goers, saying they were not welcome—the night was specifically organized for asylum travellers from Iran—and forcibly kicked them out of the night club.[56]

Conclusion

In conclusion, seeking asylum is not only an escape from the country of origin, but involves episodic, situational, flexible and spatial tactics en route to resettlement countries via Turkey. Arrival in Turkey means practicing the second bureaucratic step of the asylum journey—the liminal phase—with its bureaucratic procedures which should be performed en route to Canada to begin the incorporation phase with resettlement through the UNHCR. This is what I refer to throughout as the state of mobistasis, what travellers experience as they must stay and wait for an uncertain period during their ongoing asylum journeys.

During this state of mobistasis, asylum travellers from Iran and Iraq are mostly aware of the process thanks to the structured asylum habitus and the (mis)information that they have obtained from past and present experienced travellers. The obtained knowledge provides travellers with a sense of knowing how to get away with things within the frame of the established asylum habitus; what means of transportation to take; what cities to settle and visit in Turkey and; what phrases and codewords to adopt (and avoid) during interviews. For asylum travellers from Eritrea, Ethiopia, Somalia, Sudan, and the DRC, the practice of asylum seeking is a more tactical move, which provides 'legality' for those who arrive at the liminal space without 'legal' travel documents. Experiencing bureaucratic metamorphosis by seeking asylum offers the opportunity to be visible in their encounter with Turkey's bureaucracy, governmental and non-governmental organizations, and, more importantly, the UNHCR's resettlement programme.

Asylum travellers generally accept Turkey's geographical restriction and its correlates—the satellite city regulation limiting their movement within the liminal space, their limited access to education, the inability to obtain a valid work permit, and limited health care services during their stay while waiting for resettlement to Canada. In return, they look for the opportunity to be resettled to the third safe country to complete the asylum journey with the *incorporation phase* via the UNHCR's resettlement operation.

Notes

1 Interview, 23 June, 2014. Istanbul, Turkey.
2 Interview, 18 June, 2014. Istanbul, Turkey.
3 Most discussants refer to the UNHCR Turkey office as 'the UN'.
4 Interview, 20 January, 2015. Ottawa, Canada.
5 Ibid.
6 Interview, 6 February, 2015. Ottawa, Canada.
7 Interview, 23 June, 2014. Istanbul, Turkey.
8 The massive arrivals from Syria since 2011 have had a significant impact on the UNHCR and interview schedules due to the shortage of staff. Interview notes.
9 Interview, 22 February, 2015. Ottawa, Canada.
10 *Kimlik* is the Turkish word for ID card.
11 Interview, 15 June, 2015. Tehran, Iran.
12 Interview, 20 January, 2015. Ottawa, Canada.
13 Interview, 26 May, 2014. Istanbul, Turkey.
14 Ibid.
15 Interview, 5 July, 2014. Istanbul, Turkey.
16 Between May and September 2017, I was a research assistant for the INTEG-LOC project on Syrians run by Aysen Ustubici. We conducted interviews with Syrians who work and run their own businesses in Turkey to understand the relation between integration and entrepreneurship in the case of Syrians in Istanbul.
17 Field notes between May 2017 and August 2018, Istanbul and Aksaray.
18 According to Education Law No. 212, both primary and secondary education are mandatory for everyone residing in the country. If an asylum seeker wants to pursue post-secondary education, she or he is subject to same regulations as a

Turkish citizen. That is, the university entrance exam, which is conducted in Turkish, must be successfully completed.
19 For information about the rights and obligations of asylum seekers and the services that refugees can access in Turkey, visit https://help.unhcr.org/turkey/ For information on registration with the Turkish authorities, visit https://help.unhcr.org/turkey/resettlement/ For information about resettlement to a third country, see https://help.unhcr.org/turkey/information-for-syrians/reception-and-registration-with-the-turkish-authorities/
20 www.hayatadestek.org/refugee-support/?lang=en
21 www.tohav.org/eng/
22 www.hyd.org.tr/tr/calismalar/multeciler-ve-dayanisma
23 www.caritas.org/where-we-are/europe/turkey/
24 http://en.sgdd.info/?p=1143
25 When I was conducting my interviews for my master's thesis in 2012, a field worker informed me that there are around 50 convention refugees living in Turkey. I did not conduct interviews with these individuals who are likely to obtain Turkish citizenship.
26 Interview, 8 January, 2015. Ottawa, Canada.
27 Interview, 25 February, 2015. Ottawa, Canada.
28 Interview, 2 February, 2015. Ottawa, Canada.
29 Ibid.
30 Interview, 10 July, 2014. Istanbul, Turkey.
31 Chaldean Assyrian International Humanitarian Association (KADER) is one of most important organizations for asylum travellers from Iraq. For more details, see http://kader-turkey.org/
32 Interview, 10 July, 2014. Istanbul, Turkey.
33 Interview, 6 February, 2015. Ottawa, Canada.
34 One patent irony about the song—which is not about surveillance *per se*, but rather a man who continues to pine for a lost love—is that the band's composer and drummer, Stewart Copeland, is the son of the CIA agent Miles Copeland.
35 Interview, 25 February, 2015. Ottawa, Canada.
36 Interview, 19 January, 2015. Ottawa, Canada.
37 Interview, 8 January, 2015. Ottawa, Canada.
38 According to a report published in September 2017, Turkey plans to transfer almost 300,000 Syrian children to official schools from temporary education centres with a three-year plan. https://reliefweb.int/report/turkey-reveals-how-660000-syrian-refugee-children-will-move-state-schools (accessed 24 April, 2018).
39 http://carnegieendowment.org/sada/74782 (accessed 24 April, 2018).
40 Information based on interview in ASAM Istanbul Office, 10 July, 2014. For further information, www.egm.gov.tr/Sayfalar/iltica-goc-islemleri.aspx
41 Interview, 23 June, 2014. Istanbul, Turkey.
42 *Çabuk* means fast. Travellers call jobs in sweatshops and small textile factories '*çabuk çabuk*' since the employer always pressures them to finish the job quickly.
43 Interview, 14 June, 2018. Aksaray, Turkey.
44 Interview, 7 May, 2017. Istanbul, Turkey.
45 www.tepav.org.tr/upload/files/1533018887-4.TEPAV_Suriyeli_Sirketler_Bulteni__Haziran_2018.pdf
46 Interview, 20 January, 2015. Ottawa, Canada.
47 Interview, 6 February, 2015. Ottawa, Canada.
48 Interview, 5 July, 2014. Istanbul, Turkey. She should have been paid around TL200 (US$40). In 2014, most employers paid around TL30 (US$5) for a day's work by unskilled and irregular workers.
49 Interview, 22 February, 2015. Ottawa, Canada.
50 Interview, April 2012. Isparta, Turkey.
51 Interview notes with locals in Istanbul and Aksaray, 2017 and 2018.

52 Interview, 17 June, 2014. Istanbul, Turkey.
53 One tragic example is the death of Festus Okey, an asylum seeker from Nigeria. In 2007, Okey was arrested by Turkish police, and was then killed in detention by a police officer at the Beyoglu Police Station in Istanbul. The police officer was not held responsible for Okey's death by the court for more than four years. Due to the lack of identity information the court did not sentence the police officer. Migrant Solidary Network, an activist group, became very active in the court process and in 2011, the police officer was sentenced to four years imprisonment for 'reckless homicide'.
54 Interview, April 2012. Isparta, Turkey.
55 Interview, 24 June, 2014. Istanbul, Turkey.
56 Interview, 17 June, 2014. Istanbul, Turkey.

5 The journey of hope and the incorporation phase of the asylum journey

Upon the completion of the liminal phase of the asylum journey under conditions of mobistasis in Turkey, travellers who have successfully convinced the UNHCR to assign them refugee status—and Canada to resettle them—are ready to take the next bureaucratic step of the journey: the *incorporation phase*. In detailing this phase, the present chapter begins with the asylum travellers' image of the UNHCR as the 'legal' transnational travel agency for resettlement to Canada. It then outlines how the incorporation phase for the selected UNHCR-referred refugees begins in their last three days in Turkey with the IOM's cultural orientation programme in Istanbul, which is sponsored by Canada's Citizenship and Immigration Canada (CIC). Finally, the chapter concludes with a discussion of the practices and experiences of asylum travellers in Canada through a detailed empirical analysis of their integration narratives.

Figures 5.1 and 5.2 summarize the steps taken through the travellers' odyssey—from the arrival in Turkey to resettlement in Canada—which I call the incorporation phase of the asylum journey. Bureaucratically speaking, this phase commences when the traveller is invited to the resettlement interview at the Embassy of Canada in Ankara. However, at the personal level it often begins much earlier, sometimes en route to Turkey during the separation and liminal phases. For instance, Kim described her feeling of having begun her 'journey of hope' on the train travelling from Iran to Turkey. Her mental image of Canada and the expectation of resettlement provided Kim with this sense of 'hope',[1] well before the bureaucratic process had even begun. Another early sign of becoming or feeling ready for the incorporation phase

Figure 5.1 Tracing the transnational refugee mobility to Canada via Turkey

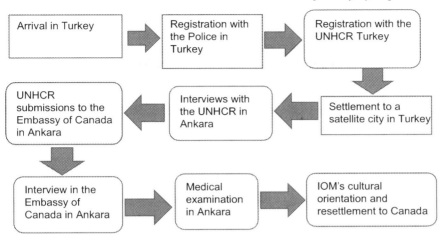

Figure 5.2 Asylum process from arrival in Turkey to resettlement in Canada

is captured in the picture of little four-year old Alex—dressed in the jersey of the Calgary Flames (a Canadian hockey team)—boarding the Turkey-bound train in Iran in the separation phase as his grandfather holds a piece of paper with the UNHCR's Ankara address on it.

The UNHCR as the 'legal' transnational travel agency

UNHCR Turkey has a special function for asylum travellers en route to Canada. Its role is not only to determine the status of travellers, but also to act as a broker in the resettlement process—a transnational travel agency, if you like—by legalizing the journey (and the traveller making it) en route. This motivates asylum travellers in taking the journey towards Canada via Turkey. Most respondents regard the UNHCR in this way—i.e., as a kind of travel agency—even though it is the IOM that has traditionally been the organization responsible for dealing with the travel logistics of resettlement to Canada. For instance, in our conversation, Travis noted that 'the UN [sic] is the easiest, most supportive, and safest way' to move to a third country—in his case, Canada.[2] At the end of our interview, he qualified this depiction of UNHCR Turkey's role as travel agency, noting that while it is certainly the easiest and safest, it is also 'the longest way' to get to Canada.

Under conditions of mobistasis in Turkey, when they arrive in Ankara for UNHCR interviews, asylum travellers inform UNHCR staff about their preferred country of resettlement. For instance, when I asked Ahoo about why she had nominated Canada, she stated: 'Everybody knows Canada is safe [...] For the USA, you don't have to have a family member or sponsor; Canada asks for a sponsor but it is just a name; Australia asks for a sponsor, [and the sponsor's] name, address [and] occupation'.[3] Even though my informant's belief is confirmed by fieldworkers,[4] having a sponsor does not guarantee entry to the resettlement countries. The information/misinformation Ahoo shared with me does not necessarily comport with the precise reality of resettlement to third countries, since the source of information she was relying on was unofficial. In other words, her information comes from what she has been told by asylum travellers she knows from Iraq and her relatives in Canada who were settled there before Ahoo began the incorporation phase. While still in Iran, she had planned to nominate the USA as her preference for resettlement, based on the information she had obtained. However, when she was on the phone talking to relatives in Canada, they informed her that 'Ottawa is a family city'—leading Ahoo to alter her preferences. Indeed, for Ahoo, Ottawa is even more a 'family city' given that so many of her extended family have settled there, having already been granted asylum via the UNHCR in Turkey. Thus this notion—of the 'family city'—takes on multiple meanings in the (re-)production of knowledge during the resettlement phase and acts as a signifier of the shared knowledge among potential asylum travellers and resettled refugees.

Adopting the UNHCR as the travel agency involves several bureaucratic procedures, including interviews for status determination and submission of the cases to the resettlement country as documented in Chapter 4. Of those who have convinced the UNHCR to grant them 'genuine' refugee status, a smaller subset is invited for an interview at the Embassy of Canada in Ankara in order to be assessed for potential resettlement to Canada. At this point, they need to convince the Embassy staff that they are a 'suitable' candidate for resettlement. The various criteria taken into consideration by visa officers makes Canada's resettlement programme quite selective. Self-sufficiency and personal abilities are important signifiers of 'suitability' for resettlement. More concretely, eligibility is based on personal abilities—including education and language skills (French and/or English)—as well as assessed capacity for self-sufficiency. Thus, candidates with family and/or friend networks in Canada have a greater chance of resettlement under the family reunification scheme within the resettlement programme.

The interview at the Embassy differs significantly from interviews with the UNHCR. An asylum traveller is expected to convince the UNHCR staff that she is *vulnerable and badly off*—namely, that she has been compelled to leaver with a 'well-founded' reason that grounds her genuine 'fear of persecution'. Once invited to qualify for resettlement in Canada, however, the very same person needs to 'turn on a dime', as it were, and prove how *effective, qualified and capable* she is. They must show they are a 'best fit' for resettlement, with the language and educational capacities to thrive in Canada were she to be resettled there from Turkey. This therefore requires the asylum traveller to be able to 'switch' his or her self-representation, from *vulnerable* before the UNHCR to *valuable* before the visa officers of the Canadian Embassy in Ankara.

The journey of hope 105

At this stage of the incorporation process, Embassy staff evaluate the interviewees and confirm which cases have been selected for resettlement, based on the aforementioned criteria. After several months, asylum travellers successfully completing the interview process with the Embassy, are scheduled for a medical examination appointment upon the approval by the CIC. The medical examination in Ankara is the final bureaucratic step that the asylum traveller must take to be eligible for travel to the 'incorporation space' in Canada. This medical approval really signals the start of the *formal incorporation phase* of the asylum journey for asylum travellers under conditions of mobistasis in Turkey. Having been determined 'medically fit', the asylum traveller is now ready to participate in the IOM's cultural orientation programme in Istanbul.

While all bureaucratic 'hurdles' on the Canadian side are now essentially complete, asylum travellers who have been deemed eligible for resettlement must complete one last bureaucratic encounter before attending the IOM's cultural orientation programme. They must travel to their assigned satellite city and obtain the mandatory official *çıkış* (exit) document from the police station there. The few who have never registered or been domiciled in their designated satellite city—quite common for asylum travellers from Iraq who prefer to live out mobistasis in Istanbul as detailed in Chapter 4[5]—are required to attend in person and pay an (often quite steep) fine to obtain the exit document.

'Reducing high expectations' through the cultural orientation programme

These bureaucratic procedures increase the temporality of asylum journeys. Asylum travellers can never be certain how long all the various bureaucratic requirements will take to complete and are thus uncertain about precisely when the incorporation phase will begin. It takes roughly twenty months for asylum travellers from Iran. For Iraqi asylum travellers, it is shorter—ranging from six to twelve months—because of the United States' resettlement programme for Iraqis following the US intervention in 2003. Travellers from Africa and Afghanistan usually wait more than three years if they are granted refugee status by the UNHCR. However, they are less likely overall to be resettled than applicants of other nationalities. Janice spent more than 24 months in Turkey and observed that 'Whenever Canada announces an increase in the quota, the process can speed up'. For example, one of her friends stayed fourteen months in Turkey, while another had to wait 27 months.[6] Rachel from Iran explains that the variation in the length in waiting is because of the discretion of the resettlement country—for the USA, it is generally six to 12 months, whereas for Australia it takes up to four years.

As mentioned, the final bureaucratic procedure under conditions of mobistasis is the IOM's cultural orientation programme for those being resettled to

106 *The journey of hope*

Canada via Turkey—sponsored by the Canadian government—that runs on a large-group, workshop format. Some respondents who attended the programme describe it as being 'organized by the UN [sic] in Istanbul' in the three days before departure. However, this is another case of misinformation in the 'mobile knowledge' (re-)produced by asylum travellers. IOM Turkey is not the UN. It is the designated travel agency for those who have already been selected by the CIC for resettlement in Canada—that this, those whom the UNHCR has already recognized as refugees. The cultural orientation programme thus forms part of this 'travel agent' role.

According to my respondents, the cultural orientation programme was an exciting time since they had already obtained their exit documents and knew that they were on their way to Canada. For them, the exit document is a kind of 'mental marker' that the incorporation phase has begun, since they will collect their passports towards the end of the orientation workshops. For those who have never had a passport—or who arrived in Turkey without one—the exit document they have already obtained is a substitute document, allowing them to travel to Canada via the IOM.

In June 2014, I attended two of IOM Turkey's cultural orientation programmes for resettlement to Canada. The venue was a hotel reserved by the IOM. The aim of orientation—which provides information about financial support from the state, schooling, employment opportunities, and unemployment benefits—is quite simple: 'to reduce high and elevated expectations' among asylum travellers, many of whom have unrealistic beliefs about the resettlement country.[7] According to IOM fieldworkers, the point is 'to reduce the culture shock' conditioned by the refugees' unrealistic expectations prior to arrival. Furthermore, IOM staff informed me that most refugees resettled to Canada have close family members—sibling(s), aunt(s), uncle(s), and/or other relatives already living there.

Most attendees participating in the orientation programme that I attended during my fieldwork in Istanbul were from Iran. The first orientation class I attended comprised 35 Iranian and three Iraqi participants, while the second had around 20 Iranians and four Iraqis. Almost all attendees at both sessions reported having at least one friend, cousin, or family member living in Canada. Thanks to this, Iranian and Iraqi refugees are more likely to have basic knowledge about Canada before they arrive.

During the programme, IOM staff there ask two main questions: 'What do you know about Canada'? and 'What do you not know that you would like more information about'? Some of the most basic common knowledge the asylum travellers report back to these questions—based on what they have heard from friends and family in Canada—are the capital city, the biggest city and/or the official languages. Just as often, they relay more complex knowledge they have learned about Canada from their contacts, including the excellent employment opportunities there and the chance to earn a good wage, the welfare system, schooling and access to higher education, and the ability to live without fear of discrimination.

The journey of hope 107

Travellers were repeatedly told that once they have arrived in Canada, there would be no further access to the UNHCR or the IOM were problems to arise. IOM staff also repeatedly explained to participants that there is no 'welcome money'—a common piece of misinformation that circulates among asylum travellers prior to arrival that IOM staff wish to disabuse them of.[8] Another important warning is the necessity of learning the English and French languages to find a job and/or continue their higher education for their successful integration in the country. Asylum travellers also ask questions including baggage allowances for the flight and the possibility of bringing saffron and tobacco into Canada. This is interesting—it illustrates that smokers already know how expensive a pack of cigarettes is in Canada. Questions about what Canada will be like upon arrival are mainly about job opportunities, citizenship status, education opportunities, social and financial benefits, healthcare services, and travel to other countries including return to the country of 'origin'. The third day sees the distribution of travel documents (including passports if the traveller has a valid passport), flight tickets, and the certificate demonstrating attendance at the orientation programme.

Very early Monday morning, the inductees—now having passed the 'orientation' and with travel documents in hand—take a shuttle from the hotel to Istanbul's Atatürk Airport with IOM staff. At the airport, everyone—including security services, IOM officials, the passengers and their friends—was in a hectic rush. When I was at the airport with travellers, I realized that some were not only en route to Canada, but some also to the

Figure 5.3 Time to fly to Canada, at Istanbul Atatürk Airport
Courtesy of the author, Istanbul, Turkey. June 2014

USA. For instance, an asylum traveller who was a pastor was waiting for his flight to Canada with his family. His friends who have undertaken the asylum journey in the past and been resettled to Australia and Canada, were at the airport to say 'goodbye' to the pastor and his family's journey to Canada.

In the meantime, the IOM's security re-checked the documents that had been handed to travellers during the orientation programme. The security personnel checking refugees exit documents at the airport told me that, in one case, a person had forged IOM documents, managed to board the flight, and was only caught upon landing in Canada.[9] After the control of documents, the travellers walked towards the main security check.

At the main security point, one asylum traveller—Hassan, from Iraq—was stopped: apparently, his name had triggered a warning from US Customs and Border Protection (CBP) as a potential security risk in the USA. What was unfortunate for Hassan is that he already passed into an international zone at the airport and could not return to where IOM officers had left him. Therefore, he had to stay overnight inside the airport's international zone. I asked the IOM fieldworker about what had happened to Hassan. The fieldworker informed me that he had only been held up on a misunderstanding—it was another 'Hassan' that was on the CBP list as a potential risk—and that he had been able to continue on his travels the very next day. This digital control that I witnessed in the case of Hassan from Iraq is indicative of the proliferation of security concerns within the rise of generalized *governmental unease* in recent years, 'a type of ban-opticon dispositive' with the increased paranoia against the mobility of certain 'undesirable' people (Bigo, 2008, p. 10).

Passing through these multiple security checks and clearing the extensive digital control means travellers are ready to board the flight and depart for Canada. They have completely left the liminal phase. Now, they are all ready to enter the last phase of the journey of hope and experience the incorporation space in Canada, which will involve some final bureaucratic steps in the first few weeks after landing.

'Pretty cool, pretty cold': the Canadian experience

To recap briefly, the incorporation phase begins once the UNHCR has granted refugee status and the resettlement interview at the Canadian Embassy has been completed. In other words, as mentioned in Chapter 4, it commences in the period of mobistasis in Turkey where asylum travellers apply for asylum and wait for refugee status determination by the UNHCR. The period of mobistasis at the end of liminal phase is uncertain, as discussed on the previous pages, and depends on the discretion of resettlement countries. Once the status is granted by the UNHCR, and the Canadian authorities invite UNHCR-referred refugees for the resettlement interview at the Embassy in Ankara, the incorporation phase begins for the list of those who have 'made the list'. Travellers are ready to practice the incorporation space in Canada after the IOM's cultural orientation programme in Istanbul.

It is important to note that experiences of travellers arriving in Canada via Turkey differ significantly from travellers who have applied for asylum inland. For example, if a person arrives and seeks asylum in Canada, he or she is not eligible for the assistance programme implemented for UNHCR-resettled refugees. Practices require the asylum claimant to attend a hearing with the Immigration and Refugee Board of Canada (IRB) to determine her status as 'genuine' or 'bogus'. The individual encounters the bureaucratic asylum process by convincing a Canadian agency of the genuineness of her asylum claim. In other words, while asylum travellers arriving in Turkey for asylum journey practice the liminality and bureaucratic metamorphosis in Turkey with the hope of resettlement, inland asylum applicants of Canada experience the liminality and bureaucratic metamorphosis in Canada.

The experience of Marek from Ghana is instructive here. Marek had no knowledge about the asylum process (or any intention to seek asylum) prior to beginning his asylum journey. Eventually Marek left his 'home' country due to constant threats as he was a member of a political group. At the time of his travel, he had a Canadian visa that was valid for six months, so Canada seemed like the best place to head to. But it was not a deliberate choice as such: 'If I'd had a visa for a different country, I would have flown there [instead]'.[10] His flight was on June 20, which incidentally is World Refugee Day. Probably for that reason, when he arrived at the airport, he saw flyers and brochures about asylum seekers and refugees posted all over the terminal building. This was what gave him the idea of asylum, which proves that this idea is not always planned and is instead quite *contingent*. One week after his arrival in Canada, he went to the Catholic Immigration Centre (CCI) in Ottawa—an organization that will be discussed in further detail below—to get information about seeking asylum. Then he applied for asylum in Canada, waiting for refugee status determination as an asylum seeker.

Several months later, Marek and I were on the same bus. We talked about his case, which had been rejected; he was appealing the decision. I asked about the case of his Senegalese friend, which was still under process of status determination. Marek explained: 'Canada wants ID and official documents from him [...] My friend is supposed to go to his country's Embassy [to get these]'.[11] It is worth pausing at this point to note that here the asylum applicant is expected to travel to a location that is technically the territory of his country of 'origin'—*the place he has fled* due to a *genuine fear of persecution*. We can safely ask how reasonable such a request is, especially in the wake of the murder of Jamal Khashoggi at the Saudi consulate in Istanbul in 2018. This is critical, as people can be at risk inside the diplomatic space of their country of origin in certain cases, in a manner that cannot be downplayed. As our conversation returned to Marek's own case, he recounted how the UNHCR—in rejecting his application—had told him: 'your government can protect you [from persecution]'. Marek, however, noted how he did not share this optimistic assessment: 'no one leaves his country without a very good reason'.[12]

In the meantime, Marek recounted how he had begun taking courses on natural science subjects—biology, chemistry, and physics—as well as English at the adult high school in his area. His aim has been to familiarize himself with the Canadian curricula so that he can start a degree in medicine, which he would pursue were he granted refugee status. For Marek—or, indeed, any other inland asylum applicant—the advantage of staying in Canada while the application is being processed is that he is allowed to enrol in adult classes to gain valuable skills and improve his English language ability. That being said, inland applicants struggle under challenging living conditions—it is hard to find a job or affordable accommodation—due to 'their precarious legal status' (Jackson & Bauder, 2013, p. 360; Lacroix, Baffoe & Liguori, 2015).

Resettlement refugees are collected at the airport upon their arrival in Canada from Turkey. They are now no longer refugees, but newcomers with permanent immigrant status. They are temporarily settled at a reception centre under Canada's Resettlement Assistance Program (RAP), which still provides short-term social and financial assistance.[13] At the reception house, basic needs are addressed by case managers who distribute ID cards and help with registration for health care, language courses—the Language Instruction for the Newcomers to Canada (LINC) programme—finding permanent accommodation, and schooling for children.

At the reception centre, some respondents who made the journey alone and without extended family in Canada experienced emotional difficulties in adjusting. Respondents making the journey to Canada with their families and being resettled through family reunification understandably find it much less stressful. For instance, Janice recounted that her 'first eighteen days' in Canada—where she remained at the reception centre sharing a room with a Rwandan refugee—were 'the saddest experience' [of her life] in terms of being alone with her new status and the ambiguities this entailed. She continued 'we were both refugees and we were both alone, sad in our room […] There was nothing to do'.[14] Even though Janice was no longer a refugee at this time—but a new permanent resident making the transition—she still felt like one because of the stay in the reception house.

Having arrived in Canada in 2012, Travis described his first impression of the centre as follows:

> I remember I was very disappointed because my image of Canada prior to arriving had been different [to the reality of the centre]. Canada is a kind of dream for people outside the country […] it was my dream when I was in Turkey […] But the reception centre was [very uncomfortable and forbidding] like an old hostel.

This environment during his immediate arrival in Canada has created a disappointment of loneliness due to his image about Canada prior to his arrival. His disappointment changed when he moved to his own apartment, and when he enrolled at Carleton University in Ottawa. He further expressed how practicing Canada as the incorporation space is a 'pretty cool, pretty cold' experience in a unique and peaceful country which provides financial and social support to refugees but where the winters are much longer and, indeed, colder than he had ever experienced.[15]

Regarding financial assistance under the RAP, respondents are told that the principal applicant will be supported with benefits for one year by the CIC under the RAP. In addition, they can earn up to CAD300 per month without losing benefit from the CIC.[16] To exemplify, if the CIC provides CAD1,200, and a person finds a part-time job that pays CAD300, the CIC reduces the government payment to CAD900. They also receive assistance finding accommodation. Resettlement officers provide a list of recommended rental accommodation. Travellers not satisfied with an initial recommendation will be provided with a second option. If the traveller is still not satisfied, she is responsible for seeking her own housing. Finding affordable permanent housing is more difficult for inland refugee claimants than sponsored refugees (Murdie, 2008). All this being said, virtually all the respondents I spoke with during fieldwork reported being content with the overall process in Canada thanks to the social and financial assistance provided by the RAP.

In addition to the RAP, a translocal network of mostly locally run refugee community organizations from various origin communities exist. These provide extended social and cultural support, as well as private sponsorship for newcomers from the same country of origin by easing the transition phase in the incorporation space (Lacroix, Baffoe & Liguori, 2015). Canada's CCI[17] is one significant civil society organization that assists many resettling refugees with services. These can include finding temporary housing, helping with official forms like the application for permanent residency and social insurance number, as well as orientation programmes for education, health and employment services, and counselling. Ingrid recounted to me how she attended a maple syrup festival and an ice-skating outing as part of CCI-organized social activities. She also noted that CCI also arranged conversation groups for integration and information sessions including the use of transit and library systems in her resettlement city, Ottawa.[18] These activities are significant as they facilitate newcomers' social and cultural adaptation to their new surroundings by establishing 'social ties [...] as mechanisms for support during refugees' initial settlement' (Brunner, Hyndman & Mountz, 2014, p. 84).[19]

In the incorporation space, children under 18 are eligible to enrol in public schools. There is a key difference, however, between school attendance in Turkey and Canada. While travellers under 18 attend school simply to fill their free time in Turkey, in Canada they do so to learn and to pursue higher vocations, not least advanced education or a post-high school career. For instance, Stephanie—whose story we encountered in Chapter 4—had been enrolled in a high school during mobistasis in Turkey during the liminal phase. As discussed, she had not been allowed to progress beyond Grade 9. She arrived in Canada when she was 17 years old. From then on, however,

112 The journey of hope

she thrived, completing her high school education in Canada, and she is currently studying in the Engineering Department at Carleton University.[20] Travellers over 18 years, once they have completed the LINC programme, are able to register at adult high schools, if required, to catch up to the Canadian curricula system by taking courses based on their interests from different fields including maths, social sciences, or natural sciences. Ingrid—a second-year architecture student at Carleton University at the time of interview—first completed her LINC classes, and took classes in an adult high school, enabling her to begin undergraduate studies in Ottawa.[21] The free courses offered by the LINC programme gives travellers the opportunity to significantly improve their English and/or French and 'helps newcomers to integrate into Canada and their community'.[22] It is also an opportunity for newcomers in the incorporation space to be acquainted with their new environment and to share stories with other newcomers before starting to look for work, or registering to study at university.

It is important to note that education has a special (and spatial) significance for Baha'i travellers. In Iran, they are prohibited from enrolling in public universities due to their faith. For instance, even though she had known other people who had been resettled to Australia via Turkey, Melissa sought Canada as her resettlement country—and then moved to Ottawa—specifically to continue her university education.[23] Sarah explained one of the primary motives in her mobility decisions, both to Canada and then to Ottawa specifically, as follows:

> Because Baha'is in Iran are not allowed to enter state universities, I went to BIHE [the Baha'i Institute for Higher Education], an underground university in Iran run for Baha'is [...] I was resettled to a small city in British Columbia. Then, in September 2014, I moved to Ottawa because universities in Ottawa recognize our degree from the BIHE.[24]

Even though it is an 'underground' university, both Carleton University and the University of Ottawa accept diplomas issued by the BIHE in Iran—opening a very distinct opportunity for Baha'i travellers who intend to pursue university and post-graduate degrees. Janice, who we met before, had applied for a post-secondary degree in British Columbia where she was originally resettled. However, she could not get admission, recounting that the 'University of British Columbia asks the for Graduate Record Exam (GRE) [...] I did not get acceptance [...] But universities in Ottawa do not ask for GRE results [...] I moved to Ottawa in September to start my MA degree in legal studies'.[25] Janice's decision to move from her initial settlement site to Ottawa also demonstrates freedom to move within the resettlement country. Most respondents have stated that they moved from their initial settlement city to another city or province for job- or university-related reasons. After arrival in Ottawa, Jamie completed art, history and sport classes at the adult high school. Then, he started his undergraduate degree in the Architecture

Department at Carleton University.[26] Recently, Jamie found a job in Montreal where he currently lives and works. Attending university signifies not only the human capital and personal career issues at stake for refugees, but also provides a possible opportunity for newcomers to participate more actively in social, economic, and cultural activities. In this way, they can more readily expand their immediate social circles.

Attending university and finding a job helps travellers to adapt within the social and cultural spheres of life during the incorporation phase. It is important to emphasize again that for those newcomers with social and familial ties prior to arrival, they can access psychological support that can greatly aid 'integration'. For instance, Ahoo found a job within just under four months of resettling in Canada. During her first four months, she attended English courses, which significantly improved her level of English. She then took a job at a Subway restaurant in Ottawa run by her cousin who had charted the same asylum journey as Ahoo, having arrived in Canada via Turkey some years before. Due to her work schedule, she stopped attending the English classes. Ashley worked part time at the same Subway restaurant through her social ties while she was attending classes at the adult high school. These two examples in the incorporation space of the journey signify the importance of *familial ties and networks* in easing potential problems in the country of resettlement, namely finding work.

The interviews that I conducted suggest similar findings—namely, sponsored and resettled refugees with familial ties in their resettlement areas have less 'integration' difficulties than travellers without them. At this point, we can usefully recall how Canada retains extensive 'capacity for choice' (Lippert, 1998, p. 381) of which travellers will be resettled there, through the selective evaluation of potential candidates at the Embassy in Ankara. Each criterion signifies how Canada's resettlement programme via Turkey is *selective*—a means of governing and controlling mobility in line with neoliberal governmental rationality in which family reunification is prioritized. If a family can sponsor a refugee for resettlement, the newcomer will be more likely to find a job and accommodation instead of relying on limited financial assistance from the state. This means that social capital en route to Canada is related to the social ties and transnational networks within the structured asylum habitus. In other words, as detailed in Chapter 4, Canada's resettlement programme via Turkey with its mode of 'selective inclusion' functions as a *humanitarian channel* of labour recruitment.

Building on this, it is crucial to reiterate that the role played by the asylum traveller in the network does not end when she arrives in incorporation space. Rather, she now becomes a potential provider of knowledge for *travellers yet to begin the journey*, thus contributing to the perpetuation of the network in time and space.

The deep extension in time of the network was revealed to me one day when I stopped in a grocery store in Ottawa. The owner—Justin, an asylum traveller originally from Iraq—spoke in Turkish: he had taken the journey to resettle in Canada via Turkey more than 20 years earlier. Curious about his fluency in Turkish after all these years, I asked him whether he has been back to Turkey since arriving in Canada. He informed me that he visits almost every summer, as his relatives from Iraq are asylum travellers currently experiencing mobistasis in Istanbul. Justin is planning to sponsor his relatives to settle in Ottawa and will undertake as much of the bureaucratic legwork as he can before they arrive to support them.

The story of Mark, originally from the DRC, is also instructive in the context of asylum habitus and mobistasis. In particular, it reveals how asylum habitus is structured for prospective asylum travellers by creating familial and social ties in new country-cases. Mark arrived at the incorporation space in 2012, having completed the liminal phase of his asylum journey in Turkey. In 2017, he received his Canadian passport, which made it possible for him to travel abroad, including back to the DRC. He travelled there in late 2017 and was married. After completing the bureaucratic paperwork in Canada, he managed to bring his new wife back to Canada. This means that Mark's experience in liminal space and his existence in the incorporation space with his wife will create valuable translocal social ties for prospective asylum travellers from the DRC. In addition, it will serve to crystallize the structured asylum habitus en route to Canada via Turkey for travellers from the DRC.

Recall the statement that I raised earlier that 'Ottawa is a family city', which can have a range of meanings within the asylum habitus. One example of this is the many community-based social and cultural events that are held in the city through the year, especially by the Baha'i community.

Figure 5.4 is an image taken during a concert at the Algonquin College in Ottawa on February 2015. The headline act was a famous Iranian pop singer, Andi, who is well-known among Iranians. Along with Andi, DJ Aligator, an Iranian-Danish DJ, performed at the concert hall. More than two hundred Iranian fans attended the concert. I was invited by an Iranian asylum traveller who had used the phrase 'Ottawa is a family city' during our conversation. This image serves to capture this idea of established community ties and the events that make Ottawa a 'family city'. For instance, the University of Ottawa hosts the Center for Baha'i Studies. At the end of February 2015, the University of Ottawa launched a campaign, 'Education is not a Crime' with the collaboration of the Center for Baha'i Studies.[27] The documentary 'To Light a Candle' by Maziar Bahari, an Iranian director, was presented at the University of Ottawa where many Baha'i individuals attended. A Baha'i traveller also stated that they regularly meet every 19 days for what the Baha'i newcomers call a 'feast' in which they socialize, tell stories about Baha'i faith and culture as part of the 'within community' events.[28] This monthly gathering and other 'within community' events, as well as CCI's cultural activities underline the importance of social networks and translocal community ties in the resettlement space.

The journey of hope 115

Figure 5.4 An Iranian singer, Andi, performing at a concert in Ottawa, Canada
Courtesy of the author, Ottawa, Canada. February 2015

The established ties and community organizations within the structured asylum habitus allow asylum travellers to *know how to get away things* in Canada. A sense of belonging within the incorporation space emerges within couple months. Kim's narrative is instructive in this context. Almost a year after she resettled in Ottawa, she applied for a PhD programme in Psychology; she could not, however, reach her professors in Iran to get the two reference letters required. She recounted that the two professors had been imprisoned in Iran due to their BIHE courses. During our conversation she seemed alright with the situation, recounting:

> Yesterday I was talking with my mother (in Iran) and she told my father's best friend was imprisoned. I started to cry, and my mother said 'Don't cry. His punishment is just three months'. I felt better […] This is like people's reaction [to the weather] in Canada: when it is –5 or –10 [degrees centigrade], they feel relaxed, they start to think it is warm, it is not bad at all. It is like this in Iran about prison terms […] If someone gets three months [this] is not a big problem […] we also know where he is imprisoned [which makes it feel less bad].[29]

There are two points that interest me about Kim's statement. The first is the normalization of the 'imprisonment' experience, as well as of exclusionary politics in Iran. The second is Kim's answer to her mum linking the relativism of the Canadian winter experience with the situation in Iran as a way to relax herself. Making jokes that reference the weather is clearly connected to experiences and practices that reflect a process of 'getting used to' local life in Canada.

I was able to glean yet another crucial insight—this time coincidentally—during my fieldwork in Ottawa. As we were wrapping up our interview, I asked my respondent, Daria, if she would not mind putting me in touch with someone who had experienced a 'similar journey' as hers that I might talk to, as I was still keen to recruit more interviewees for my fieldwork. Less than a week later, Daria forwarded me the details of one of her contacts in Canada via Facebook, and I then reached out to this individual. This lady enquired after my research, and so I explained briefly that I was talking to people who had undertaken the refugee journey to Canada via seeking asylum in Turkey. To my surprise, this contact informed me she was not going to be much help to me since she had *never been to Turkey*, nor had she *ever applied for asylum*. Not a refugee, she had simply emigrated to Canada via the 'regular' channel as a permanent immigrant more than ten years ago. What is fascinating about this encounter is what it reveals about *Daria's interpretation of her own status*, having begun her new life in Canada. She had understood that I was looking for new contacts who were 'like her'—which to Daria meant finding an immigrant with permanent resident status in Canada. In other words, Daria—when picturing a 'similar case' for me to talk to—did not imagine a 'refugee', as I had supposed she would, but simply any immigrant Canadian who had permanently resettled there.

Overall, Canada has a positive image among respondents that I interviewed in both Turkey and Canada. For instance, Hassan shared his mom's phrase in our interview: 'Canada is like a dad for me, it is my family [...] They burnt my mom's house and store because she is Baha'i'.[30] Hassan's mom practiced rather positive experiences after experiencing discrimination and fear of persecution. Her phrase is very similar to the impression of Acehnese resettled refugees in Canada: 'First Allah [God] gave us life. Then Canada gives us another life' (Hyndman & McLean, 2006, p. 345).

Conclusion

The incorporation phase is the third and final bureaucratic step in the asylum journey for those seeking resettlement in Canada via asylum seeking in Turkey. It begins in Turkey when asylum travellers complete their interview at the Embassy in Ankara and—if they are selected—their medical examination and the IOM's Canada cultural orientation programme, which is held in Istanbul. Visa officers at the Embassy function as border security forces to determine who is a 'best fit' for Canada based on personal abilities and potential self-sufficiency. Canada's resettlement programme via Turkey thus selects travellers from Turkey's refugee 'bazaar'. This 'marketplace' brings together travellers hoping for resettlement and various bureaucracies—the UNHCR (which decides the genuineness of asylum applicants by granting refugee status) and resettlement countries (which filter travellers based on their demonstrated abilities and qualities). The resettlement programme via Turkey thus functions as a 'humanitarian channel' within Canada's broader immigrant-labour recruitment programme.

Then travellers take the flight through IOM towards Canada to arrive in the country of resettlement, which I have termed the incorporation space. Upon their arrival in Canada, they are welcomed by the RAP officers with their new bureaucratic status of immigrant with permanent residency. The fixation of bureaucratic status along with financial assistance by the RAP, and social and cultural activities organized by the non-governmental organizations provides a platform for asylum seekers to take a more active part in the legal and social life of Canada, with the aim of expanding feelings of attachment to the country. The prior existence of family members in the incorporation space for many—indeed most—refugees makes the refugee resettlement programme more one of family reunification. This reduces the responsibility of Canada and eases most problems experienced in the liminal space in Turkey.

Social and human capital are clearly crucial within the incorporation space—as is produced and reproduced knowledge about Canada among past, present, and future travellers. The existence of familial ties and community networks is significant for newcomers during the process of adaptation to the incorporation space. These networks and ties perpetuate translocal relations by grounding the dynamic of asylum–resettlement know-how within a structured asylum habitus. In other words, successfully resettled travellers can now pass their experiences and practices on to future travellers who are currently practicing the separation or liminal phase. Resettlement 'welcoming programmes' supported by non-governmental organizations like the CCI and the government contributes not only to making the Canadian experience better for newcomers, but also the diffusion of positive images and knowledge of Canada among potential newcomers waiting in Turkey for resettlement.

With their new status, they have a work permit, can pursue their education, and travel anywhere they like within Canada. Once they get their Canadian passports, they can travel to other countries, including the country of origin as we saw with Mark's visit to get married in the DRC, from where he had fled originally to Turkey to seek asylum. More importantly, if they feel uncomfortable in their resettlement city or province, they can move to another city or province. We saw this in the case of Sarah, who left British Columbia for Ottawa to pursue her post-graduate degree; Kim, who moved to Toronto from Ottawa to work as a clinical psychologist; and Travis, who relocated from Ottawa to Montreal to begin his career as a photographer and who now travels the world for work.

Notes

1 Interview, 23 June, 2014. Istanbul, Turkey.
2 Interview, 25 February, 2015. Ottawa, Canada.
3 Interview, 2 February, 2015. Ottawa, Canada

4 According to a fieldworker, Australia is stricter in terms of resettlement of travellers than the USA. Interview, June 2014. Istanbul, Turkey.
5 According to an IOM fieldworker, sometimes this fine paid by Iraqis can reach as much as TL60,000 based on the length of stay in Turkey (interview, June 2014).
6 Interview, 20 January, 2015. Ottawa, Canada.
7 IOM interview. June 2014. Istanbul, Turkey.
8 The money that the UNHCR recognized refugees get is the financial assistance provided by the CIC for newcomers. Generally, the assistance lasts up to a year for government-assisted resettlement refugees. In the immediate arrival, newcomers are handed the amount covering two months' assistance since they do not have a social insurance number and bank account beforehand.
9 Interview, June 2014. Istanbul, Turkey.
10 Interview, 20 December, 2014. Ottawa, Canada.
11 Interview, 14 March, 2015. Ottawa, Canada.
12 Interview, 14 March, 2015. Ottawa, Canada.
13 For the housing experiences of the government-assisted refugees in resettled in Vancouver, Canada, see Sherrell & Immigrant Services Society of BC (2009). The study finds high unemployment and layoffs among the interviewed participants. The research also signals out the widespread 'affordability challenges' among the interviewees and low income related problems in finding accommodation (ibid.).
14 Interview, 20 January, 2015. Ottawa, Canada.
15 Interview, 25 February, 2015. Ottawa, Canada.
16 Interview notes.
17 It has recently changed its name to the Catholic Centre for Immigrants.
18 Interview, 19 January, 2015. Ottawa, Canada.
19 Regarding, integration and refugee resettlement to Canada, as well as the importance of social capital, there have been several studies conducted on privately and government sponsored resettlement programme, the success of resettlement, and 'integration' success of refugees who were resettled in Canada in different timeframes. See Krahn, Derwing, Mulder & Wilkinson's (2000) study on refugee integration and labour market; Beiser's (2003) research on private sponsorship and resettlement success; Lamba & Krahn's (2003) research on importance of social capital and refugee resettlement; Simich's (2003) research on the refugee resettlement and refugees' search for social support; Brunner, Hyndman & Mountz's (2014) study on Acehnese resettlement refugees.
20 Interview, 8 January, 2015. Ottawa, Canada.
21 Interview, 19 January, 2015. Ottawa, Canada.
22 For further information, see www.cic.gc.ca/english/department/media/backgrounders/2013/2013-10-18.asp
23 Interview, 17 June, 2014. Istanbul, Turkey.
24 Interview, 6 February, 2015. Ottawa, Canada.
25 Interview, 20 January, 2015. Ottawa, Canada.
26 Interview, 22 February, 2015. Ottawa, Canada.
27 See for further details, www.notacrime.me/
28 When I asked the reason, my respondent explained the Baha'i calendar has 19 days in each month.
29 Interview, 5 February, 2015. Ottawa, Canada.
30 Interview, 7 February, 2015. Ottawa, Canada

Conclusion
The asylum journey as the 'journey of hope'

> 'Is there any remedy for nomadism? Is it not the inescapable fate of an old civilization'?
> (Edgar Salin cited in Edding, 1951, p. x)

As articulated throughout the book, the everyday activities of organizations like the IOM and the UNHCR—as well as countries of asylum and resettlement—speak to the universal interest in seeking permanent remedies for problems that asylum travellers face during their journey of hope. However, refugee mobility—especially if occurs *en masse*—has increasingly been approached within a discourse of 'crisis' (i.e., Turkey's 'refugee crisis' or Europe's 'refugee crisis'). The current situation thus closely reflects the observation of Edgar Salin above on the 'refugee problem' in West Germany during the Cold War, which linked the 'problem' with 'nomadism'. From the state-centric perspective, mobility of some is not good, if it is free—namely, beyond the control of the authorities. In other words, mobility is something to be controlled, something in need of a 'remedy'.

In one of the greatest dystopian books ever penned, *We*, Evgeny Zamyatin sarcastically depicts the Soviet ideology of control and its endeavour to reduce individuals to a homogenous and fixed *thing*:

> And then, to myself: Why is this beautiful? Why is dance beautiful? Answer: because it is unfree motion, because the whole profound meaning of dance lies precisely absolute, esthetic subordination, in ideal unfreedom.
> (Zamyatin, 1972 [1921], p. 4)

No metaphor could be better than the act of dancing in describing the beauty of 'unfree motion'. It is like a tourist's travel from one country to another, the mobility of which—at least for the tourist—feels very 'free'. However, this is just because the tourist mostly ignores the controls and checks that are essential to any legal journey. If a tourist's nomadism is 'beautiful' for states, it is because under conditions of 'absolute' control and monitoring, it is, in reality, 'unfree' motion. It is—in the end—subordinated to travel agencies, border bureaucracies, immigration regulations, citizenship regimes, and so on. When states hear about 'free' journeys in the migration domain, they immediately begin to conceive of sedentarist mechanisms to slow down and adjust 'the speed of flow'.

In the domain of migration, this sedentarist metaphysics 'is a way of thinking and acting that sees mobility as suspicious, as threatening' (Cresswell, 2006, p. 55). Writings on refugees within the frame of sedentarist thinking largely essentializes refugees as the objects of knowledge and the nation-state as the 'national order of things' (Malkki, 1995b, p. 512). As opposed to suspicion of sedentarist thinking against the mobility of some travellers, nomadic metaphysics highlights *flow, fluidity*, and *dynamism*. It links mobility to 'a world of practice, of anti-essentialism, anti-foundationalism, and resistance to established forms of ordering and discipline' (Cresswell, 2006, p. 47). Nomadic thinking explores not only the 'corporeal, imagined and virtual mobilities of people [and] the interaction between people and objects', but also 'the constitution of social identities' by underlining 'the importance of trans-national, global, forms of governance' (Cresswell, 2006, p. 43). However, it is essential to be suspicious in using some nomadic concepts such as 'nomad, maps, and travel' since these:

> are not usually located, and hence they suggest ungrounded and unbounded movement—since the whole point is to resist selves/viewers/subjects. But the consequent suggestion of free and equal mobility is itself a deception, since we don't all have the same access to the road.
> (Wolff, 1993, p. 235)

Wolff's caution is significant in juxtaposing mobility in terms of *differential access*. Education status, country of origin, gender and personal abilities impact access to the routes and travel documents travellers need to make legal journeys and shape the encounters and negotiations they have with borders and state bureaucracies along the way. In the domain of refugee journeys, thinking of the sedentarist notion does not mean that people 'stop moving altogether and that state altogether prevents circulation of goods and movements of people' (Dahinden, 2010, p. 52). In a similar vein, highlighting nomadism is not to admit that any border crossing must reflect a free and unbounded flow.

Refugee journeys are no exception. Considering both sedentarist and nomadic metaphysics, refugee journeys are more related to Paul Virilio's (2007) concepts of speed–power and politics as *dromology*, which regards the state's 'differential motility' by 'harnessing and mobilizing, incarcerating and accelerating things and people' (Virilio, 2007, p. 8). If a refugee's nomadism is free and uncontrolled, and if there is no subordination, the journey is deemed to be a 'crisis' that calls for a remedy to the problematic nomadism. We are supposed to feel fortunate(!) that we have a global refugee protection regime that controls free journeys and erects extra barriers to stop those that refuse to subordinate themselves to the individual asylum and immigration regulations of states.

The odyssey undertaken by an asylum traveller involves many separate journeys punctuated by various stops and pauses. Put differently, the state of mobistasis is a natural part of the overall journey. Therefore, 'not only curves of movement but curves *in* movement' should be grasped to reveal both governmental strategies of migration bureaucracies and tactics of travellers in understanding relations between mobility and immobility during journeys (Manning, 2009, p. 84, emphasis added). In addition, as I have done throughout the book, embracing the approach of *journey as method*—disaggregating the assembled asylum odyssey into its many routes, pathways and encounters—allows us to better understand the acceleration and deceleration of movements, and to capture both the mobility and immobility as well as encounters during journeys of asylum travellers. Approaching the journey as method 'provides productive insights on the tensions and conflicts that blur the line between inclusion and exclusion' (Mezzadra & Neilson, 2013, p. viii). It is therefore to see the asylum journey itself 'as a living, micro-cultural, micro-political system in motion' (Gilroy, 1993, p. 4). And, furthermore, it is a process of unpacking the politics of mobility—the paths taken, and the encounters experienced—in line with Walters' (2015) notion of 'viapolitics'.

This approach is also important for exposing the various labels, identities and statuses attributed to travellers en route. As has been reiterated throughout the pages of this book, the same traveller will carry a range of distinct labels, attributions and identities en route to Canada via Turkey. To reiterate a theme first introduced at the beginning of the book, migration studies has generally viewed the status of the migrant from the perspective of—and *the categories developed by*—nation-states. More specifically, if a traveller is categorized as 'irregular' en route to, say, Turkey, the literature categorizes this traveller from the perspective of the receiving country (i.e., of Turkey's system migration governance). In a similar vein, when this same person is resettled, the label she takes on is that attributed to her by the resettlement country (i.e., Canada). Since these attributions are entirely constructed—and often arbitrary—adopting the journey as method perspective opens up the field to enable migration scholars to expose and highlight the fluidity and relativity, as well as the arbitrariness, of the attributed labels.

The asylum journey is *unfree mobility* since it is grounded in bureaucratic regulations and rituals—including the various bureaucratic metamorphoses within each ritual—as well as negotiations among the various designers and managers of the system (i.e., the UNHCR, the IOM, the country of asylum and that of resettlement). It also involves negotiation between these latter agencies and travellers en route. Therefore, asylum journeys should be regarded as a series of *interactions, encounters,* and *negotiations* between asylum bureaucracies and travellers—and the strategies and tactics deployed and counter-deployed therein. The rationale in refugee governance from Virilio's perspective of dromology is to control and regulate the mobility and to accelerate and decelerate the speed and volume of mobility with certain *governmental strategies*. Negotiation among the UNHCR, Turkey and Canada makes each asylum journey an assembled one at the transnational level in the context of resettlement to Canada via Turkey. The designers of the system pose norms and certain procedures as governmental strategies for asylum travellers including Turkey's geographical limitation on non-European asylum applicants and Canada's selective refugee resettlement programme. Each procedure is a unique phase to be passed through within the frame of asylum and border bureaucracies: fleeing the country of origin, seeking asylum in the country of asylum, and resettlement in the country of resettlement. These designers exist to map abstract and formal codes that anyone undertaking a *proper* asylum journey must follow. The codes are not there to secure the paths or ease the way of asylum travellers, but to make them harder to navigate, and to differentiate 'genuine' travellers from 'bogus' ones.

On the other hand, travellers exercise their agency in periodically accelerating and sometimes decelerating the speed of their journey, stopping at certain times by devising specific *tactics* that can oppose (or comport with) the strategies imposed on them. They interact with controlling and regulating apparatuses of state and border bureaucracies in what effectively amounts to an ongoing negotiation. Travellers convert the abstract/theoretical norms of the 'proper' asylum journey to practical/empirical knowledge that is then deployed through *tactics* during the journey of hope. In other words, the codes imposed on travellers are also the guidelines for the journeys they take. The practical knowledge sometimes advises them to negotiate with the codes but at other times to subvert them during journeys of hope en route to Canada via Turkey. This practical knowledge, which takes the form of 'mobile knowledge' as Brigden (2013) suggests, perpetuates itself through time and space by establishing translocal asylum know-how networks among the past, present, and future asylum travellers.

The production of knowledge both in time and space illustrates a certain type of solidarity in the form of shared knowledge and established networks among travellers and their friends and/or family member(s) in Turkey and Canada. The knowledge produced and reproduced en route diffuses through a historically structured asylum habitus among travellers. The asylum habitus towards Canada via Turkey has perpetuated itself since the early 1980s for Iranian travellers and the early 1990s for Iraqi travellers. A structured asylum habitus among Syrian travellers began to emerge in 2015 with the initiation of Canada's resettlement programme via Turkey.

In the context of transnational refugee journeys towards Canada via Turkey, Turkey's geographical limitation creates a transnational border-crossing pattern towards resettlement countries like Canada, the United States and Australia. In other words, the discretionary power of Turkey to restrict the stay of non-European asylum applicants in the country has created a tactic and an opportunity for non-European asylum travellers to move to Canada, Australia, or the United States. The geographical limitation not only attracts asylum travellers towards Turkey, but also determines the direction of the journey towards the West. This challenges the notion of linear refugee movement—namely, from the 'refugee-producing country' directly to the 'refugee-receiving' one. The geographical limitation leads UNHCR's operation in Turkey to be actively involved in processes of the refugee status determination and refugee resettlement in Canada. The UNHCR's active involvement in resettlement to the West attracts non-European refugees to Turkey by marking the UNHCR as the safest, 'legal' transnational travel agency. UNHCR Turkey has facilitated mobility towards Turkey as the space of mobistasis since most asylum travellers are aware that resettlement to the United States, Canada, or Australia is possible via this institution. This suggests that the travel to Turkey—particularly for Iraqi and Iranian travellers—is not primarily for protection, but rather to seek resettlement via the UNHCR. It should be noted that the UNHCR's resettlement operation *does not guarantee* refugees will be resettled to Canada. The process can sometimes last more than two years—indeed, potentially forever—which means that the state of mobistasis in Turkey may turn into permanent stasis.

The geographical limitation marks Turkey not only as a country of asylum, but also a refugee 'bazaar', both for travellers and for resettlement countries. Resettlement to Canada occurs through an elimination and filtering process in which resettlement is based on the selection of individuals in terms of the existence of a family member, or personal abilities like speaking English and/or French, education, gender, and self-sufficiency. The Embassy of Canada in Ankara operates as a form of border security agency in determining who can be resettled to Canada. Therefore, resettlement to Canada via Turkey has become the safest and the most secure way of mobility in terms of control practices in which Turkey's border agencies involves during the journey's separation phase; and then, the UNHCR conducts several interviews at the liminal phase of the journey. Turkey has been convinced by asylum travellers during their temporary stay in Turkey that they are not a security threat to the society. Finally, the Embassy of Canada clears the final security and health check for the resettlement. Resettlement via Turkey using selection-based criteria is beneficial for the resettlement country—Canada—which is now able to fulfil its 'humanitarian' refugee resettlement programme since no country is obliged to resettle refugees.

In conclusion, Turkey's geographical limitation leading to the active involvement of the UNHCR has created more of a magnet effect for asylum travellers from Iran and Iraq and has historically attracted more asylum travellers for their 'journey of hope' towards Canada. In addition to Iraqi and Iranian asylum seekers in Turkey, there are other nationals who are waiting to get refugee status from the UNHCR and to be resettled to a third safe country. Every year, Canada's refugee resettlement programme settles around 700 refugees via Turkey who are mainly Iranian and Iraqi refugees with existing family or friend networks in either Turkey and Canada. Turkey constitutes a spatial refugee bazaar where resettlement countries can select those who have been marked as 'deserving' resettlement. Even though being on the route by seeking asylum in

Turkey for resettlement to Canada involves several hardships and difficulties, travellers are content with the established system thanks to the exchange of knowledge diffused among the past and prospective travellers. Stasis and stops en route to resettlement do not produce an uneasiness among travellers as they aware of the established system on the way to the resettlement country. More importantly, each traveller has arranged her existence in accordance with this established asylum habitus (i.e., stops, pauses, mobistasis and bureaucratic metamorphoses). Each has adopted a variety of tactics from beginning to end, gathering knowledge about how to navigate the process and obtaining information on 'how to get away with things'.

For travellers, what might be source of uneasiness within this long and gruelling odyssey? The answer, from my perspective, would be any attempt by Turkey to remove the geographical limitation. For any lifting to the limitation would mean the end of the historically structured asylum habitus for travellers from Iran, Iraq, Somalia, the DRC, and Sudan. Turkey is a choice for travellers from the aforementioned countries due to its geographical limitation. And, this geographical limitation creates the opportunity of resettlement to Canada.

Directions for further research

This book has focused on individually resettled refugees and their journeys to Canada via Turkey. Group-based resettlement (i.e., resettled family units) is rather missing in this research. Further research can focus on resettled refugee families to understand similarities and differences regarding the tactics of families and strategies of states in practicing the resettlement of family units to their resettlement sites. Resettlement to other countries like Australia, the United States and European countries can be designed to compare the experiences and practices of asylum travellers in other resettlement countries.

From the historical sociology perspective, any change in structure can lead to the change in habits and behaviours of actors. The institutional change in refugee status determination in Turkey from the UNHCR to the DGMM may lead to the significant outcomes in near future in terms of the asylum-seeking practices of the Iranians and applicants from Africa countries. The change can be read as an intervention at the macro level as part of the governance strategy which may create improvisations of the asylum travellers' tactics including the changing trajectories of asylum seeking in different countries instead of Turkey. It would be useful for further research to examine the reverberations of this institutional takeover in status determination process.

Istanbul and Ottawa are the two main research sites in this volume. However, asylum travellers are dispersed both in the country of asylum and the country of resettlement. Therefore, further research in Turkey's satellite cities where non-European travellers wait for resettlement to third countries and in their resettlement cities and provinces across Canada is called for. Such studies could well incorporate a quantitative research design. This would provide researchers with the opportunity to reach more travellers to interview and to make sound generalizations in relation to the problems and hardships that travellers are facing.

Finally, I have not had time to conduct interviews with Syrians who have been resettled to Canada via Turkey. With the conflict in Syria there are millions of Syrians living in camps, in neighbouring countries, and resettlement countries. Each has a different problem to deal with, and each has different journey experiences and practices to narrate. A more comprehensive longitudinal research design on Syrians and their journey of hope would be useful for policymakers, advocacy networks, scholars and civil society organizations in the field—as well as for asylum travellers themselves.

Concluding remarks and suggestions on the routes

By conducting an ethnographic journey in each site and travelling to Tehran (Iran), Istanbul and Aksaray (Turkey), and Ottawa (Canada), the main contribution of the present book has been to trace asylum journeys of non-European travellers to Canada by seeking asylum in Turkey. By tracing journeys, the research brings both a non-Western country of asylum perspective, Turkey, and a Western resettlement country perspective, Canada. It demonstrates not only asylum governance of a non-Western country and the Western system of resettlement governance, but also the micro-practices and experiences of asylum travellers.

However, asylum journeys to Canada via Turkey are not only about practicing the asylum regulations of states, but also the dangerous and deadly routes practiced and passed through by asylum travellers. I would like to underline Amnesty International's 2018 campaign '8 Ways to Solve the World Refugee Crisis'.[1] The campaign resembles a UN campaign of the 1950s, which invited the developed countries to take more responsibility for Europe's refugee crisis in finding long-term solutions and offering permanent haven to refugees following the Second World War.

The campaign of Amnesty International addresses in particular the richest countries of the world by providing statistics about the critical dimension of the world's refugee crisis. The first two solutions put forward are directly related to the context of asylum journeys and routes taken by travellers. The first suggestion is to provide secure and safe routes for refugees, while the second one is to resettle refugees who are in urgent need of a safe haven. The second solution is addressed to the resettlement countries. However, even UNHCR's *Resettlement Handbook* clearly states that 'no country is obliged to resettle refugees' (UNHCR, 2011b, p. 5). This statement functions to resettle refugees from the 'burden sharing' perspective. More importantly, the UNHCR's phrase justifies fewer resettlement numbers in the contemporary refugee resettlement system. Therefore, the Amnesty International campaign must first change the UNHCR's approach, then has to convince countries for resettlement.

126 Conclusion

Regarding transnational mobility towards Canada via Turkey, the future can be speculated that Turkey will continue to keep its geographical limitation on non-European asylum applicants both to push them towards the West and to use the geographical limitation as a political bargaining tool when necessary. However, as suggested in this book, asylum journeys mostly follow the routinized routes with the hope resettlement by seeking asylum in Turkey thanks to the structured asylum habitus. The prioritization of resettlement of some travellers will impair the resettlement of others, resulting in a longer waiting process of asylum travellers from Iran, Iraq, Afghanistan, Somalia and Sudan in Turkey. This is not to suggest that Turkey removing its geographical limitation would provide long-term solutions nor that Canada's refugee resettlement programme will not function in favour of the resettlement refugees. Rather, if the geographical limitation is removed, the route of asylum towards Canada or another third country via Turkey will be cut since many asylum applicants enter Turkey with the hope of resettlement to Canada or another third country.

If Turkey removes its geographical limitation, it is more likely to witness more 'illegal' journeys by travellers towards Europe, as we have seen with the travel of Syrian refugees by crossing the Aegean Sea through smugglers on small—often unseaworthy—boats. If Turkey maintains the geographical limitation, travellers whose resettlement process is of uncertain duration will continue to cross the Aegean Sea through 'illegal' routes and smugglers. In this sense, Turkey's decision to remove or to maintain the geographical limitation will not influence individuals' decision to continue the journey towards the West. Here, Amnesty International's third, fourth, and sixth solutions are significant to highlight. Accordingly, the third solution is to operate more efficient efforts to prevent loss of life of refugees on the route by suggesting that border crossing of refugees should be allowed by governments instead of pushing them and putting barriers against them. Thus, travellers will not need to take the route via human smugglers as travel agents and the Mediterranean Sea will not need warships to 'hunt down' smugglers and 'illegal' travellers. The fifth solution is about the prevention of smuggling networks and the exploitation of travellers by human smugglers. However, as this research has stressed, human smugglers have been an integral part of asylum journeys by functioning, at times, as a safeguard for travellers against border security forces and bandits en route.

Regarding the resettlement of refugees, there is a certain need to use non-discriminatory discourse in the domestic politics as the sixth solution offered by Amnesty International. Accordingly, the sixth suggestion puts an emphasis on governments' responsibility to fight xenophobia and racism and not to use discriminatory discourse about immigrants and refugees in terms of social, political, and economic areas. States should remind the public that the right to seek asylum is a *fundamental human right* as laid out clearly in the 1951 Geneva Convention.

Last but not least, the humanitarian refugee protection regime at the global level under the guidance of the UNHCR should be synchronized and states should not regard the refugee crisis as 'someone else's problem', as articulated aptly by Amnesty International. The seventh solution—one of the most striking realities put forward by Amnesty International—refers to the speech of the High Commissioner Antonio Gutierrez, September 2015, about the limited financial leverage of the UNHCR. The suggestion highlights the need for funds to be made available to fix the 'broken UN system'. This is to say, that if governments approach the 'refugee crisis' as their 'own crisis'—instead of articulating mere wishful promises—we can be more hopeful in finding long-term solutions to problems that refugees have faced during their 'journey of hope'.

Note

1 For further information, see www.amnesty.org/en/latest/campaigns/2015/10/eight-solutions-world-refugee-crisis/ (accessed September, 2018).

Appendix: Interview list

Asylum traveller	Journey	Transportation means	Interview date	Interview location
Mark	Democratic Republic of Congo-Turkey-Canada	plane with passport to Turkey; plane to Canada	3 June, 2014	Istanbul
Jalal	Sudan-Libya-Turkey-USA	bus without passport to Libya; boat without passport to Turkey; plane to USA	5 June, 2014	Istanbul
Sonia	Ethiopia-Saudi Arabia-Syria-Turkey	plane to Saudi Arabia; walking without passport to Syria; walking without passport to Turkey	26 May, 2014	Istanbul
Barry	Iran-Turkey-Canada	walking without passport	16 June, 2014	Istanbul
Patrick	Iran-Turkey-Iran-Georgia-Turkey-Canada	bus with passport; bus without passport to Georgia; bus to Turkey; plane to Canada	16 June, 2014	Istanbul
Melissa	Iran-Turkey-Canada	train with passport to Turkey; plane to Canada	17 June, 2014	Istanbul
Joseph	Iran-Turkey-Canada	train with passport to Turkey; plane to Canada	18 June, 2014	Istanbul
Simon	Iran-Turkey-Canada	mule/horse without passport to Turkey; plane to Canada	22 June, 2014	Istanbul
Baharan	Iran-Turkey-Canada	train with passport to Turkey; plane to Canada	22 June, 2014	Istanbul

Appendix: Interview list 129

Asylum traveller	Journey	Transportation means	Interview date	Interview location
Kim	Iran-Turkey-Canada	train with passport to Turkey; plane to Canada	23 June, 2014	Istanbul
Samantha	Iran-Turkey-Canada	plane with passport to Turkey; plane to Canada	23 June, 2014	Istanbul
Andrew	Iran-Turkey-Canada	walking/donkey without passport	24 June, 2014	Istanbul
John	Iran-Turkey-Canada	walking without passport to Turkey; plane to Canada	24 June, 2014	Istanbul
Amir	Iran-Turkey-Canada	mule/horse without passport to Turkey; plane to Canada	24 June, 2014	Istanbul
Sophie	Ethiopia-Turkey	plane with passport to Turkey	5 July, 2014	Istanbul
Mike	Afghanistan-Turkey-USA	truck without passport to Turkey; plane to USA	7 July, 2014	Istanbul
Marek	Ghana-Canada	plane with passport to Canada	20 December, 2014 and 14 March, 2015	Ottawa
Stella	Iran-Turkey-Canada	train with passport to Turkey; plane to Canada	7 January, 2015	Ottawa
Amanda	Iran-Turkey-Canada	train with passport to Turkey; plane to Canada	7 January, 2015	Ottawa
Stephanie	Iran-Turkey-Canada	train with passport to Turkey; plane to Canada	8 January, 2015	Ottawa
Elif	Iran-Turkey-Canada	train with passport to Turkey; plane to Canada	19 January, 2015	Ottawa
Ingrid	Iran-Turkey-Canada	train with passport to Turkey; plane to Canada	19 January, 2015	Ottawa
Janice	Iran-Turkey-Canada	train with passport to Turkey; plane to Canada	20 January, 2015	Ottawa
Natasha	Iran-Turkey-Canada	plane with passport to Turkey; plane to Canada	20 January, 2015	Ottawa
Ashley	Iran-Turkey-Canada	train with passport to Turkey; plane to Canada	20 January, 2015	Ottawa

Appendix: Interview list

Asylum traveller	Journey	Transportation means	Interview date	Interview location
Azadeh	Iran-Turkey-Canada	train with passport to Turkey; plane to Canada	21 January, 2015	Ottawa
Lena	Iran-Turkey-Canada	train with passport to Turkey; plane to Canada	22 January, 2015	Ottawa
Kim	Iran-Turkey-Canada	train with passport to Turkey; plane to Canada	25 January, 2015 and 5 February, 2015	Ottawa
Cher	Iran-Turkey-Canada	train with passport to Turkey; plane to Canada	2 February, 2015	Ottawa
Ahoo	Iran-Turkey-Canada	train with passport to Turkey; plane to Canada	2 February, 2015	Ottawa
Ramon	Iran-Turkey-Canada	walking/mule without passport to Turkey; plane to Canada	5 February, 2015	Ottawa
Sarah	Iran-Turkey-Canada	train with passport to Turkey; plane to Canada	6 February, 2015	Ottawa
Hassan	Iran-Turkey-Canada	train with passport to Turkey; plane to Canada	7 February, 2015	Ottawa
Jamie	Iran-Turkey-Canada	train with passport to Turkey; plane to Canada	22 February, 2015	Ottawa
Ahmed	Iran-Turkey-Canada	walking/mule without passport to Turkey; plane to Canada	25 February, 2015	Ottawa
Travis	Iran-Turkey-Canada	train with passport to Turkey; plane to Canada	25 February, 2015	Ottawa
Ali	Iran-Turkey-Canada	walking/mule without passport to Turkey; plane to Canada	2 March, 2015	Ottawa
Mehdi	Iran-Turkey-Iran	train with passport to Turkey; train to Iran	15 June, 2015	Tehran
Steve	Iran	no	16 June, 2015	Tehran

References

Abass, A. & Ippolito, F. (2014). *Regional Approaches to the Protection of Asylum Seekers: An International Legal Perspective*. Surrey: Ashgate.
Acikgoz, M. (2015). Turkey's Visa Policy: A Migration-Mobility Nexus. *Turkish Policy Quarterly*, 14(2): 97–107.
Adelman, H. (1991). *Refugee Policy: Canada and the United States*. Toronto center for Refugee Studies: York University.
Adelman, H. (2001). From Refugees to Forced Migration: The UNHCR and Human Security. *The International Migration Review*, 35(1): 7–32.
Agamben, G. (1998). *Homo Sacer: Sovereign Power and Bare Life*. Stanford: Stanford University Press.
Agier, M. (2002). Between War and City: Towards an Urban Anthropology of Refugee Camps. *Ethnography*, 3(3): 317–341.
Althusser, L. (2014 [1971]). *On the Reproduction of Capitalism: Ideology and Ideological State Apparatuses (Lenin and Philosophy and Other Essays)*. London: Verso.
Andersson, R. (2014). *Illegality, Inc.: Clandestine Migration and the Business of Bordering Europe*. California: University of California Press.
Arendt, H. (1973). *The Origins of Totalitarianism*. London: Harcourt Brace & Company.
Ashutosh, I. & Mountz, A. (2012). The Geopolitics of Migrant Mobility: Tracing State Relations through Refugee Claims, Boats, and Discourses. *Geopolitics*, 17(2): 335–354. DOI: doi:10.1080/14650045.2011.567315
Baban, F., Ilcan, S. and Rygiel, K. (2017). Syrian refugees in Turkey: pathways to precarity, differential inclusion, and negotiated citizenship rights. *Journal of Ethnic and Migration Studies*, 43(1): 41–57.
Bagelman, J. (2016). *Sanctuary City: A Suspended State*. New York: Palgrave Macmillan. DOI: doi:10.1057/9781137480385
Bataille, G. (1991 [1976]). *The Accursed Share: An Essay of General Economy. History of Eroticism and Sovereignty*, Volume 1, 2, and 3. New York: Zone Books.
Baubock, R. & Faist, T. (2010). *Diaspora and Transnationalism: Concepts, Theories and Methods*. Amsterdam: IMISCOE Research-Amsterdam University Press.
Beiser, M. (2003). Sponsorship and Resettlement Success. *Journal of International Migration and Integration*, 4(2): 203–215.
BenEzer, G. & Zetter, R. (2014). Searching for Directions: Conceptual and Methodological Challenges in Researching Journeys. *Journal of Refugee Studies*, 28(3): 297–318. DOI: doi:10.1093/jrs/feu022

Biehl, S. K. (2015). Governing Through Uncertainty: Experiences of Being a Refugee in Turkey as a Country for Temporary Asylum. *Social Analysis*, 1: 57–75. DOI: doi:10.3167/sa.2015.590104

Bigo, D. (2008). Globalized (in)security: The Field and the Ban-opticon. In D. Bigo and A. Tsoukala (Eds), *Terror, Insecurity and Liberty: Illiberal Practices of Liberal Regimes After 9/11* (pp. 10–48). London: Routledge.

Bourbeau, P. (2011). *The Securitization of Migration: A Study of Movement and Order.* London: Routledge.

Bourdieu, P. (1977). *Outline of a Theory of Practice* (R. Nice, Trans.). Cambridge: Cambridge University Press.

Bourdieu, P. (1990). *The Logic of Practice.* Stanford, California: Stanford University Press.

Brewer, K. T. & Yukseker, D. (2006). *A Survey on African Migrants and Asylum Seekers in Istanbul* (MiReKoc Research Projects 2005–2006). Istanbul: Koc University.

Brigden, N. K. (2013). *Uncertain Odysseys: Migrant Journeys and Transnational Routes.* (Doctoral dissertation). Retrieved from ProQuest Dissertations Publishing (3576386).

Brigden, N. & Mainwaring, C. (2016). Matryoshka Journeys: Im/mobility During Migration. *Geopolitics*, 21(2): 407–434. DOI: doi:10.1080/14650045.2015.1122592

Brunner, L. R., Hyndman, J. & Mountz, A. (2014). 'Waiting for a Wife': Transnational Marriages and the Social Dimensions of Refugee 'Integration'. *Refuge*, 30(1): 81–92.

Canguilhem, G. (1991 [1966]). *The Normal and The Pathological.* New York: Zone Books.

Casas-Cortes, M., Cobarrubias, S. & Pickles, J. (2015). Riding Routes and Itinerant Borders: Autonomy of Migration and Border Externalization. *Antipode*, 47(4): 894–914. DOI: doi:10.1111/anti.12148

Cheran, R. (2006). Multiple Homes and Parallel Civil Societies: Refugee Diasporas and Transnationalism. *Refuge*, 23(1): 4–8.

Chimni, B. S. (2009). The Birth of a 'Discipline': From Refugee to Forced Migration Studies. *Journal of Refugee Studies*, 22(1): 11–29. DOI: doi:10.1093/jrs/fen051

Clifford, J. (1992). Traveling Cultures. In L. Grossberg, C. Nelson & P. A. Treichler (Eds), *Cultural Studies* (pp. 96–116). London: Routledge.

Clifford, J. (1994). Diasporas. *Cultural Anthropology*, 9(3): 302–338.

Collyer, M., Düvell, F. & de Haas, H. (2012). Critical Approaches to Transit Migration. *Population, Space and Place*, 18, 407–414. DOI: doi:10.1002/psp.630

Coutin, S. B. (2005). Being En Route. *American Anthropologist*, 107(2): 195–206.

Crawley, H. & Skleparis, D. (2018). Refugees, migrants, neither, both: categorical fetishism and the politics of bounding in Europe's 'migration crisis'. *Journal of Ethnic and Migration Studies*, 44(1): 48–64. DOI: doi:10.1080/1369183X.2017.1348224

Cresswell, T. (2006). *On the Move: Mobility in the Western World.* London: Routledge.

D'Addario, S., Hiebert, D. & Sherrell, K. (2007). Restricted Access: The Role of Social Capital in Mitigating Absolute Homelessness among Immigrants and Refugees in the GVRD. *Refuge*, 24(1): 107–115.

D'Orsi, C. (2016). *Asylum-Seeker and Refugee Protection in Sub-Saharan Africa: The Peregrination of a Persecuted Human Being in Search of a Safe Haven.* London: Routledge.

Dahinden, J. (2010). The Dynamics of Migrants' Transnational Formations: Between Mobility and Locality. In R. Baubock & T. Faist (Eds), *Diaspora and Transnationalism: Concepts, Theories and Methods* (pp. 51–72). Amsterdam: IMISCOE Research-Amsterdam University Press.

de Certeau, M. (1988). *The Practices of Everyday Life* (S. Rendall, Trans.). Berkeley: University of California Press.

References 133

De Genova, N., Mezzadra, S. & Pickles, J. (2015). New Keywords: Migration and Borders. *Cultural Studies*, 29(1): 55–87. DOI: doi:10.1080/09502386.2014.891630

Diken, B. (2004). From Refugee Camps to Gated Communities: Biopolitics and the End of the City. *Citizenship Studies*, 8(1): 83–106. DOI: doi:10.1080/1362102042000178373

Düvell, F. (2012). Transit Migration: A Blurred and Politicized Concept. *Population, Space and Place*, 18: 415–427. DOI: doi:10.1002/psp.631

Edding, F. (1951). *The Refugees as A Burden, A Stimulus and A Challenge to the West German Economy*. The Hague: Springer.

Edkins, J. & Pin-Fat, V. (2005). Through the Wire: Relations of Power and Relations of Violence. *Millennium: Journal of International Studies*, 34(1): 1–24.

Erdogan, M. (2014). Syrians in Turkey: Social Acceptance and Integration Research. Hacettepe University Migration and Politics Research Centre (HUGO) Report, available online at: http://fs.hacettepe.edu.tr/hugo/dosyalar/TurkiyedekiSuriyeliler-Syrians%20in%20Turkey-Rapor-TR-EN-19022015.PDF

Faist, T. (2010). Diaspora and Transnationalism: What Kind of Dance Partners?. In R. Baubock & T. Faist (Eds), *Diaspora and Transnationalism: Concepts, Theories, and Methods* (pp. 9–34). Amsterdam: IMISCOE Research-Amsterdam University Press.

Fassin, D. (2013). The Precarious Truth of Asylum. *Public Culture*, 25(1): 39–63. DOI: doi:10.1215/08992363-1890459

Featherstone, D. (2008). R*esistance, Space and Political Identities: The Making of Counter-Global Networks*. Oxford: Wiley-Blackwell.

Fitzpatrick, P. (2001). Bare Sovereignty: *Homo Sacer* and the Insistence of Law. *Theory and Event*, 5(2).

Foucault, M. (2003). *Society Must Be Defended. Lectures at the College de France 1975–76*. New York: Picador.

Gapelli, G., Tazzioli, M., Mezzadra, S., Kasparek, B. & Peano, I. (2015). Militant Investigation. In N. De Genova, S. Mezzadra. & J. Pickles (Eds), New Keywords: Migration and Borders (pp. 63–65). *Cultural Studies*, 29(1): 55–87. DOI: doi:10.1080/09502386.2014.891630

Garwood, P. (2011). Rites of Passage. In T. Insoll (Ed.), *The Oxford Handbook of the Archaeology of Ritual and Religion* (pp. 261–284). Oxford: Oxford University Press.

Gibney, M. J. (2004). *The Ethics and Politics of Asylum: Liberal Democracy and the Response to Refugees*. Cambridge: Cambridge University Press.

Gibney, M. & Hansen, R. (2003). *Asylum Policy in the West: Past Trends, Future Possibilities* (Discussion Paper, No. 68). Helsinki: UNU/WIDER.

Gilroy, P. (1993). *The Black Atlantic: Modernity and Double-Consciousness*. London: Verso.

Goldberg, D. T. (2008). Racisms without Racism. *Modern Language Association*, 123(5): 1712–1716.

Goldberg, D. T. & Solomos, J. (2002). General Introduction. In D. Goldberg & J. Solomos (Eds), *A Companion to Racial and Ethnic Studies* (pp. 1–12). Oxford: Blackwell.

Goodwin-Gill, G. S. (2008). *Convention Relating to the Status of Refugees Protocol Relating to the Status of Refugees*. Available online at: http://legal.un.org/avl/pdf/ha/prsr/prsr_e.pdf (accessed March, 2015).

Haddad, E. (2008). *Refugee in International Society: Between Sovereigns*. Cambridge: Cambridge University Press.

Hall, S. (1990). Cultural Identity and Diaspora. In J. Rutherford (Ed.), *Identity: Community, Culture, Difference* (pp. 222–237). London: Lawrence & Wishart.

References

Hamlin, R. (2014). *Let Me Be a Refugee: Administrative Justice and the Politics of Asylum in the United States, Canada, and Australia.* Oxford: Oxford University Press.

Hanafi, S. & Long, T. (2010). Governance, Governmentalities, and the State of Exception in the Palestinian Refugee Camps of Lebanon. *Journal of Refugee Studies*, 23(2): 134–159.

Hathaway, J. C. (1988). Selective Concern: An Overview of Refugee Law in Canada. *McGill Law Journal*, 33: 676–715.

Hathaway, J. (1991). Reconceiving Refugee Law as Humanitarian Rights Protection. *Journal of Refugee Studies*, 4(2): 113–131. DOI: doi:10.1093/jrs/4.2.113

Hathaway, J. (2007). Forced Migration Studies: Could We Agree Just to 'Date'?. *Journal of Refugee Studies*. Debate. 349–369.

Hein, J. (1993). Refugees, Migrants and the State. *Annual Review of Sociology*, 19: 43–59.

Hess, S. (2012). De-naturalizing Transit Migration: Theory and Methods of an Ethnographic Regime Analysis. *Population, Space and Place*, 18: 428–440. DOI: doi:10.1002/psp.632

Hoerder, D. & Macklin, A. (2006). Separation or Permeability: Bordered States, Transnational Relations, Transcultural Lives. *International Journal*, 61(4): 793–812.

Hyndman, J. (1997). Border Crossing. *Antipode*, 29(2): 149–176.

Hyndman, J. & McLean, J. (2006). Settling Like a State: Acehnese Refugees in Vancouver. *Journal of Refugee Studies*, 19(3): 345–360. DOI: doi:10.1093/jrs/fel1016

IOM. (1993). *Transit Migration in Romania: Annex to the IOM Study: Profiles and Motives of Potential Migrants in Romania.* Geneva: IOM.

IOM. (1994a). *Transit Migration in Hungary.* Geneva: IOM.

IOM. (1994b). *Transit Migration in Bulgaria.* Geneva: IOM.

IOM. (1994c). *Transit Migration in the Czech Republic.* Geneva: IOM.

IOM. (1994d). *Transit Migration in Poland.* Geneva: IOM.

IOM. (1995). *Transit Migration in Turkey.* Geneva: IOM.

Jackson, S. & Bauder, H. (2013). Neither Temporary, Nor Permanent: The Precarious Employment Experiences of Refugee Claimants in Canada. *Journal of Refugee Studies*, 27(3): 360–381. DOI: doi:10.1093/jrs/fet048

Joly, D. (1996). *Haven or Hell?: Asylum Policies and Refugees in Europe.* London: MacMillan.

Kafka, F. (2009 [1915]). Metamorphosis. In R. Robertson (Ed.), *The Metamorphosis and Other Series* (pp. 29–74). New York: Oxford University Press.

Kaya, I. (2009). *Reform in Turkish Asylum Law: Adopting the EU Acquis?* (CARIM Research Report, 16). Florence: European University Institute.

Kaytaz, S. E. (2016). Afghan Journeys to Turkey: Narratives of Immobility, Travel and Transformation. *Geopolitics*, 21(2): 284–302. DOI: doi:10.1080/14650045.2016.1151874

Khosravi, S. (2010). *Illegal Traveller: An Auto-Ethnography of Borders.* New York: Palgrave MacMillan.

Kirişci, K. (1991). The Legal Status of Asylum Seekers in Turkey: Problems and Prospects. *International Journal of Refugee Law*, 3(3): 510–528.

Kirişci, K. (1996a). Is Turkey Lifting the 'Geographical Limitation'? – The November 1994 Regulation on Asylum in Turkey. *International Journal of Refugee Law*, 8(3): 293–318.

Kirişci, K. (1996b). Refugees of Turkish Origin: 'Coerced Immigrants' to Turkey since 1945. *International Migration*, 34(3): 385–412.

Kirişci, K. (2000). Disaggregating Turkish Citizenship and Immigration Practices. *Middle Eastern Studies*, 36(3): 1–22.

References

Kirişci, K. (2007). Turkey: A Country of Transition from Emigration to Immigration. *Mediterranean Politics*, 12(1): 91–97. DOI: doi:10.1080/13629390601136871

Kjaergaard, E. (1994). The Concept of 'Safe Third Country' in Contemporary European Refugee Law. *International Journal of Refugee Law*, 6(4): 649–655.

Koser, K. (2008). Why Migrant Smuggling Pays. *International Migration*, 46(2): 3–26.

Koslowski, R. (2013). Selective Migration Policy Models and Changing Realities of Implementation. *International Migration*, 52(3): 26–39. DOI: doi:10.1111/imig.12136

Krahn, H., Derwing, T., Mulder, M. & Wilkinson, L. (2000). Educated and Underemployed: Refugee Integration into the Canadian Labour Market. *Journal of International Migration and Integration*, 1(1): 59–84.

Lacroix, M. Baffoe, M. & Liguori, M. (2015). Refugee Community Organizations in Canada: From the Margins to the Mainstream? A Challenge and Opportunity for Social Workers. *International Journal of Social Welfare*, 24: 62–72. DOI: doi:10.1111/ijsw.12110

Lamba, N. K. & Krahn, H. (2003). Social Capital and Refugee Resettlement: The Social Networks of Refugees in Canada. *Journal of International Migration and Integration*, 3: 335–360.

Landman, T. (2008). *Issues and Methods in Comparative Politics: An Introduction*. New York: Routledge.

Lefebvre, H. (1991). *The Production of Space* (D. N. Smith, Trans). Oxford: Blackwell.

Li, P. (2003). Deconstructing Canada's Discourse of Immigrant Integration. *Journal of International Migration and Integration*, 4(3): 315–333.

Lippert, R. (1998). Rationalities and Refugee Resettlement. *Economy and Society*, 27(4): 380–406.

Loescher, G. (1994). The International Refugee Regime: Stretched to the Limit?. *Journal of International Affairs*, 47(2): 351–377.

Loescher, G. (1996). *Beyond Charity: International Cooperation and the Global Refugee Crisis*. Oxford: Oxford University Press.

Loescher, G. (2001a). *The UNHCR and World Politics: A Perilous Path*. Oxford: Oxford University Press.

Loescher, G. (2001b). The UNHCR and World Politics: State Interests vs. Institutional Autonomy. *International Migration Review*, 35(1): 33–56. DOI: doi:0198–019183/00/3501.0133

Loescher, G., Betts, A. & Milner, J. (2012). *UNHCR: The Politics and Practice of Refugee Protection*. New York: Routledge.

Macklin, A. (2002). Mr. Suresh and the Evil Twin. *Refuge*, 20(4): 15–22.

Macklin, A. (2005). Disappearing Refugees: Reflections on the Canada-U.S. Safe Third Country Agreement. *Columbia Human Rights Law Review*, 36: 365–426.

Macklin, A. (2009). Asylum and the Rule of Law in Canada: Hearing the Other (Side). In S. Kneebone (Ed.), *Refugees, Asylum Seekers, and the Rule of Law* (pp. 78–121). Cambridge: Cambridge University Press.

Macklin, A. (2013). A Safe Country to Emulate? Canada and the European Refugee. In H. Lambert, J. McAdam & M. Fullerton (Eds), *The Global Reach of European Refugee Law* (pp. 99–130). Cambridge: Cambridge University Press.

Mainwaring, C. & Brigden, N. (2016). Beyond the Border: Clandestine Migration Journeys. *Geopolitics*, 21(2): 243–262. DOI: doi:10.1080/14650045.2016.11656755

Malkki, L. (1992). National Geographic: The Rooting of Peoples and the Territorialisation of National Identity among Scholars and Refugees. *Cultural Anthropology*, 7(1): 24–44.

References

Malkki, L. (1995a). *Purity and Exile: Violence, Memory, and National Cosmology among Hutu Refugees in Tanzania*. London: University of Chicago Press.

Malkki, L. (1995b). Refugees and Exile: From 'Refugee Studies' to the National Order of Things. *Annual Review of Anthropology*, 24: 495–523.

Manning, E. (2009). *Relationscape: Movement, Art, Philosophy*. London: The MIT Press.

Massey, D. (2005). *For Space*. London: Sage.

Mercer, K. (1990). Welcome to the Jungle: Identity and Diversity in Postmodern Politics. In J. Rutherford (Ed.), *Identity: Community, Culture, Difference* (pp. 43–71). London: Lawrence & Wishart.

Merriman, P. (2012). *Mobility, Space and Culture*. New York: Routledge.

Mezzadra, S. (2004). The Right to Escape. *Ephemera*, 4(3): 267–275.

Mezzadra, S. & Neilson, B. (2013). *Border as Method, or, the Multiplication of Labor*. Durham and London: Duke University Press.

Mezzadra, S., Neilson, B., Riedner, L., Scheel, S., Gapelli, G., Tazzioni, M. & Rahola, F. (2015). Differential Inclusion/Exclusion. In N. De Genova, S. Mezzadra. & J. Pickles (Eds), New Keywords: Migration and Borders (pp. 79–80). *Cultural Studies*, 29(1): 55–87. DOI: doi:10.1080/09502386.2014.891630

Mezzadra, S., Neilson, B., Scheel, S. & Riedner, L. (2015). Migration/Migration Studies. In N. De Genova, S. Mezzadra. & J. Pickles (Eds), New Keywords: Migration and Borders (pp. 61–63). *Cultural Studies*, 29(1): 55–87. DOI: doi:10.1080/09502386.2014.891630

Moffette, D. (2014). Governing Immigration through Probation: The Displacement of Borderwork and the Assessment of Desirability in Spain. *Security Dialogue*, 45(3): 262–278. DOI: doi:10.1177/0967010614530457

Mountz, A. (2010). *Seeking Asylum: Human Smuggling and Bureaucracy at the Border*. Minneapolis: University of Minnesota Press.

Murdie, R. A. (2008). Pathways to Housing: The Experiences of Sponsored Refugees and Refugee Claimants in Accessing Permanent Housing in Toronto. *International Migration & Integration*, 9: 81–101. DOI: doi:10.1007/s12134-12008-0045-0

Nyers, P. (2006). *Rethinking Refugees: Beyond States of Emergency*. New York: Routledge.

Nyers, P. (2008). No One is Illegal: Between City and Nation. In E. Isin & G. M. Nielsen (Eds), *Acts of Citizenship* (pp. 160–181). London: Zed Books.

Oelgemoller, C. (2011). 'Transit' and 'Suspension': migration management or the metamorphosis of asylum-seekers into 'illegal' immigrants'. *Journal of Ethnic and Migration Studies*, 37(3): 407–424.

Oelgemoller, C. (2017). The Illegal, the Missing: An Evaluation of Conceptual Inventions. *Millennium: Journal of International Studies*, 46(1): 24–40.

Oran, B. (2004). The Story of Those Who Stayed: Lessons from Article 1 and 2 of the 1923 Convention. In R. Hirschon (Ed.), *Crossing the Aegean: An Appraisal of the 1923 Compulsory Population Exchange Between Greece and Turkey* (pp. 97–116). New York: Berghahn Books.

Owens, P. (2009). Reclaiming 'Bare Life?': Against Agamben on Refugees. *International Relations*, 23(4): 567–582. DOI: doi:10.1177/0047117809350545

Papadopoulou, K. A. (2008). *Transit Migration: The Missing Link between Emigration and Settlement*. London: Palgrave MacMillan.

Papadopoulos, D., Stephenson, N. & Tsianos, V. (2008). *Escape Routes: Control and Subversion in the 21st Century*. London: Pluto Press.

Phillimore, J. & Goodson, L. (2008). Making a Place in the Global City: The Relevance of Indicators of Integration. *Journal of Refugee Studies*, 21(3): 305–325. DOI: doi:10.1093/jrs/fen025

Pieters, J. N. (2002). Europe and its Others. In D. T. Goldberg & J. Somolon (Eds), *A Companion to Racial and Ethnic Studies* (pp. 17–24). Oxford: Blackwell.

Pitkanen, P., Icduygu, A. & Sert, D. (2012). Current Characteristics of Migrant Transnationalism. In P. Pitkanen, D. Sert & A. Icduygu (Eds), *Migration and Transformation: Multi-Level Analysis of Migrant Transnationalism* (pp. 205–224). New York: Springer.

Portes, A., Guarnizo, L. E. & Landolt, P. (1999). The Study of Transnationalism: Pitfalls and Promise of an Emergent Research Field. *Ethnic and Racial Studies*, 22(2): 217–237. DOI: doi:0141–9870

Provine, D. M. & Sanchez, G. (2011). Suspecting Immigrants: Exploring Links between Racialised Anxieties and Expanded Police Powers in Arizona. *Policing & Society*, 21(4): 468–478.

Quayson, A. & Daswani, G. (2013). Introduction – Diaspora and Transnationalism: Scapes, Scales, and Scopes. In A. Quayson & G. Daswani (Eds), *A Companion to Diaspora and Transnationalism* (pp. 1–26). Oxford: Blackwell.

Rajaram, P. & Grundy-Warr, C. (2004). The Irregular Migrant as *Homo Sacer*: Migration and Detention in Australia, Malaysia, and Thailand. *International Migration*, 42(1): 33–64.

Richard, N. (2000 [1986]). Margins and Institutions: Performances of the Chilean *Avanzada*. In C. Fusco (Ed.), *Corpus Delecti: Performance Art of the Americas* (pp. 183–197). New York: Routledge.

Rodriguez, N. (1996). The Battle for the Border: Notes on Autonomous Migration, Transnational Communities, and the State. *Social Justice*, 23(3): 21–37.

Rose, N. (1993). Government, Authority and Expertise in Advanced Liberalism. *Economy and Society*, 22(3): 283–299. DOI: doi:10.1080/03085149300000019

Sartori, G. (1970). Concept Misformation in Comparative Politics. *The American Political Science Review*, 64(4): 1033–1053.

Sassen, S. (1999). *Guests and Aliens*. New York: New Press.

Schapendonk, J. (2016). African Passages through Istanbul. In M. van der Velde & T. van Naerssen (Eds), *Mobility and Migration Choices: Thresholds to Crossing Borders* (pp. 235–249). New York: Routledge.

Schuster, L. (2003). *The Use and Abuse of Political Asylum in Britain and Germany*. London: Frank Cass.

Sert, D. & Yıldız, U. (2016). Governing without Control: Turkey's "Struggle" with International Migration. In C. Ozbay, M. Erol, A. Terzioglu & U. Turem (Eds), *The Making of Neoliberal Turkey* (pp. 53–71). Surrey, UK: Ashgate.

Sherrell, K. & Immigrant Services Society of BC. (2009). *At Home in Surrey? The Housing Experiences of Refugees in Surrey, B.C* (Final Report). Vancouver: Immigrant Services Society of BC.

Shields, R. (1991). *Places on the Margin: Alternative Geographies of Modernity*. London: Routledge.

Simich, L. (2003). Negotiating Boundaries of Refugee Resettlement: A Study of Settlement Patterns and Social Support. *Canadian Review of Sociology*, 40(5): 575–591.

Şimşek, D. (2018). Transnational Activities of Syrian Refugees in Turkey: Hindering or Supporting Integration. *International Migration*. DOI: doi:10.1111/imig.12489

Soto, L. (2016). The Telling Moment: Pre-Crossings of Mexican Teenage Girls and Their Journeys to the Border. *Geopolitics*, 21(2): 325–344. DOI: doi:10.1080/14650045.2016.1157787

Soykan, C. (2012). The New Draft Law on Foreigners and International Protection in Turkey. *Oxford Monitor of Forced Migration*, 2(2): 38–47.

Squire, V. (2009). *The Exclusionary Politics of Asylum*. New York: Palgrave Macmillan.

Squire, V. (2016). Governing Migration through Death in Europe and the US: Identification, Burial and the Crisis of Modern Humanism. *European Journal of International Relations*. DOI: doi:10.1177/1354066116668662

Stone-Cadena, V. (2016). Indigenous Ecuadorian Mobility Strategies in the Clandestine Migration Journey. *Geopolitics*, 21(2): 345–365. DOI: doi:10.1080.14650045.2016.1147028

Suter, B. (2017). The Logics of Transit: The Anticipation of Onward Mobility and Its Consequences for Social and Economic Relations in Istanbul. *International Journal of Migration and Border Studies*, 3(2–3): 158–173. DOI: doi:10.1504/IJMBS.2017.083233

Swartz, David. (1998). *Culture and Power: The Sociology of Pierre Bourdieu*. Chicago: The University of Chicago Press.

Tete, S. Y. A. (2012). 'Any place could be home': Embedding the Refugees' Voices into Displacement Resolution and State Refugee Policy. *Geoforum*, 43: 106–115. DOI: doi:10.1016/j.geoforum.2011.07.009

Thrift, N. (2008). *Non-Representational Theory: Space, Politics, Affect*. London: Routledge.

Tsianos, V. & Karakayali, S. (2010). Transnational Migration and the Emergence of the European Border Regime: An Ethnographic Analysis. *European Journal of Social Theory*, 13(3): 383–387. DOI: doi:10.1177/1368431010371761

Turner, V. (1977). *The Ritual Process: Structure and Anti-Structure*. New York: Cornell University Press.

Turton, D. (2003). *Conceptualizing Forced Migration* (Working Papers, No. 12). Oxford: Refugee Studies Center.

UNHCR. (2011a). *The 1951 Geneva Convention Relating to the Status of Refugees and Its 1967 Protocol*. Geneva: UNHCR.

UNHCR. (2011b). *UNHCR Resettlement Handbook: Division of International Protection*. Geneva: UNHCR.

UNHCR. (2013). *UNHCR Resettlement Handbook Country Chapter: Canada (Revisited in 2013)*. Geneva: UNHCR.

UNHCR. (2014). *UNHCR Country Chapter: Canada*. Geneva: UNHCR.

van Gennep, A. (1960 [1908]). *The Rites of Passage*. Chicago: University of Chicago Press.

Vertovec, S. (2001). Transnationalism and Identity. *Journal of Ethnic and Migration Studies*, 27(4): 573–582.

Virilio, P. (2007 [1977]). *Speed and Politics*. Los Angeles: Semiotext(e).

Vogt, W. (2016). Stuck in the Middle With You: The Intimate Labours of Mobility and Smuggling along Mexico's Migrant Route. *Geopolitics*, 21(2): 366–388. DOI: doi:10.1080/14650045.2015.1104666

Walters, W. (2002). Social Capital and Political Sociology: Re-Imagining Politics? *Sociology*, 36(2): 377–397.

Walters, W. (2004). Secure Borders, Safe Haven, Domopolitics. *Citizenship Studies*, 8(3): 237–260. DOI: doi:10.1080/1362102042000256989

References

Walters, W. (2008). Acts of Demonstration: Mapping the Territory of (Non-) Citizenship. In E. Isin and G. M. Nielsen (Eds), *Acts of Citizenship* (pp. 182–206). London: Zed Books.

Walters, W. (2015). Migration, Vehicles, and Politics: Three Theses on Viapolitics. *European Journal of Social Theory*, 18(4): 469–488. DOI: doi:10.1177/1368431014554859

Walters, W. (2015). On the Road with Michel Foucault: Migration, Deportation and Viapolitics. In S. Fuggle, Y. Lanci and M. Tazzioli (Eds) *Foucault and The History of Our Present*, (pp. 94–110). New York: Palgrave Macmillan.

Watson, S. D. (2009). *Securitization of Humanitarian Migration: Digging Moats and Sinking Boats.* London: Routledge.

White, M. A. (2013). Ambivalent Homonationalisms: Transnational Queer Intimacies and Territorialized Belongings. *Interventions*, 15(1): 37–54. DOI: doi:10.1080/1369801X.2013.770999

Wimmer, A. & Schiller, G. N. (2002). Methodological Nationalism and Beyond: Nation Building, Migration, and the Social Sciences. *Global Networks*, 2(4): 301–334. DOI: doi:10.1111/1471–0374.00043

Wissing, M., Düvell, F. & van Eerdewijk, A. (2013). Dynamic Migration Intentions and the Impact of Institutional Environment: A Transit Migration Hub in Turkey. *Journal of Ethnic and Migration Studies*, 39(7): 1087–1105. DOI: doi:10.1080/1369183X.2013.778026

Wolff, J. (1993). On the Road Again: Metaphors of Travel in Cultural Criticism. *Cultural Studies*, 7(2): 224–239. DOI: doi:10.1080/09502389300490151

Xiang, B. & Lindquist, J. (2014). Migration Infrastructure. *International Migration Review*, 48(1): 122–148. DOI: doi:10.1111/imre.12141

Yıldız, U. & Sert, D. (2019). Dynamics of Mobility-Stasis in Refugee Journeys: Case of Resettlement from Turkey to Canada. *Migration Studies*. DOI: doi:10.1093/migration/mnz005

Zamyatin, Y. (1972 [1921]). *We.* New York: Batham.

Zetter, R. (1991). Labelling Refugees: Forming and Transforming a Bureaucratic Identity. *Journal of Refugee Studies*, 4(1): 39–62.

Zetter, R. (2007). More Labels, Fewer Refugees: Remaking the Refugee Label in an Era of Globalization. *Journal of Refugee Studies*, 20(2): 172–192. DOI: doi:10.1093/jrs/fem011

Index

1967 Additional Protocol 7, 15, 38, 40, 45, 46

accommodation 97
Afghanistan 48, 98, 106
Agamben, G. 22, 23, 99
Althusser, L. 94
Amnesty International 37n5, 126, 127
anti-mapping 7, 13
Arendt, H. 22
Aristotle 99
asylum habitus 3, 9, 34, 35, 65, 66, 82, 93, 115
asylum journey 3, 4–5, 6, 9, 11, 30, 38, 63, 66, 81, 122; journey of hope 64, 103
asylum seeker 8, 41, 61n4, 87
asylum traveller 8, 9, 12, 28, 35, 100, 105
Atatürk Airport 108
autonomy of migration 24, 26, 30, 34

Baha'i 64, 69, 88, 113, 115
Bataille, G. 33
BIHE 96, 113, 116
boat people 60n1
border as method 11
Bourdieu, P. 3, 9, 34, 35
bureaucratic metamorphosis 84, 87, 89, 91, 100, 110

Canada 14; CIC 52, 54, 103, 106, 112; designated countries of origin 54, 62; IRB, 52, 110; IRPA 52, 53, 56, 58, 62; RAP 111, 112, 118; resettlement country 2, 10, 15, 34, 39, 59, 107, 108, 110, 113, 115, 117, 122, 124, 125, 126; resettlement governance 10, 15, 29, 33, 51, 52, 54, 56, 58, 59, 60, 84, 105, 117, 119n19, 127

Clifford, J. 27

de Certeau, M. 29, 64
differential inclusion 33
DRC 95, 115
dromology 121, 122
Dublin Convention 53

employment 96
EU Acquis Communautaire 61n13
exclusionary inclusion 33, 44, 46, 51, 58, 59, 60

family reunification 54, 56, 105, 114
forced migration 6, 23, 25, 26

Geneva Convention 7, 21, 38, 40
geographical limitation 2, 7, 15, 20n1, 33, 34, 39, 45, 48, 51, 60, 96, 123, 127
Gilroy, P. 3, 27, 81, 122

habitus 3, 9, 34, 66, 93
homo sacer 22, 99

incorporation phase 6, 19, 31, 39, 103, 109, 117
integration 31, 56, 58, 108, 119n19
IOM 5, 10, 107, 118; cultural orientation programme 16, 59, 103, 106, 107, 109
Iran 2, 34, 83n9, 85
Iraq 2, 34, 46, 93
Istanbul 13, 20n5, 70, 81, 86, 93, 94, 97, 106

journey as method 9, 11–12, 27, 122

Kafka, F. 87

Index 141

Lefebvre, H. 13
LGBTQ 64, 68, 99
liminal phase 6, 19, 31, 84, 91

methodological nationalism, 24
migration infrastructure, 26, 67
militant investigation 11, 12
mobile knowledge 3, 5, 65, 75, 123
mobistasis 8, 59, 66, 82, 84, 92, 93, 122, 124
multi-sited ethnography 6, 13, 16, 126

nomadic thinking 35, 36, 121

odyssey. *See* asylum journey
Ottawa 13, 105, 111, 113, 114, 117

political imagination 25, 26, 36

refugee 7; blended visa office-referred refugee 54, 56; conditional refugee 39, 45, 46, 47, 61n11; government-assisted refugee 2, 15, 54, 119n8; privately sponsored refugee 2, 54; subsidiary protection 50, 51, 61n14; UNHCR-recognized refugee 10, 52, 54, 119n8
resettlement 62, 119n19
Resettlement Handbook 41, 59, 126
rites of passage 19, 31, 63

satellite city 20n5, 47, 92; Aksaray 13, 18, 90, 98; Denizli 96, 99; Eskisehir 86; Isparta 97, 99; Kastamonu, 99; Kayseri 13, 86, 92, 95; Kirsehir 99; Nevsehir 92; Yalova 95, 98

schooling 95, 100n18, 101n38, 112
sedentarist thinking 35, 36, 121
selective inclusion 33, 51, 58, 60
separation phase 6, 19, 31, 39, 63, 65, 82
strategy 29
Syria 34, 50; guest 51

tactic 30, 99, 123
Tehran 13, 15, 75, 83n19, 88
temporary protection 50
three phases of asylum journey 19, 31, 32
transit migration 28
transnational refugee governance 32, 33, 38
transnationalism 23, 24
transportational momentum 73
Turkey 85, 92; 1934 Law of Settlement 44, 61n6; 1994 Asylum Regulation 47; asylum country 2, 10, 14, 59; asylum governance 10, 44, 45, 46, 47; DGMM 3, 17, 51, 91, 125; LFIP 45, 61n10, 91
Turner, V. 31, 84

UNHCR 2, 10, 20n2, 38, 40, 44, 59, 88, 104, 105, 107, 124; Georgia 80; Malaysia 83n27
United States of America 40, 41, 58, 60, 67

van Gennep, A. 31, 63, 84
viapolitics 11, 12, 73
Virilio, P. 121

Zamyatin, E. 120